CITIES, COUNTIES, KIDS, AND FAMILIES

The Essential Role

Sidney L. Gardner

University Press of America,® Inc.
Lanham · Boulder · New York · Toronto · Oxford

Copyright © 2005 by
University Press of America,® Inc.
4501 Forbes Boulevard
Suite 200
Lanham, Maryland 20706
UPA Acquisitions Department (301) 459-3366

PO Box 317
Oxford
OX2 9RU, UK

Library of Congress Control Number: 2004116240
ISBN 0-7618-3094-4 (paperback : alk. ppr.)

For
Nicholas Sidney Owen

May he live in a world where children are always valued
Where the little girl in the red coat always has a protector
And where governments measure their worth
By what they do for children, not just incumbents.

TABLE OF CONTENTS

vi

viii

LIST OF FIGURES

LIST OF TABLES

A PERSONAL PREFACE

So you've just been appointed Special Assistant for children and youth issues to the Mayor or the City Manager. Good job, a chance to work with several city agencies and with a lot of outside groups.

So what do you do next?

This book is aimed at answering that question, not only for our hypothetical assistant to the Manager, but for thousands of people in local government with similar jobs. My conviction is that people with this kind of job have the best opportunity of anyone in local government to see the whole picture of the future of local government. They can be part of the decisions that will determine whether cities and counties will meet what I believe to be their most important test: responding more effectively to the needs and aspirations of the nearly 80 million children and youth in this country.

That conviction arises in part because I began my own career in such a job—pretty much clueless about how to start and what to do next. Fresh out of a first-rate graduate education in public affairs, I was nevertheless unable to put what I was doing into any framework or to relate it to any larger picture of what was happening in the city where I was working.

Today, thirty-eight years later, I hope I have learned something that could be helpful to my counterparts as they begin their careers in local government. This is the book I wish someone had given me when I started to work in a local government. It is written for Dan Nguyen-Tan, Larry Agran, Bill Steiner, Grantland Johnson, Nick Carbone, Joe Simitian, Otis Johnson, Rob Richardson, Margie Wakeham, all four of my siblings who have held local office, and all the other elected and appointed officials who have given me hope for the future of local government. It is inspired by the memories of working for and with John Lindsay, Bob Finch, Elliot Richardson, Jack Veneman, and Tom Joe.

I should declare some premises and assumptions at the outset. I believe the 500,000 elected officials in this country are the core of our democracy—at its best and at its worst. The great majority of them serve in local governments. The appointed officials, senior and junior, who work with them and give the government its permanency and much of its purpose, are some of the most valuable players in American government. Local government is the level that has the best chance of revitalizing our system of government, not only because of the stock phrase—it is closer to the people—but also because it is closer to the kids.

And that is my final premise: local government will be where we determine whether one-third of our kids will live a stunted future, unable to fulfill their potential, or become active contributors to the 21st century.

I live today in the nation's fifth largest county and in a city of 165,000 which is among the 150 largest American cities. I began my professional career working for the largest city, and over the past several years I have worked with officials and community leaders in the largest county. But I have also lived in communities of less than 4,000 and worked with county governments in places where the livestock outnumbers the human residents. If a bias for bigness creeps into this book, it is not intended. I think often of my own city as a mid-point norm—although no university town is ever "normal."

This book is written out of respect. At hundreds of speaking engagements, I have introduced myself as a "recovering politician," and I use that label with pride as well as humor. Since walking out of graduate school into a staff role in a campaign for Mayor of New York City in 1965, I have been proud to work in and around local government and its elected officials. So if the tone of this book is occasionally critical—and it will be—it is out of a belief that local government can be better, that it has been proven that it has been better in some places at some times, and that it should be better because our kids and their families need so much more.

In my research for the chapter of this book that addresses the future of local government (Chapter 16), I came across a remarkable essay by Roger Schank in which he asks the wonderful question "what happens when the answers are in the walls?" Schank is referring to the growing capacity of computers to develop omni-present answers to a student's questions which would be "in the walls" of a library or any place of learning. He concludes that a major shift will take place in the nature of learning, in which "what will be valued will be good questions," with learning defined as knowing how to frame and ask good questions, not the possession of memorized knowledge.

I hope this book has some good questions—for today and for the future of local government. What can cities and counties do for children and families? How will they be able to afford it? Where will they find the political support they will need? I believe that we pay homage to those whose work we value by asking them hard questions, not by accepting inadequate policy and practice as the limits of what is possible. It is in that spirit that this book is written.

Sid Gardner
Irvine, California
February 2004

ACKNOWLEDGMENTS

I am indebted to several careful readers who commented in depth on this work in draft, none of whom are responsible for its errors or interpretations. They include Ira Cutler, Scott Spitzer, Cliff Johnson, and Bonnie Armstrong— thoughtful practitioners, friendly critics, and advisors to local governments throughout their professional lives. I also thank my wife, CEO, and life partner, Nancy Young, who has encouraged me to work on this book through uphill and downhill times in our remarkable organization, Children and Family Futures.

Work on this book and its editing have been supported by the Annie E. Casey Foundation, a unique institution with which I have been connected since 1986. I also received support from California State University, Fullerton, while serving as the Director of its Center for Collaboration for Children. The Foundation Consortium of California and the Walter S. Johnson Foundation have also supported portions of the book. None of the individuals and organizations mentioned in this book is responsible for my interpretations and concepts.

I also want to thank three of my superb staff during the period of writing this book: Gisela Gomez, Iris Alfaro, and James Owen. Gisela bought me some of the time I needed to work on early stages of the book while at Cal State Fullerton with her marvelous sense of organization and content. Iris has attended conferences as part of this book's preparation and worked on its chapter on family support, making major contributions to these ideas. James Owen has organized my life in the last several months and been a valued information technology advisor and much more, including father of the world's most perfect grandson, the one to whom this book is dedicated, Nicholas Sidney Owen.

FREQUENTLY USED ABBREVIATIONS AND ACRONYMS

AFDC: Aid to Families with Dependent Children (the predecessor
       program to TANF)
AOD: alcohol and other drugs
CAP: community action program
CBOs: community-based organizations
CCIs: comprehensive community initiatives
CYF: children, youth, and family
FBOs: faith-based organizations
LG: local government
NIMBY: "Not in my backyard"
NLC: the National League of Cities
NPOs: Nonprofit organizations
TANF: Temporary Assistance to Needy Families
       (after 1996, the federal welfare program)
USCM: United State Conference of Mayors

CHAPTER 1: INTRODUCTION

Most children grow up in communities, and most communities are part of cities, or towns, or counties. These local governments make up part of the backgrounds of children's lives, as they carry out the tasks of doing what governments do–collecting taxes, plowing the streets, giving out traffic tickets, and cutting the grass at the park. The lives of children and the actions of local governments intersect in many ways.

But most local governments do not act as if *policy* toward children and their families were a basic part of their mission. They operate programs for children, they sometimes seek funding for new projects for children–but they rarely debate children's policy and the strategic choices among different priorities for children and their families.

The fundamental premise of this book is that local government as a whole is less involved in children and family policy[1] than it could be or should be. Cities and counties typically do less in developing and carrying out policy affecting children than they could or should do. Their potential roles are too often token, reactive, or fragmented.

The perspective of this book may often seem "half-empty," especially by those inside local governments. But since the lives of millions of children are far from being even half-empty, it seems justified to ask what more local governments could be doing about poor outcomes for children and families. At the same time, we need to highlight what the best cities and counties are already doing.

The following examples are evidence that the process in many cities and counties is seriously flawed:

- In one city, a shooting incident at a local restaurant led to the formation of a task force on violence, which addressed a number of issues affecting youth. When the question of deployment of city police officers to elementary school campuses to operate a widely discredited drug prevention program was raised, it was ruled out of order, along with other proposals for assessing the effectiveness of the several prevention programs already funded in the city. Partial programs were put in place, largely determined by what external funding would support, and evaluation plans were shelved for lack of funding or interest.

- In another county, a working group on the underlying causes of the problems of children and youth developed a draft document that identified poverty, racism, drugs, and the level of violence tolerated in the community. A lengthy debate ensued, in which influential leaders of local child abuse prevention groups pointed out that child abuse was left off the list. They were unwilling to consider the point that child abuse is a derivative of the other problems already on the list. "Their" problem was not being named, and they were unwilling to go further with the process if it was intended to develop real priorities. So they didn't.

- In another county, a discussion of why children should be identified at the earliest possible point for developmental delays was effectively derailed by a member of a local commission on children's issues who argued against funding programs that would identify new cases, "because if we diagnose them, then we would have to do something about them."

As made clear by these examples–all genuine, all recent–many cities and county governments respond to children and family issues along four fragmented, largely reactive pathways:

1. *Grant-driven priorities*: we will focus our efforts on doing what someone else– another level of government or a private donor–gives us a grant to do, because externally funded projects are all we feel we can afford;
2. *Crisis-driven priorities*: we will do what we have to when there is a local crisis, but will respond only to that crisis because we lack resources to do more, and we'll stop when it stops being perceived as a crisis;
3. *Accountability avoidance*: (a) we will operate programs for children and families, but we will not examine their effectiveness in enough depth to reallocate resources away from the least effective programs, toward the most effective; (b) we will blame state and federal governments for programs' ineffectiveness and our own lack of resources;
4. *Structural "solutions"*: we will set up an office that is given nominal responsibility for children and youth, but it will operate under the three above guidelines.

But it is not only that local governments ask too little of themselves. Funders, local service providers and advocates often ask too little of local government, too. These children and youth-serving organizations usually under-emphasize what local governments can do, asking for minimal or grant-focused responses, rather than pressing for action along the full continuum of potential local roles in addressing the problems of children and families.

Why is local government's role in children's issues minimized?

Children's policy is often invisible in local government. What those governments do that is most visible are the functions of public safety, zoning, and environmental policy—trash collection, snow removal, and street sweeping. In such cities and counties, parks and recreation and law enforcement are the major intersections between the accepted functions of the local government and impacts on children and youth. Families are affected by larger cities' roles in housing and job development.

In county-dominant states, where the county has a major role in health and human services, the effects of children's policymaking are more visible. Decisions about health coverage or child welfare get implemented in these local governments because they have major accountability for results for such programs.[2] But even in these counties, issues are more often framed as "health policy" or "welfare" than as policy about children and families. Most local governments cannot document what they spend on children and youth, while they know their health and welfare costs to the penny–both their own funds and that which comes to them from state and federal sources.

And that is the second major reason why children's policy is sometimes invisible in local governments–because it is seen as the province of state and federal decision-making. State and federal policy affecting children and families has indisputably important impact. However frustrating it may be to seek coherent action from either level, it is undeniable that welfare reform, state education standards, and state responses to new child welfare legislation, to take just a few examples from the last half-decade, have had profound effects on millions of children. Some of those effects can be argued to be bad, some good, some uncertain—but there have been major effects.

> **Accountability**
>
> A favorite story of mine confirming the unique accountability of local government came out of the first local government I worked for–a good-sized jurisdiction in the Northeast known as New York City.
>
> It was New Year's Eve, 1966, and the City was paralyzed by the threat of a subway strike. John V. Lindsay had just been inaugurated as Mayor of New York and had taken office a few hours before. The night was cold, the streets were icy, and a citizen was heading down the subway stairs when he slipped on a patch of ice. His instant reaction, according to a staff member who briefed the Mayor the next day, was to utter a mighty oath and shout "that damned Lindsay!"
>
> The story may be apocryphal–although the Mayor told it for years after. But it serves well to highlight how quickly Harry Truman's proverbial "buck" stops at the desk of local elected officials.

Excellent books have been written about social policy affecting children, but few of them discuss local government in much depth.[3] Frederick Wirt, in a fine book about politics in San Francisco, described the role of city government in the federal system as making "residual policy," meaning that cities do what is left over where state and the federal government leave off.[4] In the arena of children's policy, the observation seems even more apt for many observers of local government.

But Tip O'Neil was also right in his elegant formulation that "all politics is local." And that is a powerful reason to take local government seriously, despite the obstacles just described. In making children's policy real in American communities, local politics and the policies that result from it have critical effects on the tasks of carrying out state and federal policy toward children and youth. For the vast majority of state and federal programs, in many cities and counties, these are the levels of government that implement the policy, they carry it out on the ground, and they are where the policy meets the customers in the community.

What do cities and counties do that affects children and families?

In 2000 there were 243 cities over 100,000 population (68 of them over 250,000), including approximately 60% of the nation's population. There are sixty-seven counties with a population over 750,000. Together, these 310 jurisdictions make up the largest local governments in the nation.

Treating these local governments as junior partners to the state and federal government obscures the immense scale of what they do. Local governments employ more than 5 million workers. If we define school districts as an element of local government, 6.1 million more workers are added, who are teachers and other public school employees. Local governments include the vast majority of the half million elected officials in the country, and they spent a total of $966 billion in 1999-2000, compared with $1.08 billion in state spending. Of this total local government spending, $406 million was local spending (exclusive of state funds) for elementary and secondary education, underscoring the critical role of school districts and local funding for schools.

In county-dominant states, only 6-10% of most cities' budgets is devoted to expenditures directly supporting children and youth-specific programs, because counties carry out some of these functions. But between them, both kinds of local governments spend up to 30% of their total budgets on child- and family-specific policies, exclusive of the entire budgets of local school districts.[5]

To summarize, city and county government spend significant levels of funding on children and family services, but do not typically devote proportionate amounts of their policy-making to these issues; they spend more of their money than their policy-making time on children and family issues. A significant portion of their budgets is made up of agencies and programs that address children and family problems, but nowhere near this same level of attention is given to any specific children and family issues, with the possible exception of youth crime when these issues break into public view.

It is not just their spending, however, that matters. Cities and counties affect children and families in many other ways:

- *Their core local governmental roles affect children and youth*: In most parts of the country, they have primary responsibilities in the areas of law enforcement, the criminal justice system, housing, employment and training, parks and recreation, land use planning, zoning and licensing. Each of these affects children and youth directly, in ways we will explore in later chapters.
- *Their health and welfare roles are largely targeted on children and the elderly*: As noted, in states covering about 40% of the nation's population and most of the large industrial states, counties are in charge of administering the health and welfare programs of the state and federal governments. Nearly 60% of all welfare cases are concentrated in 89

large urban counties. [6] The typical county with a welfare administration role devotes approximately one-third to one-half of their resources to services, cash assistance, and in-kind benefits aiding children and lower-income families. With increasing devolution of authority in welfare to the state level, some states have given cities and counties further discretion in designing income support programs. How local governments exercise these responsibilities can affect whether children and families are adequately connected with the income support and in-kind benefit programs for which they are still eligible. Local governments also have substantial environmental powers that affect the health and safety of children and youth. And even in those cities that do not have direct welfare administrative roles, the fact that so many children in welfare and working poor families live in cities means that urban areas are a special focus of the "next stage of welfare reform: making work pay for the working poor." [7]

- *They have extensive impact on the nonprofit sector*: In programmatic areas where some public and private funds flow directly to nonprofit agencies, such as child care and youth prevention, cities and counties are key stakeholders, because their regulatory powers, their law enforcement roles, and their other activities affect the ultimate success of nonprofit agencies. In homelessness—a policy area where cities have special responsibilities—children and families are an increasing focus of local government policy.[8] Cities and counties can also do a great deal to energize and mobilize the voluntary, "third sector" in their regions.

- *They are unavoidably—and increasingly—involved in education*: In education, a few cities and counties are directly involved in governing school systems, through budget powers or the appointment of their boards by the Mayor, or in other ways. In a larger number of cities and counties, the trend in recent years has been for mayors and county commissions to become more, not less involved in school issues. [9] This issue is discussed further in Chapter 12.

- *Their other governmental functions affect families—all families in some cases, only families categorically defined as eligible for services, in others*. Their decisions about taxation, to the extent that they have control over those decisions, affect families' decisions about where to live. Their enforcement or lack of enforcement of anti-discrimination legislation also affects where families can live. And their hiring and contracting decisions may affect how much lower-income parents can take home in wages to support their families.

In this book, local government is defined primarily as cities and counties. School districts are unquestionably part of local government, but the literature on schools and school reform is already voluminous, compared with that on cities and counties as they affect children's policy. School districts do not debate whether their roles in responding to children should be extensive—their roles are by definition broad and deep. But in cities and counties the question is less settled and far less strategically assessed. So our concern is primarily with how cities and counties interact with and seek partnerships with schools, rather than how school districts function to address children's issues.

Different levels of children and family issues: direct, cross-cutting, and outer ring issues

"Children's issues" is a term that needs more precision, distinguishing between three different kinds of issues:

1. There are *issues that affect children and families directly*, through programs and services that aim at improving their life chances. These are the issues that providers, advocates and their supporters are most concerned with—they are the focus of children's advocacy. Foster care, delinquency prevention, and special education are examples.

2. There are also *cross-cutting issues*—issues that are arise in the first kind of programs, but that transcend separate programs such as child care, foster care, or delinquency to focus on the connections or lack of connections among these programs which help or weaken their effectiveness. Early childhood investments, the connections between child abuse and substance abuse, and after-school youth development programs sponsored by non-educational agencies are examples of such issues.

3. Finally, there are *issues with indirect but important impact on children and families*. These are less often the concern of advocates and providers, but in some cases their impact on children and families is more profound. These include the state's tax structure, the impact of technology on family life and youth options, energy, environmental disparities, and the economics of affordable housing. These "outer ring" issues are much less visible in local policy, but to leave them out entirely may shrink the arena of children and family issues and thus miss the opportunity for strategic thinking.

What are the current and potential roles of local government?

Given these effects of local governments on children and policy, why are their roles so fragmented and incoherent? In part it is because the prevailing view of local government among providers and advocates has come to be a simplistic, bipolar choice. The first role defines the role of local government primarily as providing funding, equating cash with leadership. The second, opposing role sees local government as a target of outside groups, because local government is viewed as a passive actor or because its role is restricted to token programs funded by external sources.

But the potential role of local government is much richer and more nuanced than this simple bipolar perspective allows. Those cities and counties that have shown wider and more sophisticated leadership in children and family policy have played multiple roles at different times and on different issues. The chart which follows sets forth a widely varied range of roles, all of which have the potential to affect children and families. This matrix could be used by local groups who are attempting to understand the full potential of the roles of their local government in addressing children and family problems. Local officials could also use it as a self-assessment tool to review the roles they are now playing, and those that they could play. Generally speaking, it moves from those roles which are least involved to those that commit the most local resources—both financial and political.

Table 1: Local Government Roles Matrix

Local Government Role	General	Youth Development	Health and Mental Health	Education
1. Participation in coalitions	Healthy Cities	Prevention coalitions	Immunization campaigns	Joining reform coalitions
2. Convening stakeholders	Children's summits			Lobbying for education grants
3. Endorse grants Sought for providers from state, federal and private sources	Support for CCI* grants	Seek state and federal funding: Safe Schools	Support for systems of care grants	Lobbying for education grants
4. Seek funds from private sources	Prepare grants for LG* units for local NPOs* and CBOs*	Scholarship funds for foster youth	Negotiate for grants/staffing from hospitals and HMOs with public benefit requirements	Assist education foundations
5. Collect/Provide Information: for planning; on programs costs & impact; for annual report cards; from citizen feedback on agencies' performance; study commissions: spotlight issues	Children's budgets Geo-coded data	Arrest data Sites for after school programs	Use of Healthy People 2010 goals as benchmarks	Promoting report cards by school and district Feedback on afterschool behavior by students
6. Provide residents with information: connections with family income and work support programs	Family Economic Self-sufficiency checklist or software	Enlist youth in community data collection efforts	Medicaid and CHIP enrollment	Publish regular reports on comparable schools; seek disaggregated data
7. Training and staff development	Training in policy development for CYF* issues Creating multi-disciplinary service teams	Parks and recreation workers trained in Asset Development concepts	Retrain maternal and child health/public health nurses and staff assigned to home visiting Recruit community para-professionals	Teams of school and police community service officers

8. Intergovernmental advocacy: evaluate effectiveness of state and federal programs; propose redesign of state and federal programs; develop state legislative agenda, provide support for federal policy changes with key legislators	Lobby for program design changes Blended funding proposals	Spotlighting costs of state and federal legal mandates for criminal detention	Publicizing negative formula effects on local allocations	Lobbying jointly with school officials at state budget hearings
9. Use local regulatory powers: zoning, planning and land use, cable oversight	Lower-income family access to broadband	Youth access to cable for youth programming	Health education programs in multiple languages	Child care zoning Cable education programs
10. Use local economic role: purchasing, hiring and personnel policies, investments and economic development, capital budget/bonding/construction, and renovation of facilities	Livable wage campaigns and contracts Dependent care leave and benefits	Community service jobs for youth in public agencies and contractors Recreation/early care/after school centers built into new schools	City contractor requirements to provide health coverage	City and county child care centers
11. Model employer policies	Pay levels	College information and support for part-time youth leaders	Inclusive health benefits	Released time for parent-teacher conferences Provide employers with developmental child care benefits, not custodial
12. Taxing role	Tax incentives for community services	Developer tax incentives for youth centers in new tracts	Differential taxing for employers with health coverage	Negotiated property tax incentives for community facilities in schools
13. Use local police powers: patrol, detention, and diversion	Identify disparate arrest and disposition outcomes by race and ethnicity	Identifying likely repeat offenders	Training police to work with homeless family members with mental illness and substance abuse problems	Continuation and "second chance" schools
14. Fund services provided by other organizations	Allocation of federal block grants	Family support programs	Medicaid reimbursements for administrative expenses of school-based health clinics	School crossing guards

15. Provide service directly with LG staff: from LG's own $ or from state/federal $	Use local budget to frame priority choices in CYF programs	Support family resource centers from federal child welfare funding	Public health nurses outstationed in schools	Wide range of education finance roles

* CCI=Comprehensive Community Initiatives; NPOs=nonprofit organizations; CBOs=community-based organizations; CYF-children, youth, and family; LG= local government

At least three points implicit in this matrix need emphasis:
- The first point is that although these roles move generally from those that involve less to those that require more local government power and influence, within each category there are important gradations. For example, starting out with the city or county convening other major stakeholders may simply be "providing the table," but if discussions do not go well or reach sticking points, there may be a natural tendency to bring the local government into the talks as a mediator—a much more elaborate and exposed role.
- In an information age, providing information may be as important in the long run to organizations serving children and families as providing cash. Tracking the progress made by children and youth requires information from the institutions that serve them–or the institutions we hope they will not re-enter once diverted–schools, child welfare agencies, police departments, probation agencies. "Data treaties" may yield children-serving agencies more long-term power to achieve sustainability than a small, one-time grant for a pilot project, by proving that their programs really make a difference. And providing information to working lower-income families about the income benefits programs and child care assistance programs may be far more valuable than other, softer-service forms of "family support" that do not support families in securing the income benefits to which they are entitled.
- "Filling in the boxes" of all fifteen categories does not necessarily guarantee strategic policy–it may make it harder. Strategy results from the choices made by local policy leaders among roles and the concentration of effort on a few of them, not the attempt to do a little in a lot of places. Elsewhere, this has been described as seeking the answer to the question "where is Normandy?" evoking the choice made by Eisenhower and his planners in deciding where to invade France. They did not choose several places and then divide their forces along many fronts–they invaded in force at one place judged to be critical and winnable. Chapter 3 discusses strategic policy in greater depth.

The use of pilot projects as though they represented new policy is especially problematic for local governments. Token efforts and pilot projects that address children's needs with symbolic allocations and the formation of new agencies can have three results: they cost credibility as they are eventually recognized to be merely palliative; they dissipate scarce citizen energy and social capital; and they detract from advocacy efforts aimed at the ripest private and intergovernmental targets.

How can the roles of local governments be widened and deepened?

So there are multiple roles which local governments can play, and which some of them have played. But how can more of them be helped, persuaded, or pressured to adopt such roles?

The good news is that an increasing number of cities and counties have gone beyond the four minimal positions described at the beginning of this chapter, and have begun to utilize a wide array of policy tools to address wider roles in children and youth policy. A recent assessment of local government and its receptivity to systems reform pointed out that four traditional roles of local government—controller, regulator, funder, and service provider—have been joined by four newer roles:

> **Family income support as a critical role**
>
> Local governments can make a big difference in the lives of their working lower-income families by connecting those families with the income benefits they are eligible for but do not receive. In some counties, as many as 50% of all families eligible for the Earned Income Tax Credit do not receive it; food stamps, Medicaid, and child care assistance are also under-utilized by millions of working families who do not receive these benefits due to them as a part of the commitment to "make work pay" made in welfare reform. Outreach and tracking the enrollments of their residents are critical roles for local governments to play. These benefits can provide as much as $5,000 in annual income benefits for some families.

- convener: bringing groups together to work jointly on issues;
- facilitator: helping groups resolve conflicts and reach consensus;
- catalyst: making change happen;
- partner: combining government resources with others.[10]

These newer roles, while described too vaguely to enable assessment of whether specific cities and counties are measuring up to these roles, are more challenging for local government. But these authors felt that a growing body of practice was a resource for cities and counties that were trying to move in these directions, and cited some examples in support of their contention. They and others have also described some of the tools used by local government in developing children and family policy. These tools include both information tools and tools that can be used in building wider consensus about values, and will be reviewed in depth in Chapter 4.

Two major resources: The NLC and USCM projects

The National League of Cities (NLC) has for many years provided city governments with information and networking opportunities focused on issues affecting children and youth. In 2000, NLC launched a new Institute for Youth, Education, and Families to build upon and dramatically expand the earlier work of its Children and Families in Cities Program, which had existed since 1986. Boston Mayor Thomas M. Menino, a leader in the Institute's creation, describes this new entity as "an action tank, not a think tank."[11]

The Institute has established the following five "core program areas" to guide and focus its early efforts:

- education
- youth development
- the safety and protection of children and youth
- early childhood development
- family economic security

These five items make up a much broader agenda than the typical local government, and represent one of the most comprehensive visions ever set forth of what local government's role should encompass in dealing with children and families.

Using this broad agenda as a starting point, the Institute is a national resource to local elected officials and other community leaders. It provides guidance and assistance, compiles and disseminates information on promising strategies and best practices, builds networks of local officials working on similar issues and concerns, and conducts research on the key challenges facing municipalities in these core program areas. It collaborates with a broad range of national partners and works with the nation's 49 state municipal leagues to reach local officials in up to 18,000 cities and towns across America.

Through the Institute, municipal officials have direct access to a broad array of strategies and tools that can help them strengthen families and enhance the well being of children and youth. Action kits have been developed, technical assistance projects have been launched, and a website and audio conferences have spotlighted what cities are actually doing. The NLC has emphasized the issues of improving public schools, early childhood programs, enhancing after school programs, developing transitional jobs programs, and promoting youth leadership.

The NLC has also produced some of the most useful documentation of local governments' roles toward children and families. In 1989, several hundred cities and towns responded to a survey about the needs of children and families. In 1995, 780 cities responded to an updated version of the survey, which was summarized in the 1996 NLC report *Critical Needs, Critical Choices*. A set of targeted telephone interviews in 1999 was the basis for a new report issued the following year by the Institute, *City Voices, Children's Needs: New Ways of Taking Action*. Conferences have been held every two years since 1993 on the theme of "Your City's Families," with an emphasis upon model programs and exchange of ideas among city governments.

Since 2002, the United States Conference of Mayors (USCM) has operated a similar project, with support from the Annie E. Casey Foundation and other sources. In May 2003, the USCM Partnership for Working Families published a report on Working Families, with 39 examples of family programs and policy from 27 different cities.[12] The USCM project has emphasized Earned Income Tax Credit campaigns and other measures of direct benefit to lower-income working families.

The challenge in such projects, based upon past experience with public interest groups, is the need for a balanced picture of both accomplishments and shortcomings. We do not live in Lake Wobegone, where "all children are above average" and where all governments can pretend to be above average. Without honest criticism of well-intentioned efforts that fall short of their goals—or those that set goals far short of the possible—there is no way to fully appreciate the very real accomplishments of those cities and counties that have taken risks, demonstrated leadership, and allocated non-token resources to children and family issues. Some cities and counties do a lot better than others, and deserve credit for their efforts. And some undeniably do a lot less, and deserve more accountability for what they fail to do—or fail even to try to do.

Cities and counties are far more engaged with children and family issues than they were nearly four decades ago when federal programs for local government began expanding. Some cities and counties were still refusing federal aid for human services programs in the mid-1960's. Local governments have come a long way since then, to be sure. But it does no disservice, and may even give fuller credit to those cities and counties that have led this progress, to contrast them with the norm: far less activism than is needed, possible, or desirable.

What about the states?

Cities and counties are creatures of the states, legally, although home rule and charter status give some cities and counties greater powers than their counterparts may have in other states. But the state legal

> **Strategic Planning: A Preview**
>
> The primary tasks in taking strategic planning for children and families seriously at the local level include:
> 1. An assessment of the universe of need among all children and families
> 2. An assessment of current programs that address that need: their goals, scale, and measures of effectiveness
> 3. A review of current spending (a "children's budget")
> 4. A review of non-financial assets in the community that address children and family needs
> 5. A review of current indicators of the well-being of children and families (a "score card")
> 6. Involvement of key stakeholders in an assessment of current programs' adequacy: parents, youth, policy leaders, officials from schools, public safety, and other public, nonprofit, and private agencies providing services
> 7. Scenarios for the future: what would happen if current trends continue, what external events or internal assets might create new opportunities to change trend lines and improve outcomes

framework is powerfully determinative of what local governments do and what they don't do. While this book is focusing on the local government role–in part because cities and counties too often wait for states to take the lead–there are recent policy changes in some states that have begun to reshape state-local relations around children's issues in those states. Chapter 7 will explore these further, arguing that fiscal inequities created and reinforced by the states are fundamental constraints for local governments in responding to children and family needs—but not adequate excuses, since there are numerous non-fiscal roles that cities and counties can and do play.

The policy context of local governments' roles is unavoidably constrained by the fiscal realities of the American federal system. No credible argument can be made for local governments to play larger roles in children and family policy if that argument ignores the fiscal strains affecting many cities and counties.

But two sets of facts strengthen the case for wider local governmental roles:

- not all local governments are in dire straits, and
- there are many important roles that can be played that are not resource-dependent—they are leadership-dependent, but not resource-dependent. The roles set forth in the matrix presented above make this clear: only two of the fifteen roles involve direct funding.

Most of this book takes as given the current level of resources available to local government, and also assumes no major changes in federal or state policy toward cities and counties. I advocate strongly for changes in both, and Chapter 7 discusses both, though briefly. In addition, a significant emphasis is given to the intergovernmental advocacy role of local government, since a critical part of local children and family policy is to seek greater equity in resources they receive. But there is little evidence that state or federal support for children and family policy will substantially increase, and the case made in this book that local government can and should do more does not rest on those contingencies.

Why and how should local policy for children and families be more strategic?

When there is a debate over "America's foreign policy," what is usually being discussed is the wide variety of different positions taken by the national government toward different countries, toward regions of the world, and on issues such as global trade, arms policy, and world health. No one of these equals foreign policy, yet it is recognized that goals in one part of the world may come into conflict with those in other regions, which creates the need for an overall framework of goals and priorities to help decide how to resolve the conflict. And usually, it is seen as better foreign policy when a reasonably coherent overview is visible in foreign policymaking than when each of these decisions is debated separately without reference to all the others.

The call for local government to be more strategic asks for a similar move toward coherence. What is sought is not a uniform, comprehensive framework into which every policy and program neatly fits, but a move in the direction of seeing connections where there is too often isolation and insularity. In Chapter 3 we set forth a more detailed argument for strategic policy, but its major ingredients can be summarized here.

Strategic policy includes:

- *Priorities* based on targeting clients who need the most help, clients who *can* be helped, ethnic, gender, or geographic focus, or some other defensible criterion of priority-setting;
- An effort to coordinate above the level of individual projects, seeking to determine how different programs might *fit together* and reinforce each other's goals;
- An effort to determine the *effectiveness* of resource allocations and to *shift resources over time* from less effective to more effective programs, including an assessment of whether a program has an adequate *dosage* of services to make an impact, rather than allocating token levels of resources for maximum visibility;
- Programs and policy designed to address the *root causes* of problems, not just their symptoms, and the collection of adequate information to determine which forces are most powerful in creating the problem;
- Resources strategies that seek to *leverage other agencies' funding as well as to mobilize social capital at the community level;*
- A policy which looks past children to address *family issues* as well, taking a two-generation (and sometimes three-generation) approach to programs and recognizing the crucial importance of parents and caretakers in determining the life chances of children;
- An effort to escape the boxes of children, youth, and family policy to assess impact on the cross-cutting realms of *race and culture, community and neighborhood development;*
- An effort to use the *roles matrix* in this chapter (or another one) to consider how a local government might play more than one role in a program and which roles would be most effective in achieving its goals.

The case for being strategic rests on three primary arguments:

1. Without strategy in the form of sustained priorities, every program for children and families is equally important, and local government is at risk of being merely reactive to the latest crisis or the latest external funding source.
2. Without strategy, each new program has an equal claim to continue, resulting in a patchwork of programs that represent nothing more than an obsolete map of past good intentions, without any direct connection with the needs of the future.
3. Strategy demands clarity about intended results, and sets up a feedback loop in which appropriate evaluation of whether those results were achieved can lead to better use of scarce resources.

To summarize, strategic policy for children and families requires a framework which allows decisions about how to provide sustained services and supports to children and their parents to be made across programs over time, rather than in a single isolated program arena in a single year, with a single grant or line item. For example, a children's policy that addresses issues of early childhood from birth to school necessarily depends upon efforts in more than one system, such as well-baby care, developmental disabilities, or preschool. To be strategic in making early childhood policy would require an effort to make decisions in light of the reality that children move from one system to another, while others may be served by more than one system at a time. As a result, different roles are necessary for different government bodies to respond to these multiple needs. At the local level, a city may change its zoning to encourage child care centers, a county may distribute state and federal funds for child care for welfare-leaving parents, and a school district may design new school buildings so that preschool centers can be placed adjacent to elementary schools. To address early childhood policy as though it "belonged" to any one system, such as maternal and child health, or child care providers, would overlook the multiple needs of the children who need the most help.

Often, policy is confused with the much simpler task of launching new *programs*. A local or state government may announce a new initiative that is heralded as a policy change, and attention shifts to that program. The deep categorical bias of American pragmatism and the geography and legal structure of American politics combine to create much more powerful incentives to start new programs than to reconcile old ones, which is the real challenge of making policy. Policy made by the accretion of layers upon layers of separate programs is part of the problem faced by local governments. *But policy is not just new programs.* Policy deals with how programs fit together, which programs are given priority, which are given new and flexible resources, and how feedback on programs' effectiveness is used in budgeting and planning new programs. Chapter 3 discusses how city and county policy can be more strategic, and defines what being strategic means in the context of policy for children, youth, and families.

Children and youth as a focus vs. families as a focus: which "handle"?

There are two overlapping "handles" for addressing the question of what cities and counties do for children and families: approaches from the perspective of children and youth or from the perspective of families and parents. The arguments for each are set forth briefly below:

Why Children and Youth?	Why Families?
Tracking outcomes for children and youth is the best way to measure longer-term outcomes—do they get better? do they succeed in school and later life?	The attributes of parents—their income and education, their parenting skills, their behavior, health, addictions, and aspirations—all combine to make up the most profound influences on any child's life outcomes.
A significant number of children do not live with their biological parents and their life chances depend upon the services and supports they receive and their own qualities of resiliency.	Many services and supports for children and youth require active parental involvement for entry, eligibility, and success.
The problems of a single child referred "into the system" are often the windows into working with a "whole family."	The family as a microcosm of society needs to be seen as a basic unit of social policy.
Assessing the level of children's needs is the best lever for policy change, by showing how many children are affected by an issue.	Intergenerational (or "two-generation") programs have proven to be the most effective ones in improving the long-term futures of children.

This framework should not mistakenly convey that this is an either-or choice. The ideal policy process includes both—starting with an entry point that focuses on either children or parents, but adding the missing pieces to ensure that policy is broad enough to make a difference. Using such an approach would neither exclude children in addressing family issues, nor exclude parents in addressing children and youth issues.

Yet the fragmentation of the policy process in most local governments creates a continuing risk that the entry point may become the *only* point and that policy will fade away in favor of a few projects. And so a "children's office" or initiatives aimed at developing "family policy" concentrate their work primarily on only one side of the equation. Offices for child care coordination, for example, rarely address family income supports, although they can be the most important determinant of whether a family can afford higher-quality child care.

And many treatment programs for substance-abusing parents make no provision for the children of these parents; some treatment data systems don't even record whether clients have children.

It is not just administrative fragmentation; there are also political reasons that family policy is separated from policy affecting children and youth. Younger children are less threatening, less subject to blame, as Americans revert to their deep historical view of the "deserving and undeserving poor." Older youth are more threatening, as their behavior and opposition to authority comes into view, and parents are seen as even more accountable for their behavior. In addition, the arena of "family values" is highly charged politically, affected by the tangled tasks of defining what is a family and which lifestyles are acceptable and which are not. All these make local officials at times more reluctant to venture into family policy.

Yet there are countertrends, which we will examine in later chapters, especially Chapter 8 on families and generations. The Bush administration is comfortable addressing issues of marriage and parenthood, and earlier administrations have put the issue of child support—clearly a family issue in part—in a much brighter spotlight than it previously had. There is increasing discussion of what to do about the growing number of lower-income working families at the bottom of the economy, including an approach we will look at in this book which seeks to ensure that they receive the full array of income work supports for which they are eligible.

Family policy: An overview

Local government can't affect family policy at certain fundamental points:
- It can't redistribute income to lower-income families
- It can't easily change state and federal policy without developing a strong consensus among most local governments and finding other political allies
- It can't reverse broad social trends by itself, such as those that result in one-third of all births to unmarried mothers, or those that create a continuing demand for illegal drugs

But it can play a vital role in several other areas affecting families:
- It can *implement* state and federal policy toward families in ways that increase families' access to existing benefits and family supports
- It can plan and administer local programs to take family needs and assets into account, such as designing family-friendly facilities
- It can actively consider both parents and children in the design and implementation of two-generation programs
- It can advocate for policies and programs that incorporate the above goals and principles.

In later chapters, the challenges of addressing family policy issues will be reviewed further.

Children and family policy as policy about poverty

Ultimately, the question of the role of local government in children and family policy can be reframed as a simpler question: what can local government do about poverty?

- On fundamental redistribution of wealth, the answer is not much.
- On connecting families with benefits, the answer is quite a good deal.
- On improving the earning power of families, the answer is more than most of them are doing, through a combination of active roles in job training and economic development and increased attention to vocational and adult education.
- On giving children a better shot at the best possible school readiness and K-12 academic achievement—which have unquestioned impact on eventual family income—local governments can, if they sustain their role, be a powerful force for accountability by developing their own benchmarks of reasonable progress for schools and then annually reviewing those benchmarks.
- On tracking the results of state and federal policy that aims at poverty reduction, local governments have excellent resources for monitoring progress over time: they have a ringside seat at the fight, they can see and annually report on the outcomes, and they can point to fair and unfair tactics being used by the participants. They can take sides, and call upon other actors in the federal system and in the local polity and economy to do their part, while local government is doing its part.

So the question is not whether local governments should be held solely responsible for poverty in their cities and counties. The structural barriers to reducing poverty at the local level are formidable, summarized by Kubisch and her colleagues at the Aspen Institute:

> ...deeply embedded racism, changes in the political and funding climates, population mobility, and public policies and investments that isolate poor people in the inner cities.

Cities and counties do not control the underlying causes of these forces—although they can take action in each of these areas. The debate is over whether they should try to reverse these powerful forces—it is whether they acknowledge their existence and play the roles described above where they *can* make a difference.

And so it is completely fair to ask what local governments are doing to play these other roles that are consistent with their powers, resources, and authority. As the Aspen Institute staff put it in their recent assessment of community initiatives:

> The solution...involves working more deeply within communities and more aggressively beyond their bounds.[13]

While these words were written of comprehensive community initiatives, they are equally true of cities and counties. Working more deeply within city and county boundaries, and more aggressively in intergovernmental advocacy are appropriate goals for local governments.

But poverty is a problem that is almost untouchable at times in local government. It is as though there are some problems that must not even be discussed because admitting the issue is real will require a response. Sometimes even mentioning the issue causes groups and leaders to recoil in a kind of fear that they may be held accountable for the problem.

Three examples, drawn from two different counties within a recent week's time may illustrate this aversion:

- A county agency had concluded a strategic planning exercise that had identified as a high priority issue the growing economic segregation of the county into haves and have-nots. But when this result was taken to members of the agency's board, the reaction was that the agency should not address it. One member said "We can't do anything about equalizing incomes."

- Second example, different county: A planning group was discussing how to ensure that clients of a drug treatment program—women with their children in residential treatment with them—would have adequate aftercare services to prevent relapse. The group agreed that a recurring problem for the women was the lack of adequate housing and the low wages earned by graduates of the program once they went to work. But the consensus of the group was that the agency could really do nothing about either the wages or the housing gap. One member commented, "These women are just going to have to get it together themselves—we can't give them services for the rest of their lives."

- Third example: in reviewing a countywide report card that used multiple measures of child poverty in contrast to the number of children who were no longer enrolled in welfare, a county official argued that children in poverty should not be listed as an indicator, since there was no mandate in the welfare reform legislation to address poverty and "I've never heard of any law that says we're supposed to reduce poverty."

All three of these policy discussions were essentially about poverty. In all three cases, the group or individuals involved became anxious once poverty was identified as the issue, and sought to rule the topic out of order as "something we really can't do anything about." A tactic used in all three cases is to argue against a polarized, straw man position that had never been proposed: "equalizing income," or "serving them for the rest of their lives." Using these tactics, local governments retreat from addressing poverty as an issue because they do not understand how to develop a way to address those finite pieces of the problem which local government really can do something about.

Ethical dimensions of policy

Policy also means making hard choices among different values. After the best possible technical data collection and analysis has been carried out, there will still be important choices among competing values that the numbers won't answer.

Cities and counties make ethical choices at many levels. Cities and counties both fund hospitals, directly or indirectly, and in many of those hospitals a new profession has grown up in the past twenty years–the hospital ethicist who helps doctors and families frame and think about critical choices, often end-of-life choices. But local governments also face ethical issues in many other non-health arenas, though not always as visibly.

Strategy is about choice, and so is ethics: choosing the good, the fair response to need. Raising to visibility and debating the ethical choices made every day in local government budgets and operations would help frame strategic choices better. For example, a hidden ethical choice is often made that many programs should each get a little funding for political reasons. The unspoken premise of that policy choice is that programs' effectiveness in improving children's lives does not matter as much as their political effects. There is clear ethical content to that kind of decision. Similarly, the issue of how much "dosage" a program requires to be effective, choices about where to concentrate resources, decisions about which children and families to target with limited resources, choices about who should get "second chance" programs, where to draw the line and remove children from their family based on abuse and neglect, decisions about how long to keep silent about the evidence that a program is failing to use its scarce resources effectively–all of these are ethical choices. But policy leaders and front-line staff both prefer at times to frame these as issues of resources and programmatic operations, rather than as ethical choices. We will explore these issues further in Chapter 5.

Race and culture in children and youth policy

In addressing the needs of children and families, the issues of race and culture are inextricably caught up with public policy. Parents from different cultures socialize their children to different values, they discipline their children differently, they view education and schools' responsibilities differently, and they hold adolescents accountable in different ways. All of these cultural underpinnings of family make culture a critical part of policy making–but many cities and counties make policy for racial and linguistic groups by allowing officials with too little understanding to make such decisions for parents, rather than with them. The issues of race and culture deserve greater attention than they typically receive in making policy for children and youth. Being strategic about policy for children and youth requires more than a thin layer of talk about diversity or an in-service workshop on "cultural competency." It requires a policy process that considers the cultural sensitivity and racial impacts of policy and program design as important as its fiscal design, and consults widely with parents and other community members in developing both programs and policies.[14] These issues will be discussed further in Chapter 9.

Communities, neighborhoods, and citizens: Missing players?

This chapter began by describing the setting of communities as a place where children grow up. But policy making at times ignores this important geographic base of policy. The extent of citizen, parent, and community involvement in policy for children and youth is a critical variable, to which lip service is more often paid than serious resources are devoted.

Yet here, too, exemplary cities and counties have done much more than the norm in reaching out to their citizens and to parents and other community members. While a requirement for "citizen participation" has long been a feature of federal and foundation funding, local governments can observe these requirements minimally with little fear of federal response. But some cities and counties have gone well beyond these minima to create new forms of decentralized governance, to cooperate as equal partners in local collaboratives, and to provide basic information about local government operations to community-based organizations.[15] In other cities and counties, the leadership is clearly at the community and neighborhood level, with local government at the table of stakeholders but not a leader and, at times, not even an active partner.

The geography of place is unavoidably caught up with the sociology and the economy of race and culture as they affect children and families. A rich new literature of community development and the dynamics of community-based organizations, including comprehensive community initiatives (CCIs), has emerged and has much to say about the intersection of children and family policy with community development policy.[16] We will explore these different responses to community initiatives in Chapter 10.

Conclusion: Remembering our history and creating our future

Remembering our history

Theda Skocpol has provided an immense service in reviewing the history of social programs in the U.S. in light of contemporary efforts to build social movements. Robert Putnam's controversial remembrance of things past in *Bowling Alone*, while far from a consensus view, has reframed aspects of the loss of community that Robert Nisbet and earlier writers linked to the decline of the city. Geraldine Youcha's poignant recalling of child care arrangements from colonial times to the present is largely set in American cities.[17]

We need to remember that the history of American cities is significantly the history of what happens to children and youth. Our cities are historic in their functions as places where children were educated, became orphaned, were removed from "incompetent" parents, became delinquent, tried alcohol, tobacco, and other drugs–and succeeded in great majorities in becoming middle class enough to move away from central cities or rise to political and economic power within them. Huck Finn and Tom Sawyer notwithstanding, many of the great coming of age novels in American literature are set in cities, stories of youth affected by the sweeping changes in their cities. Holden Caulfield wanted to be in the rye, but he roamed around New York, Bigger Thomas was from a vital part of Chicago, Philip Roth has told and re-told the stories of growing up in

Newark, and Victor Villaseñor has written movingly of the vitality of youth in the barrios of Southern California.

But it is not only the fictional history of cities we need to remember–it is also the programmatic and policy history. It is an inevitable and perhaps self-interested point for a sometimes policy wonk whose career dates back to the mid-60's to point out that many younger professionals are largely unaware of the more recent history of their fields. But it has the advantage of being true.

The community action program, Model Cities, Neighborhood Services Programs, the quest for intergovernmental coordination machinery, urban decentralization, neighborhood city halls, the waves and "ladders" of citizen participation, the income vs. services debate, the waves of devolution and block granting, along with decategorization and recategorization, and the ever-present overlay of the civil rights movement, immigration, and attitudes toward poverty–all these make up the recent environment of children's policy. But the vast majority of local officials seem to have little awareness of how these pieces fit together or how they make up the historic layers of their own cities' recent history.

For example, in the past five years or so, several reports have come out describing family resource centers as a major innovation, without placing them in the context of settlement houses or the 3,000 multi-service centers that existed decades ago at the peak of the Great Society (as documented by numerous federal studies). New proposals for governance changes have often ignored the literature and practice of neighborhood government and decentralization efforts of the past forty years. And discussions of citizen participation have ignored the seminal earlier work of Joyce Epstein and Sherry Arnstein on categories of citizen participation in community and education settings, as we will discuss further in Chapter 10.

But why does it matter? It matters because the leaders and staffs of local governments, if they do not understand the barriers encountered in the last four or five attempts to decentralize city government and create true neighborhood governance, will blindly and needlessly repeat many of the same mistakes. And that will be another setback for the cause of children and family policy in cities and counties.

The challenge here is to academic institutions, in-service training institutions, and the human resources staffs of local government: how do we train and re-train workers at both policy and front-line levels to understand the history of what they are trying to do with children and families? More broadly, there is a role for providing the same awareness of history to the nonprofit and community-based children's services staff who are often lower-paid and less frequently part of ongoing staff development investments than public service professionals.

The trends creating our future

What are the reasons for optimism? And what are the best places to begin?

In some cities and counties, the beginning of a strategic policy effort has already happened. In others, it will take connections among now-separate efforts to begin to move from the tactical to the strategic. Further good news is visible in an emerging set of trends, some of which are increasing the relevance of children and youth issues, while others are expanding the tools available to respond to those issues in a less fragmented way.

- Immigration will continue to add children to the population–both the children of highly educated professionals who can buy their way into the high ranges of the economy and the children of lower-skilled workers who will have to learn their way into the economy. But the needs of both kinds of children will add to the demands on local government to address children and youth policy more coherently.

- Demographic change will mean that the *relative* size of the youth cohort will shrink as aging becomes a longer process and more old persons stay alive longer. But the role of youth in an aging society will remain important, and potentially more important, because of tensions between the needs of youth and the needs of the older population–who vote in disproportionately higher amounts than other adults. Intergenerational political and intra-community tensions will both increase, as conflict among age groups assumes some of the same perceived zero-sum nature of inter-ethnic conflict in an earlier era.

- The continuing refinements of software and the use of the internet as a tool for data collection will in the next 5-10 years provide far better data on program effectiveness than has been available to most local governments. This will create a further knowledge management barrier, as raw data flows in and must be synthesized to help make decisions about funding and program design. Yet the increase in information power will bring new accountability for results to programs for children and youth, which may accelerate the process of weeding out the least effective programs in favor of the most effective ones.

- Privacy and confidentiality issues will be addressed repeatedly by local government as it decides how to protect the data it collects about its residents who use public services, while at the same time using new methods to connect families with the services they need.

- Cyberdemocracy raises fascinating questions for local governments. We will see the wider use of the Internet to communicate citizen preferences and the capacity of governments today to take a daily poll of all connected residents on any subject, post the survey on the web, and allow citizens to see daily updates of the survey results. But for children and family issues, the question may be how to filter immediate reactions about youth violence or egregious incidents of child abuse so that they lead to thoughtful policy responses rather than emotional lunges toward the most simplistic options available.[18]

- The trend toward privatization of services will continue to affect children's services, such as schools, corrections facilities, child welfare agencies, child care, and a host of other program areas yield to the initial hopes of achieving either cheaper programs or better results. But the accountability trend mentioned above seems likely to raise the stakes for privatized firms, with both the public and policymakers better able to

monitor bottom line results for children and youth, as well as profits for
these firms.

- The arguments over parent choice in education and other services are
  unlikely to decline in volume or importance; they may be joined by
  growing debates over choices being made by parents in early care for
  their children, with an increasing body of evidence that the expanded
  national investment in early care for welfare-leaving and working poor
  families has led to an expansion of the lowest quality care as a direct
  result of parents' perceptions of what is available to them.

- Biotechnology, an exploding scientific arena whose effects on national
  policy debates are highly visible, will raise numerous issues that will
  play out in local governments. The ability to influence the behavior of
  children and youth will increase with biotechnology and other
  technological advances, and the debate over what methods of control
  and treatment are ethically acceptable in criminal justice, mental health,
  and special education systems will outspeed the legal system's ability to
  regulate policy toward youth behavior. Loss of privacy for youth with
  law violations, electronic surveillance of child care facilities, invasive
  surgery and compulsory medications for youth with violent offenses,
  home detention through electronic means–there are a host of behavior-
  altering interventions that will be debated, and local government will be
  the arena in which many of these debates take place.

Several of these issues underscore the degree to which ethical frameworks
may help local governments address these issues more thoughtfully. The arenas
of data privacy, biotechnology, and cyberdemocracy are unavoidably ethical in
nature.

Are local governments ready for these new waves of children and youth
issues? Ready or not, these issues are emerging rapidly, and some are already
here. It seems clear that in at least some cities and counties they will compel a
different style of policymaking from that of the reactive, tactical past. That could
be a very good thing for the visibility and effectiveness of policymaking toward
children and youth.

NOTES

[1] In this book, the word *policy* is used to mean deliberate action by local general
purpose governments–cities and counties (but not school districts)–to benefit children and
families through use of the legal powers and the financial and political resources of those
governments and their officials.

[2] The thirteen states (including the District of Columbia) where local government
handles these children's services functions include a large portion of the lower-income
children in the nation, since these include the largest and most diverse states in the nation.
These states include California, Colorado, New York, Minnesota, New Jersey,
Wisconsin, Ohio, Illinois, Maryland, North Carolina, and Virginia.

[3] One collection of articles on children's policy published by Brookings in 1996 included an index entry for federal and state government, but none for cities or counties. Local government was discussed primarily in terms of the geography of inner city youth problems; seven programmatic areas were highlighted as the key arenas for social policy affecting children: economic security, education, child care, youth employment, health care, crime and delinquency, and child abuse. Irwin Garfinkel, Jennifer Hochschild, and Sara McLanahan, eds. *Social Policies for Children.* (Washington, D.C.: Brookings Institution, 1996).

[4] Frederick Wirt, *Power in the City: Decision Making in San Francisco.* (Berkeley, Ca.: University of California Press, 1974).

[5] These estimates have been developed through review of city, county, and education budgets in California over the past five years by the Center for Collaboration for Children at California State University, Fullerton.

[6] Bruce Katz and Katherine Allen, "Cities Matter: Shifting the Focus of Welfare Reform," *The Brookings Review.* (Summer 2001):30-33.

[7] Katz and Allen, "Cities Matter," 32.

[8] Francine H. Jacobs & Margery W. Davies (eds.), *More than kissing babies? Current child and family policy in the United States.* (Westport, Ct: Auburn House, 1994).

[9] Paul T. Hill and Mary Beth Celio, *Fixing Urban Schools.* (Washington, D.C.: The Brookings Institution, 1998).

[10] William. R. Potapchuk, Jarle P. Crocker, and William H. Schechter, *Systems Reform and Local Government.* (Washington, D.C.: National Civic League, 1998).

[11] National League of Cities, "Council on Youth, Education, and Families," http://www.nlc.org/nlc_org/site/programs/ (April 12, 2003)on Youth, Education, and Families," at http://www.nlc.org/nlc_org/site/programs/

[12] Conference of Mayors, "Working Families," http://www.usmayors.org/uscm/uscm_projects_services/workingfamilies/ (April 12, 2003).

[13] Anne Kubisch, Patricia Auspos, Prudence Brown, Robert Chaskin, Karen Fulbright-Anderson, and Ralph Hamilton. *Voices from the Field II. Reflections on Comprehensive Community Change.* (Washington, D.C.: The Aspen Institute, 2002), 17.

[14] Hedy Nai-Lin Chang, *Community Building and Diversity: Principles for Action.* (San Francisco, Ca.: California Tomorrow, 1997).

[15] Robert Chaskin and Clark Peters, *Decision Making and Action at the Neighborhood Level: An Exploration of Mechanisms and Processes.* (Chicago: Chapin Hall Center for Children, 2000)

[16] The Aspen Institute, *Voices from the Field I* (Washington, D.C.: The Aspen Institute, 1997). Kubisch et al. *Voices II.* Ronald F. Ferguson and William T. Dickens, eds. *Urban Problems and Community Development.* (Washington, D.C.: The Brookings Institution, 1999). Lisbeth Schorr, *Common Purpose.* (New York: Anchor Books, 1997).

[17] Theda Skocpol, *Social Policy in the United States: Future Possibilities in Historical Perspective.* (Princeton, N.J.: Princeton University Press, 1995). Robert Putnam, *Bowling Alone,* (New York: Simon and Schuster, 2000). Geraldine Youcha, *Minding the Children: Child Care in American from Colonial Times to the Present.* (New York: Scribner, 1995).

[18] Cass Sunstein, *Republic.com* (Princeton, N.J.: Princeton University Press, 2001).

STRATEGY AND THE REALITIES

Focusing on the structure and process of children and family policy can sometimes cause a drift away from its realities. This section summarizes briefly the very real problems we continue to face, as well as the significant progress we have made in responding to the aspirations and the needs of American children and their families.

The realities of life for the children and youth living in U.S. cities and counties range from very good to very, very bad.[1]

- 16% of American children—almost 12 million—live in poverty, meaning their parents' income is at or below the federal poverty level. Though a lower percentage, this is about the same number of children who lived in poverty in 1980.
- 7% of America's children—5 million—live in extreme poverty. This is a 17% increase from 2000. The parents of these children make half the federal poverty level, or $8,980 for a family of four.
- While the child poverty rate has been reduced by more than one quarter since it peaked in 1993, the decline stalled in 2001. The recent economic downturn has already led to increases in child poverty in several states.
- Research shows that, in most areas of the United States, it takes roughly double the federal poverty level to provide a family with the basic necessities of life like food and housing. But 38% of American children—27 million—live in low-income families below the level of 200% of the poverty level. This is a 3% increase from 2000.
- African American and Latino children live in low-income families in significantly higher rates than white children.
- 57% of African American children are low-income (down 3% from 2000), 64% of Latino (up 7%), and 34% of white children (up 3%) are low-income.
- Almost one in five young children (18 percent in 2000) in the United States lives in poverty during the early years that are so important to their future life chances. The 2.1 million children under age three who are poor face a greater likelihood of impaired development because of their increased exposure to a number of factors associated with poverty.
- An estimated 7.8 million children lacked health insurance in 2002.
- 2.8 million cases, involving about 5 million children, were referred for possible child abuse and neglect in 2000. Of these, 879,000 were

---

[1] Data in this section is drawn from a number of sources, including the National Center for Children in Poverty report *Low-income Children in the United States* (2003); Child Trends reports at www.childtrends.org; and CWLA's Fact Sheet at http://www.cwla.org/advocacy/nationalfactsheet03.htm

substantiated as abused or neglected, while a total of 550,000 children were in foster care as of September 30, 2000.

- 2.4 million grandparents were raising their grandchildren in 2000.
- Between 1.5 million and 3.3 million children witness some form of violence at home each year.
- In 2001, 11 percent of people aged 16 to 24 had dropped out of high school, compared to 15 percent in 1972. The dropout rate for Hispanics has declined significantly since 1972, when it was at 34 percent, but remained extremely high in 2001 at 27 percent. The dropout rate for Hispanics born outside the U.S. was nearly three times that of first-generation Hispanics born in the U.S. (43 percent compared to 15 percent).
- Among 12th-grade students, rates of binge drinking fell from a high of 41.4 percent in 1981 to 27.5 percent in 1993, but have remained steady at around 30 percent through 2000. Having an alcoholic beverage on one or more occasions in the previous 30 days was reported by 52 percent of 12th-grade students in 1998 but dropped slightly to 50 percent in 2000.
- A total of 2.5 million juveniles were arrested in 1999.
- National estimates of use of illicit drugs and alcohol by pregnant women range from 3% up to 17%; the most knowledgeable source estimates 8-15% use of illicit drugs and the most recent study (by the Center for Disease Control and Prevention) found that 12.8% of pregnant women consumed some alcohol during the previous month.
- A total of 1.5 million children are prenatally exposed to alcohol, tobacco, and illicit drugs.
- Of all school-age children, 650,000 (1.3%) are limited in mobility, 470,000 (0.9%) have a self-care limitation, 2,743,000 (5.5%) have a communication limitation, and 5,237,000 (10.6%) have a limitation in learning ability. Overall, 6,075,000 school-age American children (12.3%) have some type of functional limitation.
- American students consistently test lower than their peers from other nations in standardized tests.
- If the strictest states' high school exit exams were applied to all high school seniors, as many as three-fourths of all students could not pass the exam.
- By 2000, eight years after most of the 1988 eighth grade cohort had graduated from high school, only 29 percent of them reported that they had attained a bachelor's degree or higher, in an economy that increasingly requires four years of college or its functional equivalent for adequate wages.
- Mayors estimate that as many as half of the persons requesting emergency food and shelter in their cities are families with children.
- Despite a decline since a peak in 1990, there were 455,000 births to teen parents in 2001.

These problems create many policy challenges. The tendency of local officials is at times to read such statistics and either

- Give up on making more than token impact because the problems are so big and they perceive their resources to be so small;
- Respond to whatever a "higher" level of the federal system is funding at present, adopting that fundable item as their agenda, or
- Use a specific "handle" or entry point for policy across these areas.

Any one of these statistics provides a justification for a programmatic intervention. But local governments adopt either tokenist or strategic responses based on the extent of their visions of a longer-range horizon and their staying power in moving from an entry point project to a wider policy intervention. Those with shorter time horizons settle for projects; those with an eye for the longer-range may begin with a project but move into implementation with some idea in view as to what the next steps might be.

In choosing different entry points for moving from projects to strategic policy, cities and counties must recognize that none of these are "the right one." Each responds to a local reality, building on hot issues, the significant infusion of new resources, or a unique form of local leadership. A carefully selected entry point may prove to be strategic—or may be degenerate under pressure into just another project.

A part of being strategic is looking beyond these strategic opportunities, rather than being driven by the issue of the moment or the latest grant announcement. Strategy includes springboarding from whatever is on the six o'clock news to a wider, longer-range perspective on how these immediate events create negotiating room or political capital for longer-range action. In the next section, we explore the parameters and tools of policy.

Introduction to Section 2:

Section 2 comprises four chapters that describe the tools and frameworks of policy-making in local government:

- Policy tools, including methods of using information and values in making decisions;
- Ethical factors that need to be used in framing and weighing decisions about children and families;
- Budgeting and fiscal analysis frameworks; and
- The nature of city and county government themselves as similar, but distinct policy settings, as well as a brief review of special districts and public authorities, and state and federal roles in policy.

Each of these provides context and capacity for local governments' efforts to make more strategic children and family policy; each demands stretching the current capacity of what most cities and counties are now doing.

Chapter 2: Missing from Theory and Practice: The Role of Local Government

The vast majority of books on children's policy place their emphasis on federal or state policies; the vast majority of books on local government mention children's policy not at all or very briefly; and the vast majority of books on community development, community building, and community capacity mention local government only in passing.

So this book either exists in a vacuum that no one much cares about—or we are trying to fill a significant gap that affects what 80 million children and youth get from the communities where they live and grow up. Obviously, I choose to believe the latter. But it is not enough to say most scholars and practitioners who care about children and family policy neglect local government. We need to answer two questions before prescribing what local governments should do about children:

1. Why have highly reputable writers and scholars neglected the role of local government or concluded that it is not a significant source of children and family policy?

2. What is the case against taking local government seriously as a source of strategic policy for children and families—and how can those arguments be answered?

Of the hundreds of books written on children's policy, local government, community development, and family services reform, several seem to best exemplify what thoughtful writers across these fields have said—or not said—about the subject we are addressing in this book.[1] This section will review each of these as they address or fail to address local governments' roles in children and family policy.

These works fall into three broad categories: those that largely ignore or dismiss the role of local government, those that mention it in passing or treat it primarily as an obstacle, and those that describe it as either a potential change agent or an important target for other change agents. In the section that follows, we will review different works that fall into the categories of the *dismissers*, the *mentioners*, and the *targeters*.

The Dismissers

One of the most negative prognoses comes in one of the few books that addresses the connections between local government and children's policy explicitly: Kahn and Kammerman's 1996 edited collection, *Children and Their Families in Big Cities: Strategies for Service Reform*.[2] They found

> ...no illustrations of cities that had successfully confronted [children's]
> problems on a citywide basis ...subsequent studies have searched in vain
> for big-city service exemplars.

Kahn and Kammerman emphasize larger cities, which they define as over 500,000 (29 cities) or 1 million (9 cities). If the thirty-four counties over 1 million are added, the definition covers only 63 jurisdictions, although they include 25.4% of the nation's population. They further restricted most of their discussion to community building initiatives in these cities, rather than the full range of city and county policy affecting children and families. Interestingly, in a work two years later, they concluded that

> Cities are the sites of programs and of delivery systems. It is they who
> can point the way, pilot the initiatives, or give states the benefit of their
> experience.[3]

Focusing on the effects of welfare reform, and based on discussions and field work in six cities that took place during 1995-97, this compilation highlighted the critical role of states and the political and financial disadvantages faced by big cities (and counties, in the case of Philadelphia, New York, and Los Angeles).

In a book on the social environment of children and families:

> Local governments figure prominently in discussions of decentralized
> services and informal supports. This will continue to be volatile as states
> and localities engage in new forms of budget battling...in the face of
> economic downturns and many a state's penchant for balancing deficit-
> ridden budgets by skimming inordinate proportions of [funds] truly
> intended for localities, many cities, towns, and neighborhoods will be
> required to fight even harder than before to maintain acceptable levels of
> funding.[4]

This is the only reference to the role of local governments in the book, with the exception of a paragraph suggesting the ways in which cities are anti-child and anti-family.

Another recent text on civic innovation deals only in passing with local governments' roles, and does so far more often in negative terms than positively.[5] And the recent assessment of community capacity-building undertaken by Robert Chaskin and his colleagues at Chapin Hall mentions local government in passing in discussing "exogenous influences and constraints," stating that building community capacity

> will require a broader shift in power, resources, and influence that allows
> communities to take advantage of opportunities and buffer themselves
> against *calamities born of actions by government* and business at the
> metropolitan level and beyond.[6]

In a provocative and wide-ranging monograph, Charles Bruner has described five different theories of change used in attempting to reform social services in poor neighborhoods.[7] In each of them, there are important roles for local government that affect the potential for enacting children and youth policy; yet Bruner does not often refer to local government in his discussion of the five approaches. The review of the five roles that follows suggests how each of these roles *could* impact local government.

   1. Prevention
      a. Local government's role in prevention includes the "primary systems" categorized by Richman and his colleagues from Chapin Hall as being the bottom level of services to children and families: parks and recreation, Little Leagues and soccer leagues, etc.[8]
      b. Local government operates and funds youth development programs and governs the siting and licensing of child care programs
      c. Local government is involved in various forms of family involvement and parent empowerment initiatives as prevention programs
      d. Local governments in some cities and counties focus on neighborhood improvement efforts targeted on lower-income neighborhoods and communities
   2. Services integration
      a. Local governments in some areas attempt to link families with income benefits through one-stop centers
      b. Local governments have provided facilities and out-stationed staff for siting co-located services
   3. Changing Front-line Practice
      a. Some of the staff these approaches propose to train and re-train currently work for cities and counties, and some work for agencies they fund or co-fund
      b. Local governments fund their own staff training and in-service education
      c. Some local governments have been involved in promoting interprofessional education for their own employees[9]
   4. Results-based accountability and comprehensive planning
      a. This is possibly the largest role for local governments, because they are the level of government closest to those programs that need results-based accountability
      b. Local governments have included provisions for results-based accountability outcomes as a base for funding their contract providers
   5. Building Grass-roots Capacity
      a. Local governments have opened their decision-making processes to wider community involvement, through community advisory groups
      b. Local governments have convened community organizations and coalitions, enabling them to make effective contact with each other, as modeled by the Beacons Schools project in New York City and the intermediary role of the Youth Development Institute[10]

But overall, as mentioned, the role of local government is rarely referenced in Bruner's monograph.[11]

Finally, in recent years, family policy has been discussed as an example of an area where it may be impossible to develop coherent federal governmental policies that reconcile widely differing views on the definition of a family, what government should do that families cannot do for themselves, and other broad areas of disagreement.[12] A counter-argument is that very powerful family policies already exist in the form of public subsidies for some kinds of families (those with mortgages who can deduct them from their taxes, for example) and biases that make it more difficult for some families to enter housing markets in many parts of the country. Just as in foreign policy, there are areas where inconsistency prevails over the attempt to be uniform, and family policy is certainly one of those arenas as well.

The Mentioners

In Ferguson and Dickens' edited collection on community development issues, several of the authors refer to local government as it affects power alignments and community development efforts. Ferguson reviews the prospects for what he calls (following Clavell, Pitt, and Yin's discussion in a separate article)[13] "the community option," which he summarizes as "more frontline functions of city government and some from the private sector...handed off to community-based organizations." Ferguson concludes that the community option needs challenging, but does not reject it. He calls for "more mixed alternatives" that combine front-line for-profit and government organizations.

In a section on youth and family development, Ferguson presents some of the closest links in any recent work between urban policy and children and family policy, using the example of the Beacon Schools in New York City as a model. It is worth noting, in making the case for local government as one of the important players, that the Beacon Schools were initiated by an agency of the city government, provided technical assistance support through a nonprofit entity, the Fund for the City of New York and the Youth Development Institute, and operated by neighborhood nonprofits. It is a solid example of a mixed strategy that makes clear what city governments can do to initiate and fund the start-ups of such projects, while encouraging other players to take an active role as well.[14]

One issue underscored by Ferguson and others in this collection is the great importance of public safety and schools in community development strategies. These twin drivers of family housing choice are both children's issues, as well as community development issues.[15] They build a foundation for a needed emphasis on public safety as a children's issue. Safety and the perception of safety affects where they can play, how far they can go to attend schools out of their own neighborhoods, and how safe they feel coming home from school and making acquaintances with adults in their own neighborhoods. Local governments who separate crime and children's policy into isolated compartments miss the payoffs of safe streets and sidewalks in the lives of children.

The income level of families matters in targeting resources on families. Ferguson notes that

> mayors across the nation share the goal of attracting and retaining middle-income residents to the inner city and are willing to spend public resources to achieve it.[16]

Again, he further suggests that "schools and safety" are the two most critical disadvantages of inner city neighborhoods that city officials care about changing to attract middle-income residents. But this is not entirely a zero-sum game, since attention by local governments to these two issues can make a big difference to lower-income families as well. Ferguson adds that the loss of middle-income families has a special negative effect on the socialization of youth, pointing to a further connection between income stability and children and family impact.

Ferguson notes that the role of local government is "rule-making," which echoes the emphasis in other frameworks of collaboration on changing the rules of local governance and systems as a higher-order form of collaboration that has more value than merely operating joint projects with external funding.[17] Ferguson repeatedly makes the point that trust is at the heart of collaboration and governance changes that build up the capacity of community groups.

A major publication of the Aspen Roundtable on Comprehensive Community initiatives—a policy forum that has sought closer links between the community development and children and families fields more fully than most other groups—refers to local government as part of an overall tension between "inside-outside" forces, within the neighborhood and outside it.[18] But in discussing governance issues as they arise in community initiatives, local government is listed simply as one of the stakeholders, without any detailed reference to its particular role. It should be noted that this source is primarily a compilation of the perspectives of those within CCIs, and this reflects their view of local government at the periphery of what they do, rather than a normative role by the authors. One respondent, however, did comment that "change insulated from the 'systems downtown' is nothing but therapy."

In a later work, the Aspen writers devote an entire chapter to the "outside game" for community initiatives, discussing the "localism" tactic that ignores local government and other external resources. In this work, the Aspen group certainly falls into the "targeter" classification, rather than merely mentioners.[19]

The Targeters

The third group of writers and reviewers of local initiatives goes beyond mentioning the role of local government to seeing its role as one of several critical elements of a comprehensive strategy aimed at changing systems, rather than merely running projects or joining coalitions. Nelson, for example, describes the Casey Foundation's continuing belief that a major investment needs to be made both at the neighborhood/community level and in the public systems changes that will open local government to more community action.[20]

Kagan and Pritchard emphasize the potential role of local government in services integration, noting that

Diminished optimism in efforts to link services has been accompanied by minimized faith in the federal government as a central catalyst for change. As a result, the locus of momentum has shifted from the federal to state and local efforts. Overall, recent efforts at linking services have strong local flavor, with impetus, planning and support coming from states, municipalities, the private sector, and professional organizations.[21]

They cite family resource centers and school-linked services as models of such locally based coordinative efforts.

Robert Chaskin's assessment in 1997 of local governments' roles in community-building directly addresses the different roles played by local governments in the seven cities they reviewed.22 While its subject remains community building and not children and family policy, it focuses more upon local governments' reactions to neighborhood-based governance than to its need to respond with its own actions. We will return to this tension between reactive and proactive roles in Chapter 10 when we focus directly on communities and neighborhoods. Chaskin summarizes the relationship of city governments with their neighborhoods as "with rare exception, distant at best and highly contentious at worst...across the cities surveyed."

Although Lisbeth Schorr refers to several model projects that have succeeded in replicating their efforts without more than passing reference to local governments' roles, like Ferguson and others she mentions the critical role of the city government in New York in expanding the Beacon Schools.[23] And in the monograph already mentioned in Chapter 1, William Potapchuk and his colleagues discuss at length the critical role of local governments in systems reform.

Local government in "best practices" and model programs

There are a number of model programs that have received a great deal of attention from students and observers of children and family policy in recent years. For the most part, these are not linked with the local jurisdictions in which they occur, although there are some important exceptions. One of the best known of these, reviewed by Lisbeth Schorr in both her landmark books on innovation, is the Sunset Park Center for Family Life. While not featured in description of its services, it has ties through the Beacon Schools program with the City and with state-local child welfare programs operated by the city. It is an example of a community-based program that is not dependent on local government, but that has developed close working relations with it and receives direct help from it in helping families.

Very few of these innovations, however, "belong to" city and county government. Reviewing the innovation awards of the Kennedy School/Ford Foundation innovation awards program since 1986, most of the awards given to local governments have been for non-human services programs, although in the past two years, Deschutes County, Oregon, received an award for its Commission on Children and Families and San Francisco City/County received an award for its kinship child welfare programs.

Another useful window on current practice comes from the experience of foundations as they fund and oversee projects at the local level. In a thoughtful review of their experience with the Casey Foundation's New Futures program, Don Crary and Otis Johnson reviewed their hands-on roles in Little Rock and Savannah. Their comments on the local government roles in those programs are revealing, and might best be summarized by this exchange:

> **Otis**...I think we haven't been clear about the political nature of this work. People tend to work with three different models in this field, and they tend to think their model is the only one that works. One is the collaborative model, where you bring all the different stakeholders together under the assumption that they all have some common interest at heart, and they all want to do the right thing, and they'll come together and do it and everybody will be happy. Then there's the professional planners model, where you bring together experts and planners to analyze the problem and come up with solutions. And because it's all so logical and rational, everybody is going to agree to it and march off to do what's right. Then you've got the conflict model, where the assumption is that the haves and the have-nots possess diametrically opposed interests, and if the have-nots are ever going to get anything from the haves, it will only be through conflict and struggle.
> But very few people realize you need all three models to make change. And if I could go back and start over with New Futures, I'd have been much clearer up front about the importance of using all three models, and reconciling them. Right now I'm most concerned about the confrontational piece. We've built the collaborative body. Now we need an advocacy body. Power yields nothing without a demand, and if you don't have a sophisticated advocacy group, there is nobody making a strong demand on behalf of people in the low-income community....If the school system is ever going to change, it's going to come from outside community pressure, not from an internal realization that we need reform.
> **Don:** I agree we need to increase the community's voice in the process. At the same time, the community needs a strong [intermediary organization] on the other side, to meet them. Because even if you build up the community, if there isn't someone who convinces the city government and the mayor that they in fact need to be at that table, that it's in the interest of the city to be at that table, that they must work with this neighborhood organization on answers — well, I don't know, without that, how it plays out. Because there's plenty of examples of good neighborhood organizations that can't make a dent in city hall.[24]

This nuanced view of local government—neither in charge in a top-down mode, nor out of the loop completely—seems much closer to what is likely to emerge in the wide middle ground between full leadership and passive disengagement of local government. It is also at odds with much of the literature on community building and children's policy, which assumes a lesser role.

The case against local government

As revealed by this overview of recent literature and best practices materials, the case against local government's relevance is often implicit, though it occasionally rises to visibility in discussion of recent history or assessments of the power realities of community development, notably in the Ferguson and Dickens compilation. Several arguments recur, however, in dismissing or arguing against local government in children and family policy—and in other major, linked arenas such as community development.

It is important to acknowledge and respond to the case against taking local government seriously as a source of children and family policy. Cities and counties are not left out of the discussions about the future of children, youth, and family policy for idle reasons; there are structural, financial, and political reasons that local governments are overlooked or dismissed in these discussions. Without agreeing with these arguments, they must be set forth and addressed because they are so frequent.

- The argument from history is that cities and counties haven't shown a concern for a children and families agenda and at times have opposed antipoverty strategies aimed at better outcomes for families. Historically, the role of city governments has been seen as a set of classic confrontations between status quo-oriented elected officials and advocates for community change, with city leaders supporting urban renewal and displacement in minority neighborhoods, opposing the early forms of community action in which federal funding came directly to community action agencies, and defining economic development primarily in terms of downtown interests. [25]

- The real leadership for community development is not in local government; it comes from community groups, nonprofits, and foundations, rather than local governments themselves.[26] An argument can be made—and increasingly is—that local government is simply not "where the action is." This argument points to comprehensive neighborhood and community development entities, privatization and service delivery by for-profit firms, and the imperatives of decentralizing from city governments to neighborhood governance.

- Nearly all public finance literature makes the point that local government is the level at which redistributionist policies are least likely to be successful, since those who pay taxes are so mobile in the medium and long range. To the extent that children, youth, and family policy cannot avoid the interests of lower-income families, a policy emphasis upon these beneficiaries is very difficult financially, as well as politically risky for local governments.

- Turnover in local government is so great there cannot be a sustained policy leadership because most initiatives get wiped out by the next administration, and the "B team"[27] is not supportive enough or deep enough to sustain the changes.

- State and federal policy really are the drivers and local policy is merely residual. This is really Fred Wirt's argument about "residual policy" updated to the 21st century. A variation of this argument is that local policy *is* significant, but it is unavoidably focused on the economic demands of local government as the bottom level of the federal system.

This argument holds that Wirt is right about that portion of local policy affecting children and families, which is merely residual because federal and state budget-making determines whether children and family programs can be sustained.

- Children and youth as non-voters really aren't important enough in local politics and policy; it is economic elites who most often determine local policy.

- This focus on economics means that in addition to budget-making, policy is driven by economic development as the highest priority—local governments compete on which businesses they can persuade to re-locate (or not to re-locate) and what jobs can be relocated or retained. As a result, policy for children, youth, and family issues, if it exists, is subordinated to these economic development priorities.

- Local government simply isn't very important in the intergovernmental arena, because it lacks flexible funding for family-oriented programs, except at token levels. It is often noted that localities are weaker partners in the intergovernmental system, with federal aid to cities having declined by nearly 20% between the early 1980's and the early 1990's. In the past decade, this trend has continued, although Clinton-era allocations for Empowerment and Enterprise communities reversed this somewhat. Yet numerous sources cite the structural deficits built into city and county budgets, which may ease in expansionary times but remain major barriers to expanded roles in support of lower-income residents. Ester Fuchs has called this "the permanent urban fiscal crisis."[28]

These are powerful arguments, and taken together they explain a good deal of why local governments have not been a focal point for those seeking to improve governmental policy toward children, youth, and families. But each of them overlooks important realities that need greater emphasis.

The Counter-case: Why local government matters and shouldn't be ignored

What is the counter-case to this history of local governmental neglect of children and family issues? How can the positive potential of local government best be framed and justified?

In several critical areas, there is ample evidence that cities and counties recognize and are willing to act on the connection between their policies and the well-being of their youngest residents:

- Cities are moving into education as an area too important to their futures to ignore, as documented by Paul Hill and recent developments in New York City.[29]

- A number of cities and counties are developing policies and programs in the area of early care and education.[30]

- Counties, in some county-administered welfare systems, have moved to reform the delivery of child welfare services at the community level.

- Some cities and counties, using the familiar dual entry points of economic development and job training programs, have moved on from these roles to address family income policies.[31]
- Cities and counties are addressing the problem of lower-income working family income with livable wage policies, affordable housing policies, and efforts to enroll city residents in work support programs. Counties in some areas of the nation are raising the second-generation question of welfare reform: what improvement has taken place in the overall well-being of children whose parents have left welfare? In Los Angeles, for example, a major effort is under way to use welfare incentive funding from the state to reach lower-income working families with a Family Economic Self-sufficiency Initiative.
- City governments in the early 21st century are very different than they were in the mid-1960s, when there were two African-American mayors in the nation and no Latino had been mayor of a major city for over a century. Not only has cities' political makeup shifted, with Hispanic candidates running highly credible races in New York and Los Angeles and winning races in other cities, but multi-ethnic slates in some cities have altered polarized racial relations toward more complicated forms of politics in which the ins and outs are not always racially divided, but affected by patterns of immigration and historic access to political machinery by different ethnic groups.
- The redistributionist point: State and federal capacity to redistribute resources is unquestionably greater than that of local government, and this argument is one of the strongest points arguing against local government's expanded role. But we have already referred to the critical part played by some cities and counties in ensuring that their residents have access to federal and state income support programs, and this role is best played by those governments whose staff and grant-funded providers are closest to their clients. In localities where the state administers most children and family programs, cities and counties have even more incentives to try to help their residents collect all they can from state programs. The argument also ignores the economic role of local government itself, as an engine of hiring, purchasing, taxing, making land use decisions, and playing roles that both create and constrain economic value. If local governments can redistribute resources to the private sector by their economic development decisions, it seems a little inconsistent to let them off the hook of responsibility for creating family economic value while they work in a regional economy to benefit the government's own revenues.
- Another partial counter to the redistributionist critique, while based more on political values than economic analysis, came in E. J. Dionne's moving (to an ex-Lindsay appointee) tribute upon the death of former Mayor Lindsay:

    It's also true that Lindsay Liberalism pointed to the limits of what a single city could hope to do to achieve social justice. It turned out that more spending by city governments meant higher taxes, which in turn meant the flight of middle-class citizens (black as well as white) and businesses. All by itself, a city government could not create an egalitarian utopia. It also turned out that city governments could not become so engaged in the work of justice that they could forget about the basic services: controlling crime, cleaning the streets, educating kids....But it would be a shame if the title of Charles Morris's thoughtful book on New York City's post-Lindsay blues, "The Cost of Good Intentions," was all we remembered of the Lindsay years. Good intentions should not be discredited just because the policies aimed at achieving them didn't always work as planned. We could use a new round of good intentions toward our poorer urban citizens of the sort Lindsay represented. We can learn from Lindsay's mistakes, but we can also learn from his energy, from his commitment to racial justice, and from his love of urban life. If Americans didn't come to the aid of "our beleaguered cities," he said, we would have to ask ourselves: "What kind of a people are we?" It's still a good question.[32]

Dionne's reflections do not overturn the anti-redistributionist argument; they do, however, pose a serious challenge to those who continue to ignore urban inequities relative to the rest of the country.

- With term limits affecting more state legislatures than city and county offices, and with the tenure of federal presidential sub-cabinet appointees approximating twenty-two months, the turnover argument is true at all levels of government. At the local level, there are still city and county governments where dynasties rule, but they are fewer all the time. The remedy for turnover is a set of framework and institutionalized structures that last beyond a single administration. And there are some cities and counties that have achieved this; San Francisco's Department of Children, Youth, and Their Families, Minneapolis' Youth Coordinating Board, Chatham County-Savannah's Youth Authority, New York City's Beacon Schools/Youth Development Institute, Hartford's Youth Services Bureau, and Boston's Mayor's Youth Council are examples of structures that have out-lasted political turnover. Numerous counties have institutionalized their children's budget and report cards—some for as long as a decade.

- Wirt is right; state and federal policy on many health and human services issues trumps local policy. But at a certain point the argument is circular: cities and counties don't pay much attention to children and family policy and as a result, states and the federal government have larger roles. Writing in 1974, Wirt also could not take into account the examples cited in this book and other cases where local government has acted over three decades to make a difference.

- Finally, even if cities and counties have not been leaders, they should not be ignored, because they make great targets when they are not leading. The response of city halls to devolution of Community Development Block Grant authority to local elected leaders in the 1970's has been cited by some historians of this era as evidence that community groups were able to pressure cities into expansion of community roles in service delivery.[33] The strongest constituencies for community building efforts, some urban historians would argue, arose in cities such as San Antonio where cities were first targets and then became more responsive to grass-roots constituencies. A more developmental view of local government is needed, rather than dismissing local government at the outset in a static assessment of local politics, which ignores the extent to which these forces are nearly always dynamic over time. Margaret Weir provides that perspective, describing three types of political response to demands for community-level changes: those governments that are elite-dominated, those that are subject to political patronage in city approaches to neighborhoods, and those that are inclusionary in their politics.[34] Clavel, Pitt, and Yin make a similar point about the variability of local governments:

> Local governments' responses vary from outright hostility to creative support of nonprofits. In between are many awkward governmental attempts that help less than intended or are actually harmful, particularly when the voluntary organization is fragile.[35]

Why is politics left out?

It is impossible to imagine that some of the "dismissing" is not a blend of disdain for local politics and a suspicion that its outcomes are solely the fault of its practitioners. It is as though outsiders and advocates conclude "Politics is messy, power is often used against the powerless—and we are not involved in either—so it must be bad." The anti-intellectual tradition in American life which Richard Hofstader told us about may be matched by an anti-politician tradition which predates the founding of the country, and which is often a good thing. Garry Wills, in his masterful *A Necessary Evil*, shows the role played by what he called the "anti-governmentalism" deep in our history, which he describes as founded on historical and constitutional arguments that are "largely bogus."[36] However bogus, they remain powerful, and they feed anti-local government sentiments that are among some groups also fundamentally opposed to governments responding to children and family policy *at all*.

But if this anti-governmentalism leads us to ignore local politics and its outcomes, hoping for state and federal saviors to rescue us—the wait may be a long one in some parts of the nation and during some presidencies. And if children and family advocates disdain the processes by which hundreds of billions of dollars are allocated because the process is political and elites often win the contests, presumably the process will remain political—and the elites will continue to win.

Conclusion

Our conclusion is that local governments are neither as irrelevant as much of the literature has made them out to be, nor as fully engaged as some of them have claimed. To make the case for the second part of this assertion, we will turn in the next section to an assessment of some of the initiatives that have occupied part of the recent spotlight on local efforts in children and family policy. Our critique of these efforts as often inadequate and non-strategic, though often attention-getting, is a further element of the case we seek to make for more genuinely engaged cities and counties.

NOTES

[1]   These include Charles Bruner's excellent summary of five contrasting service reform strategies, *Social Services Reform in Poor Neighborhoods*; Robert Chaskin and his colleagues' review of *Building Community Capacity*; Ron Ferguson's edited collection on the issues involved in community development, including his and Sara Schottland's essay "Reconceiving the Community Development Field;" and Kammerman and Kahn's edited collection from 1996, *Children and Their Families in Big Cities: Strategies for Service Reform.*

[2]   Alfred Kahn and Sheila Kammerman, (eds.) *Children and Their Families in Big Cities: Strategies for Service Reform*. (New York: Columbia University School of Social Work, 1996).

[3]   Alfred Kahn and Sheila Kammerman, *Big Cities in the Welfare Transition*. (New York: Columbia University School of Social Work, 1998), 92.

[4]   James Garbarino, *Children and Families in the Social Environment*.[2nd ed.] (New York: Aldine de Gruyter, 1992), 290.

[5]   Carmen Sirianni and Lewis Friedland, *Civic Innovation in America*. (Berkeley, Ca.: University of California Press, 2001).

[6]   Robert Chaskin, et al. *Building Community Capacity*. (New York: Aldine de Gruyter, 2001),174 [emphasis added]. It should be noted that Chaskin, in 1997 co-authored one of the most thoughtful assessments of local governments' role in community development policy, discussed below

[7]   Charles Bruner, *Social Services Reform in Poor Neighborhoods*. (Des Moines, Iowa: National Services Integration Clearinghouse, 2000). Actually, Bruner said that a better term, given the lack of depth of some of these theories, was "notions of change."

[8]   Joan R. Wynn, *Children, Families and Communities: Early Lessons from A New Approach to Social Services* (Washington, D.C.: American Youth Policy Forum, 1995).

[9]   Jacquelyn McCroskey and Susan Einbinder, *Universities and Communities*. (Westport, Ct.: Praeger, 1998).

[10]   Schorr, *Common Purpose*, 53-55, 6

[11]   It should be noted, however, that a considerable amount of Bruner's other work has addressed local government roles in children's policy, including landmark work with Allegheny County in developing long-term budgets that examine the costs of poor outcomes for children. These topics are discussed in Chapter 4 in reviewing the tools used by local governments.

[12]   Gilbert Steiner, *The Futility of Family Policy*. (Washington, D.C.: The Brookings Institution, 1981).

[13]   Pierre Clavel, Jessica Pitt, and Jordan Yin, "The Community Option in Urban Policy," *Urban Affairs Review* 32 (March 1998): 435-58.

[14]   Ronald F. Ferguson and Sara Schottland "Reconceiving the Community Development Field," in *Urban Problems and Community Development*. Ronald F. Ferguson and William T. Dickens, eds. (Washington, D.C.: The Brookings Institution, 1999), 58-60.

[15] Ferguson and Schottland, "Reconceiving," 576.

[16] Ferguson and Schottland, "Reconceiving," 576.

[17] Sid Gardner, Beyond Collaboration to Results. (Phoenix: Arizona Prevention Resource Center, 1998).

[18] Voices from the Field I (1997), 56.

[19] Kubish, et al. Voices II, 80.

[20] Douglas Nelson, "Conference on Local Social Policy," A speech by Douglas W. Nelson. Sponsored by The International Initiative and the Ministry of Health, Welfare and Sport at The Hague, The Netherlands June 1, 1999.

[21] Sharon L. Kagan and Eliza Pritchard, "Linking Services for Children and Families," in Edward F. Zigler, Sharon L. Kagan, and Nancy W. Hall, eds. Children, Families, and Government, (Cambridge, Cambridge University Press, 1996), 390.

[22] Robert Chaskin and Ali Abunimah, A View from the City: Local Government Perspectives on Neighborhood-Based Governance in Community Initiatives. (Chicago: Chapin Hall Center for Children, 1997).

[23] Schorr, Common Purpose, 53-55.

[24] Joan Walsh, The Eye of the Storm: Ten Years on the Front Lines of New Futures. (Baltimore. Md.: The Annie E. Casey Foundation, 1998).

[25] Kammerman and Kahn, Children and Their Families.

[26] Joseph McNeely, "Comment," in "Swimming Against the Tide," Ferguson, Urban Problems, 122.

[27] This is a frequent reference in administrative reform; the "B team" are those career professionals who will be there long after political appointees and elected officials have moved on, and thus hold a key role in subverting or supporting innovation.

[28] Ester Fuchs, "The Permanent Urban Fiscal Crisis," in Kahn and Kammerman, (1998) Big Cities, 43-73.

[29] Paul Hill and Mary Beth Celio, Fixing Urban Schools. (Washington, D.C.: The Brookings Institution, 1998).

[30] "Supporting Early Childhood Success," (Washington, D.C.: The Institute for Youth, Education, and Families, 2002).

[31] W. Chun-Hoon In Support of Low-Income Working Families: State Policies and Local Program Innovations in the Era of Welfare Reform. (Baltimore: The Annie E. Casey Foundation, 2003). Building Strong Financial Futures: A Framework for Family Economic Success. (Baltimore. Md.: The Annie E. Casey Foundation, 2003).

[32] E. J. Dionne, "A Pioneer Mayor," The Washington Post, December 26, 2000.

[33] McNeely, "Comment," 123.

[34] Margaret Weir, "Power, Money, and Politics," in Urban Problems and Community Development. Ronald Ferguson and WilliamT. Dickens [eds.] (Washington: The Brookings Institution, 1999).

[35] Clavel, Pitt, and Yin. "The Community Option," 453.

[36] Gary Wills, A Necessary Evil: A History of American Distrust of Government. (New York: Simon and Schuster, 1999).

STILL FRAGMENTED, AFTER ALL THESE YEARS

In 1988, with the help of a gifted editor, Bruce Kelly, I wrote an article titled "Failure by Fragmentation." It was published by California Tomorrow, where I was then working, and reprints have somehow found their way into thousands of conference and workshop packets across the nation.

It has been very gratifying to know that this article has helped illuminate the work done by thousands of people on these issues. But it is somewhat frustrating, too, to know that fragmentation is today widely acknowledged as a problem that affects children and families, but is still *so widely practiced at the same time.*

In fact, I believe it is possible to make a case that fragmentation is a more serious problem for services for children and families today than it was in 1988. Not only is the problem more evident; we are no longer taking fragmentation seriously. Instead we are taking it for granted, or we are failing to see it at all because it has become normal, like fish experiencing water. What water, say the fish? What fragmentation, say those who work with children and families? That's just the way the system *is*—now let's get on with our new initiative!

It sometimes seems that the emperors of fragmentation are walking around without a stitch of clothing on, and because they are funders, or politicians we like, or local officials we work with, we smile and say how nice their clothes look today. Those clothes take the form of each "new initiative," launched down a parallel track, as though there were no other programs aimed at that problem or those children and families.

What is the evidence for this finding of worsening fragmentation?

- Welfare reform, which is preoccupying many providers and advocates in the children and families field, is being implemented in a fragmented way in most communities and only in a few is it being used to pull programs together.
- Foundation initiatives have in some large and medium-sized metropolitan areas, begun to proliferate to a point where the locals chuckle about the latest Request for Proposals that they have received and how much it reads like the last one. A few foundations have begun to try to work together, but the norm is still taking a proposal to a board and claiming that "no one else is really trying to do this."
- Education reform is proceeding with a classroom-only focus down an almost totally separate track from the other school-based reforms aimed at career readiness, school-linked family support programs, and early childhood initiatives that seek school readiness outcomes among younger children.
- New juvenile delinquency prevention programs, or positive youth development programs, as they have been re-labeled in some communities, are launched in the form of new centers or services that

ignore all the prior prevention programs that aim at violence, teen pregnancy, alcohol, tobacco, or drug abuse, or other risky adolescent behavior. New layers of youth programs come in on top of the old layers, but very few communities yet have an annual budget for all youth spending or an annual report card for key indicators of youth problems and progress. Since 1964, more than two dozen separate prevention programs aimed at youth have been begun by the federal government alone.

- At the neighborhood level in some communities, family resource centers, family support programs, school-based centers, after-school centers, and multiservice centers housing public agency teams of workers all exist separately from each other. Sacramento County recently did an inventory of all neighborhood-based programs in the city which resulted in a matrix describing millions of dollars of staffing and facilities which no one had ever mapped or added up before.

- At a recent statewide conference aimed at moving "from pilots to policy" three legislators came to the conference armed with proposals for new categorical pilot projects. What is worse, there is increasing evidence that term limits accentuates the narrow-gauge view of categorical legislation as the way that short-term legislators can "leave their mark."

In some communities, the problem is worsened by the practice of fragmenting by ethnicity. As Keith Choy from San Francisco has put it in numerous meetings over the years, to the great amusement of some and the distress of others, "when you have to have programs for blue-eyed Samoan cross-dressers and every other imaginable group, the money gets spread very thinly."

Of course programs should be culturally sensitive to the groups they serve, and of course we should recognize how few programs today really are. We can stipulate that large public and nonprofit agencies have great difficulty responding to specific groups' needs and strengths. But a program for nearly every group, which is where the logic of some of the ethnic fund-slicing has headed, is ultimately destructive of the effort to find "common ground" as well as celebrating and understanding diversity. It also makes it far more difficult to take an excellent pilot project to scale, as we slice and dice programs across dozens of different ethnic and geographically defined groups.

The answer? It is *not* seeking the grail of fully comprehensive, coordinated initiatives. We have a categorical funding system and a federal delivery structure because we live in a large, diverse nation, which has chosen for more than a century to operate a wide variety of social welfare programs in both public and private sectors. Coordinating all of those programs with each other would be hopelessly complex and largely a waste of time. But the opposite extreme, allowing each initiative to compete or fade away as though they were brands of cereal or cars, is wasteful of scarce resources that are intended to help people. In the middle ground, between mega-coordination and the current trend toward the "initiative *du jour*" approach, there is a lot of room for improvement.

As one who has spoken against collaboration for its own sake, I believe that collaboratives and local coalitions can and will be judged by what they do to break through conventional thinking on the endemic problem of fragmentation. The good news is that technologically addressing the confusion is not difficult, with geocoding, regularly updated inventories of services, and data matching across agencies to find shared clients. But solving it politically demands leadership, not just good management. The act of leadership that is missing in most communities is the willingness to hold existing programs accountable for results, rather than launching new programs every time new resources are available. Lisbeth Schorr's book Common Purpose tackles these hard questions of going to scale and how pilot projects have become part of the problem. She and others have pointed out how often pilot projects become the method used by large institutions to insulate themselves for real change. The lessons in her book are powerful challenges to community leadership, which is where the pieces have to be put together to reverse the tides of further fragmentation.

Funders, leaders, and grantees willing to speak the truth to their sources of support—that's all we need to reverse the worst of the flow of fragmentation that is now running. It's upstream work, to be sure, but surely floating easily downstream is not how community building will happen. Building communities is finding how the people who live and work in the community and the programmatic pieces they want and need can all fit together in a greater whole, with a greater hope for a payoff for children and families.

CHAPTER 3: STRATEGIC POLICY: MOVING THE BAR UP

The task this book has set for itself is to make two cases: that local governments *could be* more strategic in making and implementing policy for children, youth, and families and that they *should be.* In making those cases, the definition of strategic policy needs to be clear, or any policy making efforts will simply be re-labeled as "strategic," and local governments will easily be able to perform up to a very low standard.

A book about children and family policy had better have a clear definition of policy, and this chapter tries to meet that challenge. Let me state my own definition of the key elements of policy as it affects children and families, and then explain its roots.

Policy is the authoritative allocation of resources by local governments in ways that affect children and families, whether that effect is intended or unintended. Its essential ingredients include:

- Priorities—a "short list" of things that matter more than other things
- Deliberate connections among programs that affect children and family, rather than isolated projects
- A budgetary dimension, answering the question "what does the policy mean to the budget?"
- Specifics about intended results that goes beyond "MAP chatter"— Motherhood and Apple Pie formulations that are so general they don't mean anything.

These ingredients raise a more demanding standard for local governmental policy for children and families—they raise the bar. They would exclude some "policy statements" developed by cities and counties in recent years. That is my intent, because these policy statements are not really statements of strategy or priorities—they are generalities intended to convince voters, residents, advocates and providers of children's services that something real is happening when it is not.

As mentioned in Chapter 1, Frederick Wirt has described the role of city government in the federal system as making "residual policy."[1] But as helpful as this concept is in clarifying roles in intergovernmental politics, it may give undue aid and comfort to the minimalist school in city and county government who resist efforts to address the problems of children and families in depth.

Cities and counties, as discussed in the first chapter, make policy all the time. Building new parks, deciding which offenses local police will not prosecute and diverting youth away from detention, establishing zoning rules for child care centers—all these are examples of local policy that affects children and families. They *authoritatively*—based on the legal powers of local government—*allocate resources*—space for playgrounds, diversion services, child care expansion opportunities.

In one of the classic public administration works of the past 25 years, Michael Lipsky wrote *Street-Level Bureaucracy* in 1980, pointing out how much discretion inheres in the daily work of local employees like police officers, teachers, public health nurses, and social workers.[2] At the "street level" where most of their jobs take place, these workers have the power to decide how to do their jobs and how to treat their customers. The fact that these are local government workers is the point—these workers have the opportunity to make a critical kind of "bottom-up policy" in which they interpret what policy really is. They work within the broad rules—a social worker cannot grant funds to a client who is ineligible under new federal or state rules, but she can decide within these broad parameters which clients she will try harder to help and which she will refer on to other agencies, or simply ignore.

Why have policy at all?

Before moving to address the case for making local policy on children and families more strategic, we need to answer the prior question—why should local governments go beyond the residual role at all? The normative case for local children and family policy needs to be understood before arguing whether it should be strategic and how to define that term. And that case must be made on both altruistic and self-interested grounds.

The argument from altruism

Local government *should* work harder to develop strategic children and family policy because it is morally right to do so. Making that case, however, is very different from making the case that it is in the political and economic self-interest of cities and counties to do more. The components of the normative case—why local government should do more—are the focus of this section.

The equity or ethical case rests on at least three arguments:

1. Children require the intervention of adults on their behalf, since they cannot act effectively on their own.
2. Poor children with disabilities or family problems that are not their own fault are deserving—on any imaginable moral grounds—of intervention to help them cope with problems not of their own making.
3. A local government has some measure of responsibility for the well-being of its residents, and its decision to provide some services and facilities for children and families require it to accept some responsibility for those children who use these sponsored services, (e.g. an open playground maintained by a city should be safe for children to use).

These threshold arguments for the moral component of policy-making for children and family do not yet reach the question of why policy should be strategic, however. To address that issue requires a fourth premise:

4. Policy that is intended to benefit children and families should actually seek to achieve those benefits, and should include efforts to assess whether the policies actually are effective; otherwise, policies may be

simply symbolic efforts to appear to benefit children and families, without actually doing so. They may also, if ineffective, waste scarce resources which are then no longer available to help children.

The self-interest case: the growing importance of children and family policy

Political self-interest arises in the *relative* importance of issues. I can tell you that ten issues are "important," but you are likely to be more interested in the ones that are growing in importance. So a part of the argument from self-interest is making the case that issues affecting children and families will become more important to elected officials and other residents of local areas.

Why will children and family issues become more important in the decades to come?

- As noted in Chapter 1, demographic change will mean that the *relative* size of the youth cohort will shrink as aging becomes a longer process and more old persons stay alive longer. But the role of youth in an aging society will remain important, and potentially more important, because of tensions between the needs of the youth and the needs of the older population who vote in disproportionately higher numbers. Intergenerational political and intra-community tensions will both increase, as intergenerational conflict assumes some of the same perceived zero-sum quality of inter-racial conflict in an earlier era.
- The marketing power of youth remains disproportionately high, as their increasing control and influence over consumer dollars rises. The marketing of music, movies, clothes, computers, and other goods and services and leisure items to youth with high disposable income—their own and their parents'—is now a very significant segment of the economy. For cities, this means that retailing and sales will have an emphasis on attracting youth to centers of consumer spending, which means malls at the moment, which creates further recreational and delinquency issues in some urban and especially suburban areas.
- The ability to influence children and family behavior will increase with biotechnology and other technological advances, and the debate over what means are acceptable ethically will outspeed the legal system's ability to regulate policy toward youth behavior. Loss of privacy for youth with law violations, chip implanting for tracking youths' location voluntarily (for safety reasons) and involuntarily (for control reasons), electronic surveillance of child care facilities, invasive surgery and compulsory medications for youth with violent offenses, home detention through electronic means—these and other behavior-altering interventions will be debated, and local government will be the arenas in which many of these debates take place. (These issues are discussed further in Chapter 5 on the ethics of children's policy and in Chapter 16 on the future of children and family issues.)

- As the ability to track long-term outcomes increases, programs for children and family will receive greater attention due to the demonstrated ineffectiveness of some programs. An example is the development in California's Proposition 10-funded programs that have set up six-year client tracking systems to follow children and their parents from birth to primary school enrollment. Along with the debates about privacy raised by this new capacity, there will also be a growth in the outcomes data that is available over time, leading to more debates in local government over why funding should go to programs that don't work. While these tools will affect all social programs, their impact on programs for children may be more profound because of the long time frame for prevention programs; if the case for home visiting programs that begin at birth rests in part of payoffs and cost offsets that happen in high school, the long-term costs of these interventions may get more of a spotlight if they prove ineffective.

The self-interest case II: the politics of children and family issues

The second part of the self-interest argument is that it is good politics to increase the importance of these issues. The projects sponsored by the National League of Cities and U.S. Conference of Mayors mentioned in Chapter 1 would not have gotten off the ground if they were politically uphill in every respect. Mayors and city councils are keen readers of the political winds, and the benefits of greater emphasis on children and families are apparent, at least to those who are actively participating in the projects, which included attendance of hundreds of participants at a national conference hosted by the NLC project in Minneapolis in May 2002.

That is not to argue that strategic policy has no political downside. Grant-driven, project-focused children's programs are an easier way to win short-run political credits, however shallow they may be, than long-term responses to the problems of children. But it is worth reviewing the case for political advantage for children and family policy, so that we can understand why and how it can be good politics.

1. Focusing on younger children enables a wider focus on all children. This is due to the political appeal of children in their preschool years, in contrast with far less popular adolescents, who can be stereotyped as gang members and teen mothers. But when children's policy places a spotlight on innocent younger children, there is an appeal to the photogenic that can be irresistible for the media—and for elected officials.

2. Focusing on the working parents of children and families enables elected officials to pay homage to one of the oldest and most powerful dichotomies in American political life: the perceived difference between the deserving poor and the undeserving poor. However stereotyped, this distinction dates back at least as far as the Elizabethan poor laws of 1602, and traveled across the Atlantic to have an even more powerful effect on our politics. Numerous historians of American social

policy have underscored the importance of this theme, and its power underlay a good deal of the political appeal of the "middle way" of the welfare reforms of 1996, with their emphasis upon "ending entitlements," while retaining and creating entitlements to a set of work supports—income benefits and supplements—intended to "make work pay" for lower-income working poor. It was that these heads of families were working that made all the difference, and a good deal of political slack for income benefits to lower-income families has been created as a result.

These two reasons provide some of the political cover needed for strategic children and family policy, and economics provides more.

The self-interest case III: the economics of children and family issues

Two components of the economics of children and family policy affect local politics: (1) the impact on city and county budgets and (2) the impact on family budgets, which in turn also affects local budgets.

1. To ignore the continuing drain of middle- and upper-income families out of a local jurisdiction is to eventually risk losing an important part of the city or county's tax base. Many cities have justified the increases in their police and corrections budgets based on the need to keep middle-income families in neighborhoods that will only hold these families if they are perceived as safe places to live. The same argument holds for schools, as we will see when we examine the bases for local officials becoming more deeply involved in education.

2. If children and family policy addresses the underlying causes of family income decline or stagnation, as a basis for connecting local children and family policy with economic and job development policies, it becomes clear that better jobs are a mobility factor that can work for or against a locality. Cities and counties find it difficult to affect their regional economies, for reasons discussed in Chapter 11. But within a given economy, cities can do a great deal to affect family income through several policies:

   a. The way they assist families in getting to jobs through transportation and job location policies;
   b. The way they assist families in connecting with the work and income supports to which they are entitled; and
   c. The way they target job and training subsidies on the families that need the most help to get into the "good-job economy"—working poor families, single heads of households, usually women, and young workers who are just beginning to start their families.

3. In the long run, if children and youth do not become productive citizens, or if they grow up to be anti-social in their behavior, it may cost the local government money. This is also true at times in the very short run, which is why some cities support after-school recreation and tutoring programs as a way to divert their youth from less desirable post-school activities. But the economic argument for such programs, as opposed to

the "get-them-of-the-street" arguments, become more powerful over the longer run, especially in cities with high concentrations of lower-income families.

In a recent column, David Broder summarized the stakes in stark language:

> The workforce is likely to grow barely at all in subsequent decades, thanks to continuing low birthrates, which means that overall economic growth will be limited. Meanwhile, lengthening life expectancy and the sheer number of boomers will cause retirement and health care costs to explode.[3]

Fewer productive workers hurt local economies in ways local officials cannot ignore indefinitely.

We may have made the case for a greater emphasis on children and family policy, but we have not yet made the case for strategic policy. That is our next challenge.

What is strategic policy?

The references to "strategic" and "policy" throughout this book are intended to suggest that what cities and counties are now doing is often neither. Based upon the best practices of exemplary local governments, it is possible to set forth standards for distinguishing strategic policy from merely tactical projects.[4]

- Policy is strategic if it rises above the level of separate projects for specific clients to ask how the needs of all clients could be met, by raising the issues of sustainability, going to scale, and replication which Schorr, Cutler, and others have discussed in depth;[5]
- Policy is strategic if it looks past a single target group—preschool children, adolescents—to address the full age cycle of children and families from birth to adulthood and to ask how one project will "hand off" children to another system as they grow older and move into other agencies' enrollments or caseloads;
- Policy is strategic if it looks past children's issues to address family issues as well, taking a two-generation (and sometimes three-generation) approach to programs and recognizing the crucial importance of parents and caretakers in determining the life chances of children;
- Policy is strategic if it escapes the boxes of children, youth, and family policy to assess impact on the cross-cutting realms of race and culture, community and neighborhood development, asking how does this project for these children affect this neighborhood or this culture?
- Policy is strategic if it uses the matrix in Chapter 1 (or another one) to consider how a local government might play more than one role in a program and which roles would be most effective in achieving its goals;
- Policy is strategic if it considers the possible effects of a given program based on the level of resources available for that project, recognizing that political forces often reward shallow investments for many projects

rather than greater concentration of resources on fewer, more effective projects;

- Policy is strategic if it builds in a genuine feedback loop to assess effectiveness of the program, including investing enough resources in information systems to be able to assess effectiveness in depth;
- Policy is strategic if larger equity issues are addressed as well as the needs of a single group of clients in a single project, assessing whether one group in the population experiences disproportionate outcomes and if those affected by the policy have a voice in planning, designing, and evaluating it;
- Policy is strategic if limits on resources are not allowed to rule out full consideration of new policy, asking whether wider partnerships and community buy-in could multiply available resources, rather than permitting budget concerns to rule out the search for enough resources to make programs effective.

These are hard tests. Policymakers should not assume that all of these tests could or should be met by a single policy or a single local government. But easy tests mean that rhetoric is allowed to substitute for making hard choices. Too often, single projects have been allowed to substitute for policy in the children, youth, and family arena, and most projects by themselves cannot meet any of these standards.

A city can adopt programs in response to a new grant source, as a tactical program innovation. Or it can move from tactical programs to a tactical policy, such as diversion of youth arrested, which is definitely a policy change. But this policy is still isolated, ignoring many related policy questions: what will we do with the diverted youth, how many of them will there be, what prevention efforts will make up the "front end" of the policy, what cutoffs will be adopted for youth whose offenses are too serious for diversion?

At a higher level of strategy, a programmatic response can be a network of programs rather than an isolated pilot project. At the highest level, a comprehensive youth development policy would incorporate the program initiatives into an overall set of goals, the tools to measure them, and a feedback loop to determine whether programs were effective.

Some examples

What examples of policy for children, youth, and family issues appear to be strategic? Some recent efforts include:

- The City of Boston has enlisted police, probation officers, health professionals, clergy, neighborhood residents, prosecutors, federal officials, psychiatric personnel, court staffs, and school officials in an interwoven network of programs to reduce gun violence, curb gang activity, teach youth how to resolve conflicts peacefully, and provide focused help for youth who are showing early signs of trouble.
- In Multnomah County, Oregon, a comprehensive plan has been developed in response to state enabling legislation which focuses

resources on home visiting programs covering 70-80% of first births, with follow-up over the first five years of a child's life.

- In Los Angeles County, the Children's Planning Council has set forth seven policy principles. These include increased emphasis on prevention and early intervention, enhancement of management information systems to support planning, comprehensive continuous case management for at-risk children, and "patching" or blending funds for services to children served by more than one department.[6]
- Houston, Texas, spent a year focusing planning on the needs of children and families. One major result was a permanent, cooperative Commission on Youth serving both the City of Houston and Harris County.
- Santa Fe, New Mexico, has developed a strategic plan with annual updates that allocate funds from a gross receipts tax and leveraged local funding to local nonprofit agencies serving children.
- Hampton, Virginia, has developed a community-wide process for strategic planning for youth policy involving youth themselves in project development.

These and dozens of other efforts demonstrate that cities and counties are attempting to be more strategic. Assessing some of these efforts in greater depth is essential as a way to test the feasibility of acting strategically in local government.

Current efforts to develop strategic policy: The glass, more than half empty

Praise is due to the impressive efforts made by hundreds of cities and counties to develop children and youth policies, and also to the work of some of these governments to add a family dimension to their policies. Against uphill barriers, as described in the prior chapters, these cities and counties have moved beyond projects, in concrete ways. They have allocated real resources from their budgets to children and family programs, and they have begun to measure the effectiveness of some of those programs. This is no mean feat, and a separate book can and should be written about that progress.

But that praise should not be uncritical, and should not overlook the shortcomings of these efforts. We may learn a good deal more from a critical analysis of these efforts than from a compilation of them without it. Most of them, after a detailed review, reveal some serious gaps:

- They are inadequately strategic, focusing upon either lengthy lists of programs or a few programs that are restricted to a single age group or programmatic area, such as child care, youth development, or loosely defined prevention efforts.
- They rarely address budget realities; many of the plans do not even add up the costs of their recommendations and very few have developed children and family budgets.

- They rarely raise issues of budget redirection and accountability, failing to define strategy as shifting resources from the least effective programs to the most effective ones, or efforts to concentrate resources in order to reach a dosage intense enough to achieve best practices outcomes.
- They rarely include targeted numbers of children and families in their discussion of the programs they recommend, making it impossible to know the scale of their recommendations.
- Their discussions of demography highlight recent changes, usually in the direction of greater diversity, but they rarely include a strategic response to disproportionate outcomes among some racial and ethnic groups.
- They fail to raise issues of targeting, referring to at-risk children and families but failing to make clear which ones are most important for the projects they recommend starting or expanding. An important exception to this, which is worth noting, are the home visiting programs, such as those in Multnomah County, Oregon, that have targeted all first births or all births with special risks, using criteria such as Hawaii Healthy Start's risk factors to target resources on those families.

Again, these local efforts deserve praise, for they have gone well beyond the norm in raising children and family issues to new visibility, they have proven that wider constituencies of support can be mobilized around new plans, and they are at least trying to do what most cities and counties have not even tried. But it is their non-strategic nature that is critical, since some of these efforts are proudly labeled "strategic plans." To assume that this is the best we can do in making strategic policy is to ignore the empty part of the glass. What is needed is an added effort to build on these important foundations to make them genuinely strategic, and thus able to command more resources in the long run.

A review of three generic "strategies"—policy statements, children's funds, and offices for children—suggests that in many cases they may be the focus of significant efforts, they may be very well-intentioned—but they aren't really strategic.

Policy Statements

Some cities and counties have developed formal policy statements that set forth goals for children and youth. There are pluses and minuses in developing such statements, similar to the pros and cons of developing a new structure—an "office for children and youth." Like these offices, policy statements can serve, intentionally or inadvertently, as diversions away from serious policy efforts that do not impact the mainstream of local budgets. A review of the pros and cons of developing such policy statements may help make clearer how such a diversion can happen.

Pros

- The policy statement may help to create a brighter spotlight on the fact that the city or county does in fact have wide effects on the lives of children and youth, which in itself is a policy message worth stating.

- The policy statement may combine separate programs that affect children in a single over-arching framework of prevention or some other cross-cutting way of describing the goals of programs for children and families. This may have the effect of rising above the programmatic grant-chasing that characterizes many local governmental efforts.
- Policy statements that set out genuine priorities (see the second "con" point below) can help rally supporters to specific tasks that are stated clearly enough to command resources. For example, there is a sizable difference between "identify children at risk at birth and provide them with resources needed to connect them with a medical home" and "support children with resources needed to live up to their full potential."

Cons
- Like the creation of a new office, policy statements can substitute for real action. "We've issued a new policy statement for children" may be placed in an annual report as a major accomplishment which may divert energy and attention from changes of real consequence for children.
- As noted above, some policy statements are merely "MAPs"—*motherhood and apple pie* statements of good things that raise no issues of choice or priority, but merely state desired goals in terms so broad as to offend no one.
- Depending on the breadth of the process involved in developing them, policy statements may be another top-down document that undermines civic engagement goals by sending a message that "Government knows best."

What would a policy statement look like if it were significant? At least five qualities seem important:
- It would signal *clear priorities*, rather than seeking comprehensiveness of rhetoric by mentioning a multitude of problems and strategies without any stated priorities among them;
- It would form a basis for *resource allocation*, aimed at budgets and other decision-making processes such as staffing, facilities planning, and intergovernmental negotiations;
- It would reflect a process wider than deliberations of the elected body or a few staff members, involving *stakeholders from throughout the community*, in a process that is not dominated by providers but also includes representatives of geographic, age-specific, and ethnic communities;
- It would begin to address issues of cause and effect—what underlying forces *cause* problems—rather than simply mentioning a long list of the symptoms of problems faced by children and youth; and

- It would be *reviewable and renewable*, rather than a one-time statement of policy that is intended to be frozen in print for all time as though conditions never changed.

Nearly all of the more than thirty policy statements reviewed were unable to meet these criteria. Among those reviewed, the Multnomah County strategic plan, as mentioned, had major strengths, as did the Los Angeles County policy statement.

The problem of local children's funds

A small number of cities and counties have created special funds or local taxes that are dedicated to children's programs. Most advocates have treated these as major policy reforms, and some national foundations have spotlighted these efforts.

But it is another glass less empty than full, in my view.

To applaud the merely programmatic and the token allocation made to a single project is to lower our sights. It is not just a matter of scale—some of the very best practices began with a very finite group of children and families. But the question remains whether a "Children's Fund" is ever aimed at leveraging a full budget, or whether a demonstration program for fifty children is ever intended to achieve replicable benefits for some significant portion of the thousands of youth who need it as much or more than the first fifty do.[7]

The question is also how much these "funds" divert scarce energy away from the "real budgets" in favor of a smaller playing field. Some have called it "sandbox politics," suggesting that children and youth advocates are easily diverted away from the real power issues into sandboxes of smaller, near-token allocations of too little money to make a difference in outcomes.

A further concern arises in the old budget adage that "floors become ceilings." This means that setting aside funds to ensure a basic level of support for a program can lead to resentment among other programs, an argument that "you already got yours," and a net result that the set-aside becomes "all you're going to get" a capped ceiling on spending for that function, in effect.

In an interview several years ago with county officials in a site where one of these dedicated taxes had received national attention, I asked whether the new funding had made any changes in the county budget. The response was that the funds were really separate from the county budget—which was my point. I again asked if there was any intended leverage effect from the new funds into the county budget, and again the answer was no. Finally I asked if they knew how the dedicated funds compared to what the county was spending in total on children and youth programs—and the answer was again negative. My conclusion was that another sandbox had been created, a fairly sizable one in this case, but without any discernible impact on "the real money."

What criteria can be set forth to guide local officials and private fundraisers considering a new matching fund effort or a dedicated tax source? At least three seem worth considering:

- Is the tax source significant enough to provide genuine matching funds for local projects operated at scale—or just enough to launch pilot projects and fund a limited number of existing programs? (At this writing, the "espresso tax" in Seattle is pending; in Seattle, espresso may be a primary source of revenue, but even so, it is not like oil in Texas or alcohol in California—it is a fringe tax, and will raise fringe funding.)

- Will the new fund be administered separately from the local budget, or will it be used for integration of new funding to be used to leverage and redirect existing funding for ineffective programs—or to connect isolated programs with each other?
- Will the fund-raising effort be focused on a single purpose so as to be less diversionary of ongoing funding, e.g. a new children's shelter or funding an endowed institution for child development training?

The common ingredient in all of these is the question "will these new funding sources drain resources from other efforts to secure wider funding for children and youth programs, or will they be used to improve the effectiveness of those programs?"

The Role of "Offices of Children's Issues" in Local Government

A number of cities and counties have adopted ordinances creating offices with specific responsibilities for children and youth issues. Sometimes these offices are created to tap state and federal funding for specific functions, such as youth employment, delinquency prevention, or child care. (I was the author of such an ordinance creating the Youth Services Bureau in Hartford City Government in 1979, which is still in existence as of late 2003.) In other cases the responsibilities given to these offices are more generic in nature.

However general their assigned roles, however, it is rare that these units ever play a genuinely strategic role in local government. At their best, they may serve to staff a broad coalition or a collaborative network of agencies. But typically, these offices have a few staff members who are not part of the core of the government, and they are often focused on projects with day-to-day operational responsibilities that leave them little time for more strategic policy roles. When they explain their functions to policy leaders, it is far more often in terms of new external funding they have brought in, rather than in terms of a broad agenda for redirection efforts aimed at more effective use of funds already in the local budget or other public and private funds already in the community.

We have said that it is rare that these offices operate in a strategic manner—but there are a few that do. Indianapolis currently has a Deputy Mayor for Policy who combines roles for community improvement and children and family policy. Los Angeles County's Children Planning Council also plays a broad role that cut across multiple county agencies and communities, as does San Francisco's Department of Children, Youth, and Their Families, and the Nashville Mayor's Office of Children and Youth. So there are some cities and counties that have worked across program areas to address strategic issues that rise above the level of program initiatives.

Typically, an office of youth policy would not meet this standard, because it usually does not address either early childhood foundations of youth policy or a focus on family economic success. This narrowing of the agenda does not invalidate what an office of youth policy could do—but it makes clear that its scope will be too confined to respond to issues from other arenas that are linked closely to youth problems.

What would it take to make such offices strategic, rather than merely new structures? The concrete evidence of strategic roles would include the following:

- Active involvement in putting together the portions of the local government budget that affect children and youth—the full budget, not just a sub-section for project grants (this issue is discussed further in Chapter 6 on budget issues);

- The ability to gather useful information on an annual basis that makes up a "score card" of the conditions of children and families in that jurisdiction;

- Sufficient credibility with other sections of the government on "middle and outer ring" issues to ensure that the office is consulted on children and family impacts of those policies;

- Depending upon the local governments' structural and fiscal relationship with local school districts, an office should have a clear policy toward partnering with the schools on children and family policy development;

> ### The question of fit and linkage
>
> How programs "fit together" can be a neglected element in strategic thinking, because the focus of planning is often only a single program. In a recent effort to develop a new child abuse prevention initiative, the most important tasks came to be ensuring that this new initiative fit into *prior efforts* that had already been funded and staffed: home visiting, family support, parent education. None of these prior efforts were labeled "child abuse prevention" but all of them, if effective, achieved that outcome. Connecting the new program with the prior ones will require formal protocols for interagency referrals, cross-training of staff, agreements for set-aside funds and earmarked slots for clients of each others' programs—and a host of other linkages that will be developed as the program begins implementation. Without these connections, the new initiative and the prior efforts will set off on diverging tracks, unlikely to ever meet and share resources, despite aiming at many of the same outcomes. Ideally, a new program provides glue that makes new connections possible.

- Sufficient credibility with state and federal government to represent the local government as part of an intergovernmental team negotiating the details of programs affecting children and families; and

- Active involvement with the community in ways that assure that there is a true constituency for the office made up of more than the providers funded through its programs.

These six preconditions for a strategic role may seem minimal to some local government practitioners—but to others they will seem far in the future.

In a detailed assessment of state governmental offices with responsibility for collaboration across children's programs, John Hutchins prepared a report for the Family Impact Seminar in 1998 which concluded that these entities had been involved in integrating services, creating state-local block grants and decategorized funding streams, establishing benchmarks and outcomes for children's services provided by state agencies, *fostering regional and local collaboratives*, evaluating programs, changing budgeting procedures, and raising the profile of children's issues[8] (emphasis added). The fourth of these is especially relevant, since state-sponsored local collaboratives (such as early care and education planning councils or local prevention councils) may in some ways become competitive with local offices, or they may provide the resources to sustain such offices. The same criteria we have suggested for local offices for children and families may be used to assess state offices and their local counterparts. But it seems fair to ask whether the best of these offices—whether locally inspired or state-stimulated—can meet the criteria suggested above.

A summary: why aren't these efforts strategic?

It may well be that these criteria for effectiveness set the bar too high. Many of the cities and counties that have attempted these strategies have been the unquestioned leaders in trying to develop and implement children's policy. But if we call any project or any publicly visible initiative a "strategy," we may have demeaned the term so much that it begins to be used for nearly any effort, however minor its impact on children. And that would really be lowering the bar, in a way that ultimately affects children and families, and minimizes what cities and counties could be doing.

So it's not strategic—So what?

The fact that local policy is piecemeal is not an abstract problem of planning methods; the critical point is that piecemeal policy will not achieve good results. Education policy that is not strategic will be ineffective, substance abuse treatment that is provided in a fragmented way will be ineffective, and efforts to get people off welfare and out of poverty that are not strategic will also be ineffective.

Fragmentation is not an issue because it is logically incoherent—it is a problem because it cripples the implementation of greatly needed programs for children and families, and it wastes resources on programs that won't work well enough to justify those resources.

Fragmentation means the right mix of services doesn't get to the kids that need them, and it also means that those services that do get delivered are often ineffective. They are ineffective because they are not combined with other resources needed by the same clients, because they are provided in a dosage too small to make a difference, and because treatment and other services are provided on a "people-fixing" basis that assumes that after three or six months of attention, clients will "get better" and not need further supports, ignoring everything we have learned about the importance of after-care and community supports.

The fundamental point is that policy that is merely tactical is merely programmatic, and is thus often ineffective in achieving the larger goals a local government should hold itself accountable for when it puts scarce resources behind a policy. So strategy matters, if our goal is achieving better lives for children and families in our cities and towns.

The scope of strategic policy: Not always comprehensive

Strategic policy need not be fully comprehensive to be strategic. It can be targeted on:

- The "whole thing:" children, youth, and family issues in their entirety, as when a city or county develops a Santa Fe-type strategic plan for children and families;
- A comprehensive age group, e.g., a strategic plan for early childhood programs, as with Proposition 10 funding in California or Smart Start funding in North Carolina;
- A cross-cutting program administered throughout a locality: e.g., a strategic plan for a county's substance abuse policies;
- A comprehensive program that serves as an entry level for wider issues, as in a child abuse prevention initiative across a city that defines child abuse prevention broadly, rather than categorically.

Each of these can be strategic, if it has some of the ingredients of strategic policy. The widest lens obviously has the greatest value, but such breadth can also be beyond the reach of some policy leaders—or may be too broad to have specific local traction. So "falling back" to a lesser scope can still represent a sizable step forward in many localities.

Strategic policy and politics: The blend of information and values

Despite these examples, inevitably, the call for local policy to be more strategic and to include clear priorities is at times met with a response something like this:

> This is a hopelessly idealistic notion, because policy is what results from local politics, media spotlights, and whatever funding is available for that year. We don't set priorities because we can't set priorities—we don't have the money to choose what we want to fund—we can only fund whatever state and federal grants (and sometimes private foundations or donors) give us new money to fund. And we can't set priorities across all the programs that affect kids because whichever groups were left out of the list would come after us for neglecting those children.

Having spent some intense time in and around local politics, I recognize that sentiment. I know enough about politics and compromises and the need to please lots of the people lots of the time to be realistic about the prospects for fully rational policy-making: they are nil.

But it is not fully rational policy-making that I am proposing; that is an easy straw man that can be quickly dismissed. What I believe is both needed and possible is movement in the direction of a *better blend of information and values* as the basis for local policy that affects kids and their families. We can seek better information to respond to local political pressures, or we can just respond with whatever loose resources are lying around and create another isolated pilot project. We can seek to build wider consensus when we see that organized groups hold opposing values on children and family policy—or we can chalk it up to basic disagreements among extreme views and try to find a middle ground that will not upset anybody very much.

When both information and values are on the table, it becomes clear that the only final basis for priority setting is a combination of community feedback on the services and supports legitimate community spokespersons want and need, combined with feedback from solid assessments of which programs are working. These are the dual sources of legitimacy—*programs that people want and programs that work.* And that is part of what it means to be strategic: strategy flows from an effort to combine community consensus on what is needed with powerful information. Such information is really *data converted to knowledge.* It seeks deliberately and in a sustained way what works to achieve community needs.

Camilla Stivers has developed a fascinating review of progressive traditions in public administration in which she views the early twentieth century as an era of innovation that included municipal research bureaus, the advent of the city manager movement, and settlement houses. What is most interesting in this is the degree to which she views these through the lens of gender, citing Jane Addams' career in settlement houses and contrasting her community-based style with that of the scientific, rational management outlook of the male administrators she discusses.[9]

If one extends this contrast to the idea of dual sources of legitimacy in decision-making and priority setting, the basis for choices in allocating resources must be a blend of the "hard" use of rational techniques in results-based accountability—the constant striving to learn and document what works—and the "softer" reliance on and trust in community responsiveness, in which there is a parallel, constant striving for active engagement of those affected by and those paying for a given program. *What works* and *what citizens want and need,* voiced through democratic processes and active listening, can together provide a much stronger basis for launching, changing and terminating programs

Checklist for Strategic Thinking

- Are we responding to the availability of an external funding source or to local needs and strengths?
- Have we set clear priorities among needs and programs based on local data, programs' growth, or other criteria that are understood by policymakers?
- Have we tried to assess what concentration of resources it would take to make a difference in responding to the problem, or have we just allocated resources to start a program, without regard for what it takes to have a real impact on children and families?

than either by itself. And that is the best ground on which to form and defend strategic policy.

For children and youth, the effort to move toward policy priorities is especially important, because of the truism that is the first phrase out of any advocate's mouth—"they don't vote." (Actually it is far more important when their parents don't vote, or when demography shifts toward the elderly and the childless in a way that relegates parents to a small minority in local elections.)

But the truism misses an important political fact: setting policy for children and family issues can be good politics, and can be done in a way that widens constituencies for the policies that are set. In the chapters that follow, we will review models of local policy-making that were good politics, as well as some less praiseworthy actions by local officials that represent some classic examples of "what not to do."

When equity is defined as each group getting a little bit of resources for its token-level programs, politics has overwhelmed the potential for policy to help children and family in non-token ways. At that point, we need to go "beyond equity," in a phrase I first heard from Doug Anglin of UCLA's Drug and Alcohol Research Center. Equity can be degraded to mean mere tokenism—a symbolic allocation for each group, never concentrating enough resources to make a difference and assuming the groups will never know the difference.

James Schlesinger calls this "the symbolism of concern," referring to the frequency with which "resources are applied thinly over a wide array of programs."[10] The political forces underlying this tendency and its longevity, however, should not obscure the new tools of analysis available as a counter-force. A critical technique is assessing whether the "dosage" of a program is adequate to achieve the results claimed for it. Opponents of the tokenist approach to diffusing resources may still not win their arguments with supporters of well-intentioned, low-resource programs, such as DARE and ten Saturdays worth of parent education, but they will have more powerful evidence to make their case.

In an earlier book, I wrote that strategic planning is an oxymoron—if it is strategic, it is more than a plan, and if it is only a plan—it isn't strategic because it doesn't lead to action. So the final filter on strategic policymaking is that it must have a bias toward action, not planning, and not hollow policy statements.

The paradox of strategy: Lofty visions and the guts of government

If strategy is defined as creating vision statements and goals at a high level of abstraction, it is unlikely that strategy by itself will lead to changing much that government does. It is within the most intricate and arcane processes of government—its budgeting, its personnel processes, and its purchasing agencies—that some of the most lasting changes can be made. But if a children and family agenda remains grant-driven and single program-based, it is unlikely to ever penetrate these inner sanctums of policy and practice, and new goals statements will be filed away and largely ignored.

Down in the guts of government is where lasting change is made, not along the tops of city and county agencies where "innovative projects" are often used as a buffer from real change. Sadly, if innovative energy is diverted to the operational details of a new grant-driven program, then it is far less likely that the hard questions will ever be asked of those who really run the government on a day-to day basis. And then a city personnel department need never look at its leave policy for single parents, and a purchasing agency need never ask who gets hired by its contractors and how much information they are given about family-based income supports.

So systems change is about knowing the insides of the government—the very guts of local agencies—so well that the workings of the system are visible, rather than hidden behind a hollow pilot project that operates on top of the system and prostects it from having to make real change. Systems change also requires a fundamental respect for those who know what happens inside the guts of the government. The kinds of people who like to work in arenas of innovation sometimes regard those who work inside the agencies in career roles as staid and resistant to change, leading to a patronizing attitude at best and an overall disdain for working with these insiders at worst. It is an expensive disdain, costing knowledge of the very systems that innovators seek to change.[11]

Tools: The how to

Finally, the tools of strategic planning also matter. Chapter 4 describes several of the most important tools that local governments have used to work on both information and values in their planning.

NOTES

[1] Frederick Wirt, *Power in the City: Decision Making in San Francisco*. (Berkeley: University of California Press, 1974).

[2] Michael Lipsky, *Street Level Bureaucracy*. (New York: Russell Sage, 1980)..

[3] David Broder, "The CEOs' Dim View of Deficits," *Washington Post*, March 5, 2003.

[4] I am using the words tactical and strategic here in their military sense, as they have been used in numerous other arenas of government. Tactics is employing forces in combat; strategy is employing all potential tools—political, psychological, and military—to advance policy. Using the hinge of American history as the example, Lee ended up in Gettysburg for strategic reasons, based on his swing north into Pennsylvania to pressure the Union to surrender; his ordering Pickett's charge at Gettysburg was tactical, intended to win that battle in that particular place..

[5] Schorr, *Common Purpose*. Ira Cutler, *The Challenge of Sustainability*. (Port Chester, N.Y.: Cornerstone Consulting, 2000).

[6] Jacquelyn McCroskey, "We Can Get There From Here: Lessons Learned from the Development and Operations of the Los Angeles County Children's Planning Council." (Los Angeles: University of Southern California School of Social Work, 2001).

[7] In *Beyond Collaboration to Results*, I cited a city in which a new $12 million fund was the primary focus of advocates' efforts while more than $100 million was being cut in children's programs in the rest of the budget. That fund is now up to $35 million, in a

city budget of $800 million—thus equaling .8% of the total budget. The point remains valid.

[8] John Hutchins, *Coming Together for Children and Families.* (Washington: Family Impact Seminar, 1998).14-15.

[9] Camilla Stivers, *Bureau Men, Settlement Women: Constructing Public Administration in the Progressive Era.* (Lawrence, KS: University Press of Kansas, 2000).

[10] James R. Schlesinger, "Systems Analysis and the Political Process," *Journal of Law and Economics,* (October 1968), 285.

[11] I accidentally learned a portion of this lesson early in my tenure at HEW on a series of sites visits to Model Cities around the county. On some of these trips, I ended up sitting next to the Assistant Secretary for Budget and Administration, James Kelly, who was a superbly experienced career civil servant. He took pity on a newly appointed Deputy Assistant Secretary and explained some of the inner workings of the Department. Ever since, I valued those sage insiders who know how the system works and can guide newcomers toward understanding where the levers of change might be—and where resistance is most likely to come.

CHAPTER 4: MAKING BETTER POLICY THROUGH TWO SETS OF TOOLS: USING INFORMATION AND SHAPING VALUES

The task of making better children and youth policy requires not only a strategic perspective on policy-making; it also requires (1) a set of policy tools, and (2) an approach to dealing with disagreements over values that arise in policy-making. As already noted, both information and values must be addressed in developing policy. Without these tools, policy will remain ad hoc and fragmented. Policy will be partial and undermined by token allocations to small projects, unless values disagreements are bridged in a way that enables clear priorities with enough resources to make a difference.

These two tasks are of equal importance: both the information tasks and the values tasks must be addressed if policy is to replace fragmented programs. Unfortunately, proponents of a mostly technical approach and proponents of what some call a "civic dialogue" have been arguing from extremes in recent years in urging local governments to adopt their respective remedies. These two approaches are typically over-polarized into a sterile debate about an overly technical "number-crunching, bean counting" effort contrasted with a "grass-roots" strategy that develops values "from the bottom up." Neither, in my view, can succeed by itself; each needs the other.

It is the combination of an information strategy and a consensus-building strategy that offers the best hope—not an either-or approach.

We live, unquestionably, in an information society. But *values matter also,* and the best hope for making better futures for children and families is to work at the dangerous, important intersection where data and values come together. The paths we choose at that intersection will determine where local governments will end up in trying to make better policy for children and families. Our planning and strategic thinking will be better to the extent that we are capable of weighing both data and values—and not pretending that data will decide or that a dozen or so community forums will come up with lasting answers by themselves.[1]

Traditionally, planes require two wings to fly (newer versions with single wings or no wings are notable exceptions!). Both "wings" of the plane of local policy-making—information and values—are needed to ensure a better chance for the children and parents we are seeking to help. But it will take both wings, and at the same time we will need a well-functioning set of connections between the two to make sure that they are headed in the right direction. The policy tools described below have the potential to form those connections.

Figure 1: Pyramid of Family Support

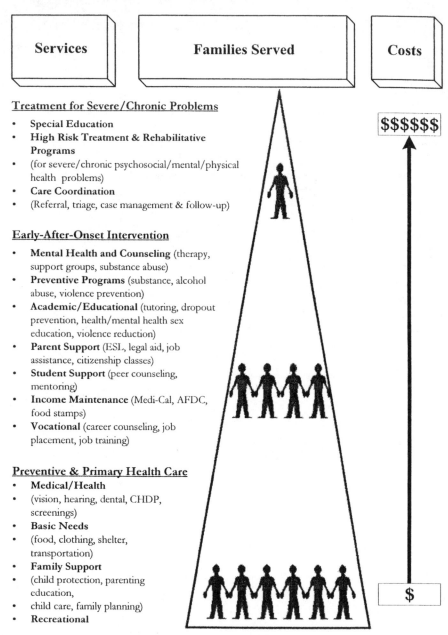

Services   **Families Served**   **Costs**

<u>Treatment for Severe/Chronic Problems</u>

- **Special Education**
- **High Risk Treatment & Rehabilitative Programs**
- (for severe/chronic psychosocial/mental/physical health problems)
- **Care Coordination**
- (Referral, triage, case management & follow-up)

$$$$$$

<u>Early-After-Onset Intervention</u>

- **Mental Health and Counseling** (therapy, support groups, substance abuse)
- **Preventive Programs** (substance, alcohol abuse, violence prevention)
- **Academic/Educational** (tutoring, dropout prevention, health/mental health sex education, violence reduction)
- **Parent Support** (ESL, legal aid, job assistance, citizenship classes)
- **Student Support** (peer counseling, mentoring)
- **Income Maintenance** (Medi-Cal, AFDC, food stamps)
- **Vocational** (career counseling, job placement, job training)

<u>Preventive & Primary Health Care</u>

- **Medical/Health**
- (vision, hearing, dental, CHDP, screenings)
- **Basic Needs**
- (food, clothing, shelter, transportation)
- **Family Support**
- (child protection, parenting education,
- child care, family planning)
- **Recreational**

$

The Ten Tools

Out of the experience of local governments throughout the nation, it is possible to derive at least ten essential tools that every local government can consider using in developing policy positions and in implementing state and federal policy concerning children and youth. This chapter will not describe any of them exhaustively, but will attempt to make clear how wide a variety of tools exist to help with the process of making strategic decisions about children and family policy. Those tools include:

The Tools of Information

1. *Taking inventory*: building a data base of funding and other resources that enables the local government to track and eventually to influence the flows of funding coming into its jurisdiction from external funding sources aimed at children and families. One way of doing this is through a *children's budget*. This topic is discussed in Chapter 6.

2. *Keeping score*: the use of citywide and countywide outcomes as community indicators which annually track the well-being of children and youth with key indicators; in some cities and counties this has taken the form of a *children's report card.*

3. *Monitoring program performance*: using outcomes at the agency and program level for both the agencies funded by local government and other jurisdictions' agencies—to determine whether programs are effective in meeting the needs of children and youth and their families. This *accountability agenda* includes *evaluating key programs* over time.

4. *Mapping the local economy as it affects families*: Understanding, reacting to, and seeking to shape the workings of the local economy as it affects and is likely to affect the children and families most likely to be impacted by that economy. This includes assessing new jobs, layoffs, family-friendly workplaces, and a shift in the kind of jobs that are being created and the skills needed for young workers to enter the regional economy, including tracking the relative success of those young people who do not go on to higher education but enter the local work force. This requires *family income monitoring and assessment.*

5. *Identifying the universe of need*: A program developed in response to a specific problem is unlikely to be strategic about how that need fits into a broader picture of the full range of needs (and strengths) of children and families. One approach that has been developed by a number of agencies, notably UCLA's Center for Healthier Children, Families, and Communities, depicts a full universe of need graphically, as shown in Figure 1. Another approach is to list a group of overlapping groups of children identified as having specific problems, as shown in the table later in this chapter.

6. *Tools for targeting*: Information tools can also be used to be more strategic in targeting scarce resources on clients and groups that can most benefit from them. *Geo-coding* data about demographic

characteristics and where service needs are coming from can help in targeting by neighborhood or community. *Data matching* can determine which clients are enrolled in multiple agencies' caseloads—or should be, because they are eligible for multiple benefits. And tracking clients over time through various forms of *"tagging"* clients each time they encounter service systems can build up information about which clients return for services and how their needs change over time.

The Tools of Consensus-building around Values
1. *Using a collaborative values inventory*:   Various tools have been developed for values clarification, using surveys of groups that are intending to work together and documenting group members' agreements and disagreements about underlying values. Some groups have used these in combination with various types of collaborative capacity self-assessments—tools used to measure organizations' or collaborative groups' readiness for serious collaboration.
2. *Framing issues in ethical terms*: As discussed in greater depth in the following chapter, tools originally developed in the health field have been adapted to children and family issues, providing another frame for the values decisions made by local governments.
3. *Structuring direct feedback processes*:   These tools include on-line citizen surveys, public opinion surveys, and other methods of gathering feedback on city and county services.
4. *Deliberative democracy methods*: These tools include several methods used to expand citizen involvement in framing and giving feedback to major policy choices. This can include working and negotiating with other local governments on those problems of children and youth for which solutions are more appropriately regional than local.

To do all ten of these would be to take seriously the need for a strategic response to the needs of children and youth. But few cities and counties have done this. For many of them, as noted above, the minimum remains the norm. Yet there are examples of several of these that have been used in developing children and family policy.

Table 2: Examples and Sources of Strategic Responses

Tools	Examples and Sources
Inventory of resources and assets Grant inventories and funding streams	Los Angeles Children's budget; Contra Costa budget, Hawaii youth asset mapping; Arizona statewide inventory of all AOD grant funding, organized by GIS
Report card—key indicators	Numerous cities and counties; the Annie E. Casey KidsCount project

Accountability agenda-outcomes monitoring & program evaluation	Numerous sources; see The Finance Project
Family income monitoring and assessment	Multnomah County use of Oregon Eligibility Estimator
Identifying the universe of need by severity of need	UCLA materials, California Proposition 10 county-level plans
Data matching	Chapin Hall review; http://www.jcpr.org/research_summaries/vol1_num4.htmlb
Geocoding needs and services data	Arizona AOD inventory [see above]
Collaborative values inventory	Strategic planning across child welfare and substance abuse agencies
Framing issues ethically	Oregon health options process
Deliberative democracy	http://www.deliberative-democracy.net/index.html

Several of these tools merit further discussion.

Healthy communities and asset-counting

Over the past ten years or so an impressive shift in thinking and writing about the problems of youth has taken place.[2] It is impressive because its perspectives have filtered into the speech and outlook of thousands of youth workers. Led by Karen Pittman of The International Youth Foundation, Peter Benson of the Search Institute, Bonnie Benard of WestEd and several others, this "movement" takes multiple forms, but its common dimensions include

- an effort to emphasize the developmental assets and resiliency of youth and their communities, not their deficits[3]
- a concern for prevention of risky behavior (somewhat at odds with the first tenet) by youth and a perspective that links multiple forms of risky behavior—unsafe and/or premature sex, smoking, violence, abuse of alcohol and other drugs—rather than setting up categorical programs for each of these
- a sustained effort to involve youth as actors in programs, not just as objects (occasionally this effort has used the refreshing, challenging slogan "It takes a child to raise a whole village.")[4]

> **Deciding without a Context**
>
> In one large county recently, a $5 million funding increase in early care and education programs was reviewed by a policy group without any consideration of the more than $120 million flowing into the county from twenty different child care funding sources—because it wasn't their funding and it wasn't part of the proposal they were asked to approve. As a result, no leveraging opportunities were framed as part of the discussion.

- an emphasis upon universal programs for all youth rather than programs targeted to groups that are especially at risk
- an effort to build "healthy communities," defined by Benson as "places with a shared commitment to care for young people."[5]

This is a good set of themes and has behind it some very solid practical knowledge and experience. But its impact on the actual workings of local government seems to be far less than its impact on the language and attitudes of youth practitioners. The problem is that this seems wholly predictable, since Benson (and others) refer to local government as "a secondary support system," devoting three paragraphs to its role in a 300-page book.[6] It is as though the billions spent by local governments on youth-related activities is invisible, or must be briefly acknowledged as part of the problem, and then ignored or written off as impossible to change.

But those billions, even if we exclude schools and early care programs—are too much to write off, by my arithmetic. Local government is non-trivial and non-marginal in children and youth policy, and to ignore *its* assets seems to miss a lot.

So there is no substitute for the hard work of assembling an inventory of local spending as well as the community-based assets which the above sources emphasize. Fortunately, we have the excellent work by Mark Friedman, Anna Danegger and their colleagues at the Finance Project to draw upon.[7] Their review of the state of the art in children's report cards makes clear how useful it can be to place a new funding stream in the larger context of the full funding available to a city or county. These issues are addressed in Chapter 6.

Keeping score: On the report card front

A city or county without a children's report card may have an excellent children and youth policy process—but it is hard to imagine how they got there without a road map of where they were going. Using the original model of the Annie E. Casey Foundation's Kidscount process at the state level, dozens of cities and counties have developed their own reports cards or conditions of children reports. Los Angeles' Children's Planning Council has been in the forefront of efforts to add family indicators and to combine negative measures of deficits with positive indicators of well-being. An important refinement of these tools is the use of baseline data to track progress and declines in all of the children, with disaggregation of the data to track disproportionate outcomes by ethnic, geographic, and other groups within the total city or county population.[8]

But report cards by themselves are not policy discussions. They can shine a brief spotlight on trends that are improving, stagnant, or worsening; they can heighten awareness of positive as well as negative indicators; and they can pinpoint areas where the data most needed is not currently available. But the policy implications of a report card are harder to frame than the numbers are to assemble. A "second generation report card" would address the policy implications rather than letting the numbers make their own case. For example, one county report card annually plots a graph showing the correlation between free and reduced lunch enrollment and test scores for each of the 300 schools in the county. Predictably, the graph shows a direct correlation, but what is equally powerful is to see the 20-30 outliers—the schools with similar socio-economic makeup that do much better or much worse than their counterparts. Yet no action has been taken by any educational institution in the county to seek more information on why these schools differ so much from the others like them.

In Philadelphia, efforts have been made to link the children's budget and the report card closely, out of a conviction that resources and results need to be tied together much more than they typically are. As the 2001 report says,

> The true measure of public investment is in the results. That is why *Children's Budget 2001* should be examined with *Report Card 2001: The Well-Being of Children and Youth in Philadelphia,* which tracks a number of indicators measuring the health, safety, and development of children and youth in Philadelphia. Together these two documents can be used to evaluate what actions and investments are necessary to improve the well-being of children and youth. Results accountability and outcomes monitoring

Whole books have been written about outcomes accountability and performance measurement; this is not one of them. But a children and family agenda demands more than indicators of child and family progress at the citywide or countywide level; it also demands the tools to monitor whether programs are in fact achieving their intended results.[9] The good news is that extensive efforts are being made in cities and counties to expand the use of performance measures, the federal government has both required and funded new state and local capacity to collect new child welfare outcomes, Head Start outcomes, substance abuse treatment outcomes, and other measures of program effectiveness, and investments in outcomes monitoring systems at the local level are increasing.

Yet the move toward outcomes, like all management reforms, can be overdone or misdirected. Some of the caveats that should be added to a strong endorsement of greater use of outcomes at the program and client level include:

- At times outcomes and indicators of performance are selected because the data is available—not because it measures the right thing;
- Outcomes can degenerate into technical debates about administrative data, rather than an in-depth discussion of an agency's or program's mission and how to measure whether the mission is accomplished;
- Some cities, in particular, have used performance measures rather than community outcomes to measure primarily what their agencies do, rather than whether communities and residents are different as a result of what agencies do;
- Recent "software wars" among vendors for automated outcomes systems have begun to increase skepticism among some cities and counties about performance measurement. Two emerging syndromes are

- understated "feeding costs," i.e. the costs of feeding useful, quality data into the system by front-line workers, and
- a failure to specify the analysis needed to determine what vast arrays of outcomes data actually *mean for policy*.

- New efforts to require agencies to collect outcomes have not been matched by efforts within the state and federal governments to rationalize these outcomes mandates, with the net result that many agencies that have successfully sought multiple funding sources have now fallen victim to multiple—and completely inconsistent—mandates for reporting differently defined outcomes to each of their funders. One agency documented use of six different outcomes "systems" for a single program.

As Paul Light has written of the tides of federal management reforms over the forty years from 1945 to 1995 (his book tracks four separate waves of reform, including various versions of performance budgeting),

> unlike the tides of the ocean which simultaneously erode and reshape the shore, the tides of reform mostly add administrative sediment, whether in the form of new statures, rules, paperwork, or administrative hierarchy.[10]

Better evaluation, not "the gold standard"

To prescribe more and better evaluation as a part of a strategic planning feedback loop may be misunderstood as calling for a level of evaluation rigor that is well beyond the reach of all but a very small minority of local governments. To urge local government to work harder at assessing the effectiveness of its programs for children and families is not to put the bar up so high that huge shifts of resources are needed from services to evaluation. Lisbeth Schorr, Anne Kubisch, and their colleagues at the Aspen Roundtable have dealt with these issues in far greater detail over the past decade than we need to in this book. They describe the "gold standard" of evaluation as those rigorous studies that use control groups, and point out how unrealistic this standard is for evaluations of community building or any integrated services strategy with multiple components, where control groups are unavailable.[11]

Here, three points need to be added to the discussion of the tools of strategic planning

- It is a straw man to argue that localities cannot afford to use control groups and expensive evaluations; most cities and counties do not even try to go beyond counting their clients at present, much less engage in serious evaluation. If they did, the DARE program would have disappeared years ago.
- Another barrier to better effectiveness evaluation is an inappropriate quest for causation and "the attribution problem," as a county official smugly described it recently in a meeting with a strategic planning team proposing wider use of outcomes. In this book, we have raised the issue

of whether any attention is given to which problem is the driver and which are just symptoms or effects of other underlying problems. Determining that with certainty would require many years and lots of funding, and might still end up with a set of ambiguous findings that only academics could love. But what is far more useful is having a serious discussion, as the Los Angeles Children's Planning Council did some years ago, about whether race, poverty, substance abuse, and the level of violence tolerated by the community were more fundamental driving causes than the host of symptomatic conditions such as child abuse and neglect, poor nutrition, and the lack of affordable child care. There is a difference between causes and effects, and the difference is worth talking about, despite the lack of certainty in answers.

- A faddish call for "evidence-based practice" is probably a net plus, in light of the previously mentioned ignoring of evidence that some programs just don't work. But it is disingenuous coming from legislatures and executive branch agencies in state governments that consistently underfund evaluations of statewide programs—and then demand evidence-based program proposals.

A deeper commitment to assessing the effectiveness of locally funded and operated programs may take the form of some fairly simple changes:

- Building outcomes into information systems—seeing how many of the youth in after-school programs do better on attendance, behavior, and performance in the classroom—rather than just counting heads
- Recognize the difference between performance measures—which lots of cities and counties do collect—and outcomes. Mark Friedman remains the clearest thinker on this issue:

  > Performance measures are absolutely essential for running programs well. But they are very different from results and indicators. They have to do with our service *response* to social problems, not the *conditions* that we are trying to improve. It is possible, even common, for individual programs to be successful, while overall conditions get worse.[12]

- Gathering qualitative as well as quantitative data—asking clients how they experienced the programs, asking community members to rate city and nonprofit services or to indicate where they would go first if their family needed help.
- Asking local academics for help in designing evaluations, in conducting them, or loaning interns to do them; lobbying national research firms that are going to do in-depth evaluations to pick your city or county as a site.
- Read: assign staff to stay current with the effectiveness literature and the many websites on promising practices.

All of these are no-cost or low-cost ways of getting better information to make decisions. None require massive longitudinal evaluations; all would improve feedback and raise it above the fairly low base in most local governments.

The universe of need approach

The universe of need is a tool that enables local government to move from generalized statements of need to specific priorities for targeted program design and implementation. It asks which children and families are most important, and why. As recently framed in one county, it proposes clear choices among:

- 12,500 births a year—which are higher-risk—why?
  - 1,073 births to teens
  - 14% of those births were to mothers who received late or no prenatal care
  - 6% were low birth weight
- At 2 years of age, 31% of children in the county were not fully immunized
- 15-21% of all children aged 0-5 had no medical insurance
- 11,000 children 0-4 were living in families below poverty
- 2,154 were special needs children, with developmental delays or disabilities
- 8,470 were living in families with one or more alcoholic or chemically dependent adults (based on a 11% national figure)
- 5,775 were born substance-exposed (based on a 7.5% figure from random screenings as part of a 1992 statewide study)
- 1,050 were the subject of a child protective services report of abuse or neglect.

Obviously many of these categories overlap. What the universe of need forces local planners and policy makers to deal with is *which* of these identifying factors are most important, and which conditions should be the targets of interventions. It also argues strongly for data matching to identify the extent of the overlap among these conditions.

Information, OK—But why values?

When we leave out values, we leave out a lot.

The values dimension is the most frequently omitted and neglected element of strategic planning. Most frameworks mention it in passing, if at all. Yet values are how we choose—whether we identify our choices as values-based or pretend that they are data-driven and fully rational. Value-based choices are not just another step in the process—they are the foundation, if the process is done well and inclusively. Leaving out the values dimension leaves out the foundation of the most important choices that need to be made: the choices that convert a list of desired outcomes into concrete priorities. To ignore value-based strategies is to pretend that manipulating the data by itself can lead to choices, when planning always reveals that the data are inadequate to ensure certainty of results. A leap of faith is often needed to go from the data to choices among priorities.

The importance of values is heightened when venturing into the arena of public policy affecting family life. Kathleen Sylvester has written a very thoughtful monograph on listening to families as a process of understanding public and private values, which makes a strong case for using values to build new and wider consensus in support of children and families programs.[13] She argues that

> Whether constant or evolving, what Americans believe about family life has come to fix the boundaries of what advocates for children and families can expect to achieve.

Values determine

- What outcomes and indicators we select as *priorities* as a response to community need;
- Which *groups and individuals* we select as the focus of our programs and interventions;
- What *data gaps* we choose to invest in improving so that we know where we are and where we are headed;
- What approach we take to the *efforts of existing agencies*—assuming that they are well-intentioned and just need more resources or assuming that they are structurally incapable of achieving better results;
- What approach we take to the *role of citizens, community groups, and parents*—whether it is to be symbolic, episodic, and token or genuine and institutionalized;
- What *sense of urgency* we have about this work—whether we are driven by a sense of the developmental clocks running in the lives of younger children or whether we adopt the slower-paced timetables of agency change.

We avoid values-talk for understandable reasons. It often raises issues of controversy, and many public meetings and advisory groups are conflict-averse. Groups often believe that conflict is a sign that the group is "stuck," rather than recognizing that if the conflict is ignored or avoided, the group is still stuck and lacks consensus, but is ignoring the lack of consensus, which is bound to affect its later work.

But in any human relationship, when there are "non-discussables," there is a lack of trust. So in collaboratives, when conflict is feared, the trust needed to move the collaborative to deeper levels is missing. A diagnostic sometimes used for healthy collaboratives is to ask "what have you disagreed about lately?" If the answer is nothing—the collaborative may have trouble getting to shared outcomes because it hasn't had the basic discussions about the underlying values that shared outcomes must rest upon.

How do we get values into the discussion? Probably not by asking everyone in the room to state their personal values. But there are at least three approaches that have been used in some collaboratives:

- A Collaborative Values Inventory is a neutral, anonymous questionnaire that can be filled out and scored so that a graphic picture of the range of agreements and disagreements on major values issues in visible to everyone in the room—without self-declarations being the starting point. Seeing a graph that shows major disagreement among members of a group shows the group that they disagree, without one person needing to dominate the discussion.[14]
- Facilitators can openly address the process of conflict management in working with collaboratives, and then work to identify areas of consensus when the signs of disagreement emerge in discussions. Sometimes this requires reframing issues, as when a group is stuck on different programmatic needs—pre-school investments versus adolescent prevention, for example, and the group can reach a consensus on identifying the facts regarding how much is currently being spent in each area as a preliminary exercise.

Issues can be framed by group leaders and facilitators so that their ethical, values dimension is explicit. Issues that always have a values dimension include:

- Targeting—which children and families should receive funding and support with limited funds? Why?
- Effectiveness—should we continue to fund programs that are ineffective when highly effective programs lack the funds they need to expand?
- Dosage—should lots of small projects be funded or fewer, larger programs with more chance of success because they have the resources they need?
- Intergenerational issues—which age group is now favored with services and supports? Which ones should be? Why?
- Race, culture, and income gaps—disproportionate outcomes analysis—which groups have caseloads larger than their percentage of the population? Why?
- Reciprocity and personal responsibility issues—what can we demand of clients in return for helping them? What standards of behavior should the larger society require of those helped, as a way of showing respect for them rather than treating them as objects of charity?

As is clear from this list, inclusiveness and diversity issues are a significant part of several of these areas where values matter. We all have trouble addressing these issues of race, class, poverty, and immigration. Yet they are unavoidable in a program that deals with children in our cities and counties, if only because those children are far more diverse than the rest of us, and because so many of the youngest children are poorer than the rest of us.

Beyond these tools, the National Civic League in their work through the Center for Community Problem-Solving has identified others. The following chapter on ethical frameworks for children and family policy also discusses some of these tools. We should also note that a growing field of the theory and practices of deliberative democracy is a resource for cities and counties that want to emulate what Oregon, Ft. Collins, Colorado, and other states and localities have been able to do in helping their communities handle fundamental values disagreements.

Deliberative democracy: an emerging set of tools for addressing values

Linked closely with what others term "the civic renewal movement," the ideas of deliberative democracy include a variety of techniques that seek
- Expanded options for citizens to participate directly in policy identification, refinement, and assessment;
- Heightened face-to-face engagement among representative groups of citizens on well-framed questions of public and community policy;
- Community involvement efforts that include more-than-typical follow-up on public forums, that attend to the likely dominance of forums by providers of services and other interest groups, rather than community residents and consumers of services;
- Adequate time and preparation for the discussion of issues to be reflective, rather than mere repetition of each group's prior arguments.

The Oregon Health Decision Process of the early 1990's is cited often as a model of deliberative democracy or civic renewal, along with environmental dispute resolution frameworks that have been used in public settings. Some practitioners and theorists link civic journalism with deliberative democracy, citing some media efforts to sponsor and cover deliberative forums of various kinds. Defined partly by what it isn't, its literature cites the Clinton health plan (and, more recently, the Bush energy plan) as archetypes of closed, non-deliberative processes.[15]

For children and family policy, these approaches offer an additional set of tools for grappling with the difficult values choices faced in policy making. They offer assurances, for local officials who want or need them, that dealing with thorny values issues need not lead to polarized, explosive sessions, but can be the basis for widening participation in a way that has definite political returns, balancing the risks of moving away from a closed-door model of allocating resources.

Universities and the tools of local government

For some cities and counties, their best chances of using some of these tools may come from a close partnership with a local college or university. Some of these tools have been developed by institutions of higher education, while others have been widely used and refined by university-based research and policy analysis organizations. Developing ties with these organizations may be worth the time it takes, as a means of extending the resources available to local governments.

In some cities and counties, ties to institutions of higher education (IHEs) have produced strong connections and solid products. These include the ties between the Los Angeles County Planning Council and the University of Southern California, long-standing links between New Jersey state and local government and both Rutgers and Princeton, and links between Chapin Hall at the University of Chicago and a variety of children and family institutions in the Chicago and Illinois areas. Some local elected officials (including some mentioned in this work, such as Mayor Bill Purcell of Nashville and Vanderbilt and Mayor Otis Johnson of Savannah and Savannah State) have moved between local government and local universities, adding value on both sides of the relationship.

What to look for in government–university linkages

Not all universities can play such a role, however, and not all local governments have the staff resources or bargaining experience needed to work out a win-win relationship with university-based research and analytical units. The list of what can go wrong on both sides is worth keeping in mind:

- Some university researchers are only able to work on their own narrow areas of specialty, rather than across agencies; the rhetoric of interdisciplinary work has expanded far more rapidly than its reality;
- Some universities are interested in serious relationships with local government only if it produces concrete resources in terms of grants or contracts, internships for students, or access to local databases that can be used for research purposes;
- Some university faculty and researchers lack experience at the practitioner level, which may be compounded by a purist research perspective on difficult issues that makes them unwilling to compromise any of their research findings by making them policy-relevant; this is referred to as "analysis paralysis" by some practitioners who have tried to work with researchers, but found them unwilling to take a final stand on a specific program's effectiveness because the information available is not completely pure.

Universities and the information tools

Some IHEs have been most effective at expanding local governments' power in the use of information, through a variety of approaches:

- Universities have housed units that develop children's report cards and first drafts of children's budgets;
- Universities have analyzed caseload data from child welfare, juvenile justice, education, early education, and numerous other areas and presented information on trends which cannot be done inside local government;

- Universities have developed analytical programs based on geographic information software, enabling city and county agencies to see where their clients live, where caseloads are densest, how far foster children live from their biological parents' homes, and a variety of other geographically specific factors that help refine program design and evaluation;

- Universities have provided evaluation feedback on local programs, ensuring that an independent perspective is available for assessing impact and effectiveness (which at times can solve the problem of who will tell proponents of a particular program that it doesn't work).

Beyond the use of these information tools, some universities have also provided neutral ground for convening parties to local disputes that affect children and families, including education reform debates between teachers' unions, local businesses, and elected school board members.

Universities and a training and education agenda

Policy tools are of little value if there is no one inside the city or county staff who understands how to use them. Well-designed in-service and pre-service education can equip staff with the ability to use and understand the potential of these tools, if it is provided by instructors who have the same understanding and experience. Many universities have contracts with local government to perform training for their staff and local agencies, using such funding sources as Title IV-E funding for child welfare, HUD funding for a variety of urban and housing-related programs, and funding from the Department of Justice for law enforcement and court personnel.

A critical dimension of training local staff to work with children and families in ensuring that training is responsive to the full array of their needs, rather than fitting training into academic and disciplinary categories. The good news is that several universities have begun to develop interprofessional training models, as described in several recent publications.[16]

Conclusion

Using both the tools of information and the tools of consensus-building may require different skills; data mavens may not be the best-equipped facilitators of consensus. Both sets of skills are needed, along with leadership that is open to both. Neither a technocratic number-crunching nor a deep faith in process for its own sake is likely to produce decisions framed so that policy leaders and community residents can join in making better choices for children and families.

NOTES

[1] This section draws upon work supported by the Foundation Consortium as part of the Results for Children initiative with Proposition 10 funds in four California counties.

[2] These issues of youth development are discussed at greater length in Chapter 15.

[3] Bonnie Benard. "Fostering Resiliency in Kids: Protective Factors in the Family, School, and Community Educational Leadership." (Volume 51, Number 3, November 1993).

[4] John P. Kretzmann and Paul H. Schmitz. "It takes a child to raise a whole village." *Wingspread.* (Racine, WI: The Johnson Foundation Inc. 1995).

[5] Peter Benson. (1997) *All Kids are Our Kids.* (San Francisco: Jossey-Bass, 1997), 21.

[6] Ibid. 117, 213-214.

[7] Mark Friedman and Anna Danegger. A *Guide to Developing Child and Family Budgets.* (Washington, D.C.: The Finance Project, 1998).

[8] Mark Friedman. *A Guide to Developing and Using Performance Measures in Results-based Budgeting.* (Washington, D.C.: The Finance Project, 1997). Jacquelyn McCroskey. *Getting to Results: Data-driven Decision-making for Children, Youth, Families, and Communities.* (Sacramento, CA.: The Foundation Consortium., 1999). *Laying the Groundwork for Change,* (1998) The Los Angeles County Children's Planning Council. Jacquelyn McCroskey et al. "Show Me the Money: Estimating Public Expenditures to Improve Outcomes for Children, Families, and Communities." (Los Angeles, CA.: University of Southern California School of Social Work, 2002).

[9] Jim Culotta. "Performance Measurement: A Tool for Managing County Governments." (Washington, D.C.: National Association of Counties, 1999). Evan Berman and XiaoHu Wang., "Performnce Measurement in U.S. Counties: Capacity for Reform." *Public Administration Review:* (Vol. 60, No. 5. September/October 2000). Theodore H. Poister and Gregory Streib. "Performance Measurement in Municipal Government: Assessing the State of the Practice," *Public Administration Review.* (Vol. 59, No. 4. July/August 1999).

[10] Paul Light. *The Tides of Reform: Making Government Work 1945-1995.* (New Haven: Yale University Press, 1997). [3]

[11] James P. Connell, Anne C. Kubisch, Lisbeth B. Schorr, and Carol H. Weiss (eds.) *New Approaches to Evaluating Community Initiatives,* Vol. 1: *Concepts, Methods, and Contexts.* (New York: The Aspen Institute, 1995).

[12] Mark Friedman. *A Guide to Developing and Using Performance Measures in Results-based Budgeting.* (Washington, D.C. The Finance Project, 1998).

[13] Kate Sylvester. *Listening to Families: The Role of Values in Shaping Effective Social Policy* (Washington, D.C.: Social Policy Action Network, 2001).

[14] A current version of the CVI, first introduced in *Beyond Collaboration to Results,* is available at www.cffutures.org.

[15] "Deliberative Democracy," Carmen Sirianni and Lewis Friedland, Civic Practices Network. http://www.cpn.org/cpn/sections/tools/models/deliberative_democracy.html
See also Carmen Sirianni and Lewis Friedland *Civic Renewal in America.* (Berkeley, Ca.: University of California Press, 2001).

[16] Jacquelyn McCroskey & Susan Einbinder. (eds.) *Universities and communities: Remaking professional education for the next century.* (Westport, CT: Praeger, 1998). Interprofessional Education Consortium, *Defining the Knowledge Base for Interprofessional Education.* (San Francisco: The Stuart Foundation, 2001). Joan Levy Zlotnick, Jacquelyn McCroskey, Sid Gardner, Myths *and Opportunities: an Examination of the Impact of Discipline-specific Accreditation on Interprofessional Education.* (Alexandria, Va.: The Council on Social Work Education, 1999).

CHAPTER 5: REFRAMING ETHICAL ISSUES IN SERVICES TO CHILDREN, YOUTH, AND FAMILIES[1]

For a majority of the nearly 77 million children in the US, the ethical boundaries of their lives are set by their parents, the rules of the communities in which they live, and the private institutions to which they belong—the Little Leagues, soccer associations, Girl Scouts, and congregations. The rules they live by and their sense of what is fair comes from these sources. While their lives are touched in many ways by public institutions and public policy, including schools, parks, and police departments, they live and play in the mainstream of their communities.

For a sizable minority of these children, perhaps as many as 10-15 million, however, their vulnerability makes them subject to ethical decisions in very different ways. For these children, ethical choices made in local government affect whether they will grow up in their birth families or be removed from them, whether they will enter the labor market able to earn a decent living for their families, whether they will be allowed in regular classrooms or assigned to special institutions, and whether they will be jailed or diverted to community programs. Social policy, whether or not ethical factors are considered explicitly, affects these more vulnerable children in far more lasting ways than it does the majority of children and youth.

Ethical decisions are especially important in services to children and youth because we act *on behalf of* those without capacity to act on their own behalf; we hold another life in our hands, literally and figuratively. Therefore such decisions have deeper consequences than acting for ourselves alone.

At the level of policy, it is common for policy debates to use ethical language in justifying an advocacy position, arguing that it is fair to provide all children or some specialized group of children new or expanded services, with arguments based on the basic rights of children to the necessities of life. At times, ethical arguments are also used to justify budget reductions, based on the conviction that the costs of programs will affect future generations.

"In the Best Interests"

My wife and I were required to attend four "training sessions" as a part of becoming foster parents for our two children, whom we have since adopted. The most memorable moment came when the trainer wrote on the blackboard the phrase "in the best interests of the child." Great, we thought, we are finally going to get into a serious discussion of how the agency will make decisions about returning the children to their birth parents. But to our amazement the trainer never spoke about what the words meant in practice or policy, and soon erased them. That was our exposure to ethical dialogue in the child welfare system.

But neither in practice or policy is there a consistent framework of ethics that can be used in addressing the hardest choices, such as allocating funds among competing programs, determining what to do about ineffective programs, or deciding which children and families should receive limited funding.

The failure to develop a consistent framework is partly a result of the frequent avoidance of ethical choices when they occur in children's policy discussions. This avoidance grows out of a concern that such debate will create conflict or that values choices are best left to the individual. Some local officials avoid framing issues in ethical terms because they fear groups with strongly held values will surface and oppose them if values choices are brought to the fore.

Ethics in local government today

In recent years, there has been increased emphasis upon ethical factors in local government. But much of this has been focused on the problem of administrators' integrity in balancing the public interest with the pressures of private interests, emphasizing areas such as practices in dealing with private contracts in an era of privatization. Procedural ethics and compliance with codes of ethics predominate in the literature, although some recent works in the public administration field have made a broader case for ethics as "morality in action," to use the phrase of Louis Gawthorp.[2]

In addressing the issues of ethics in local government, in this book I am less concerned with the highly visible issues of bioethics, genetics, and parent surrogacy.[3] As important as these issues are, they appear to be receiving far more attention at present in national policy than issues of accountability for results, the impacts of programs on children they are intended to help, and decisions about which children and families to target with scarce resources.

Categories of ethical issues

Categorizing the different types of ethical issues that affect children in cities and counties is difficult, since there are many different frameworks for child development, for the interactions among parents and children, and the legal boundaries around what children may or may not do and what may or may not be done to them or on their behalf. The four categories used to separate the illustrative issues listed below include:

- issues of programs' effectiveness,
- issues of choices among different clients,
- issues of agencies working together, and
- issues of client responsibility vs. social responsibility.

A further framework for assessing ethical issues that has been used in the health care field distinguishes among social, institutional, and individual levels of ethical analysis.[4]

It is clear that legal standards alone will not suffice in addressing ethical issues affecting children. Merely satisfying the legal requirements is insufficient to meeting ethical requirements, even though law codifies much of our moral reasoning. Acting ethically requires more than observing "the letter of the law," as long as ethical requirements are clear to the worker or policymaker who is involved.

A recent text, *Children, Ethics, and the Law,* while written primarily for mental health professionals involved in direct treatment of children, does an excellent job in its introductory chapter of clarifying how children are different as *objects and subjects* of ethical decision-making.[5] The book also discusses the contrast between *child advocacy* and *child-saving,* in which children's rights are the focus of the first approach and intention to protect specific, vulnerable children is the intent of the second.

Each of these categories is helpful in addressing issues of ethics in children's services, but clearly, all of them cannot be used at the same time. The question is what are the best tools for reframing issues of ethical choices in children's programs; is there an amalgam of these several frameworks that would be useful and comprehensible both to scholars and practitioners in the field? The list below illustrates different kinds of ethical policy choices, with examples drawn primarily from the field of substance abuse treatment.

Issues of Programs' Effectiveness
1. The use of scarce funding to support programs that seek to prevent substance abuse by adolescents–but which are widely recognized to be ineffective; the limits of a leader's responsibility to inform the public of a program's ineffectiveness if the public is paying for it through taxes or donations.
2. The unwillingness of some agencies (and their funders) to adopt client outcomes as a measure of their effectiveness in helping children and youth.
3. The ethics of professionalizing helping, i.e. when and how should professionals determine that "natural helpers" or parents are the most effective "practitioners," rather than credentialed and accredited professionals with approved academic training?
4. The ethics of "pilot projects" whose sponsors never consider operating at scale; is it ethical to measure progress against baselines of historical performance—"we saw twice as many clients as last year"—rather than measuring impact on the entire population needing services?

Issues of Choices among Different Clients
1. Choices made among different clients have obvious ethical content— whom shall we serve, and why? These include rationing decisions, whether made explicitly as in Oregon health policy debates, or implicitly, as in adjusting foster care placements to available matching funding for placement beds.
2. A bias against women and children in current allocations of substance abuse treatment funds (only 29.8% of all publicly funded treatment slots are allocated to women, and in most treatment programs, the children of parents in treatment are not even counted).[6]
3. The lack of clear distinctions among clients who are harder-to-serve and those who may need less help in achieving outcomes, which may

compromise the purpose of an outcomes-based funding system by "creaming" easier-to-serve clients and creating incentives to screen out those who are harder-to-serve. This issue appears especially relevant in light of current welfare policy changes and choices in serving the harder-to-serve clients who remain on the caseloads.

Issues of Agencies Working Together

1. The ethics of collaboration: when is it unfair or malpractice not to seek help from an outside agency that may have a different expertise needed by the client, in a climate of agency competition for resources in proving that they help clients?
2. The ethics of referral, i.e., when is referral a client-centered decision and when is it agency-centered and defensive in nature—"this is your problem?"

Issues of Client Responsibility vs. Social Responsibility

1. The ethics of "second chances:" at what point and using what standards of ethics, if any, can society and its front-line workers make fair decisions about parents at risk of losing their children or youth who are at risk of incarceration? How many "second chances" are fair to children affected by a parent's substance abuse, if the evidence is strong that more than one episode of treatment is needed for most clients? How many "second chances" are fair to parents, given the evidence that one-third of clients succeed in their first episode of treatment and half of those remaining succeed in later episodes?

Effectiveness and targeting

In local government, the first and second of these categories are the ethical choices that are most often visible. The issue of program effectiveness is a good example of a policy issue with ethical content. If scarce resources are spent on programs intended to help clients in need, the funder, the provider, and the intended beneficiary all can be said to have rights to some measure of assurance that the resources are well-used. Therefore, we believe that the efficacy argument must also be addressed in considering the ethics of services to children: programs and services must be effective and have good evidence of effectiveness to be valid ethically. Helping is not enough if there is available evidence that the programs being used will not really help children. In other words, *there is not only a moral obligation to help; there is also a moral obligation to seek effectiveness in helping.*

This proposed effectiveness principle is by no means a majority position in the human services, as Lisbeth Schorr notes in *Common Purpose*.[7] She cites Mother Teresa's quote "God has called on me not to be successful, but to be faithful," as well as Gandhi's dictum: "It is the action, not the fruit of the action, that is important." Many providers of services to children would make a similar argument that the core of good intentions is far more important than the outer circle of results or accountability for results. But if we can assume that most providers are not at the level of either Mother Teresa or Gandhi in their exemplary capacity to mobilize the best in humankind, then results do matter—especially to those we seek to help. It raises fundamental ethical questions if those who work in the "helping professions" do not measure whether in fact those we seek to help really do get better. And for local governments, the merit of good intentions is no substitute for using scarce resources from city and county budgets for programs that work.

This raises the question of whether ethical practice and policy place clients—some prefer the words community members, recipients, or other terms that are less mechanistic—at the center of things. In addressing the ethics of public policy, the means by which that policy is delivered is part of the equation of fairness. In personal ethics, if individuals act on their own behalf at the expense of another person, a judgment can be made that the behavior is wrong because it is self-centered. Institutions can be judged on their ethical behavior, too, especially if they are funded and given their legitimacy based on their supposed help for their clients. If institutions instead act primarily or solely to preserve their own well-being, rather than that of the client whom they are funded and authorized to help, then their actions can be judged to be institutionally-centered in ways that can be questioned and contrasted with more client-centered action.

In the field of health care, hospital ethics committees date from the 1970s, and have evolved in the 1990s in some institutions into a wider concern for "organizational ethics" which move beyond decisions about individual patients to issues of institutions' responsibility to their wider community and the whole society.[8] In addressing children's issues, these organizations have focused primarily upon the rights of newborns with disabilities, rather than the issues of health care for uninsured children, the needs of immigrant children, or intergenerational issues. Recently, however, some hospital-linked ethics centers have begun to address this wider circle of issues that go beyond the patients already in the hospital's care to questions about those who *could be.*

In framing ethical judgments, institutional practices rest significantly upon the *adequacy of program effectiveness information.* Ethical reasoning requires adequate information, and an effort to get that information is itself an ethical practice. Some proposals for health care rationing, for example, suggest doing so based on "marginally beneficial services" in which costs and benefits can be calculated with some precision. It is argued that:

> Physicians should not be expected to perform cost-effectiveness studies at the bedside. Rather, they should become familiar enough with the concepts of cost-effectiveness so that they can more accurately identify marginally beneficial health care services.[9]

If we extend this analysis to local government support for and children's services beyond the health care arena, we can see the further ethical importance of insuring that adequate information is available to make judgments about programs' effectiveness. Local policymakers and their staffs need to go beyond simply measuring what programs do to assessing whether clients and communities improve. Subjecting client information systems to this test would find many of them inadequate, in that they do not track clients long enough to determine whether they really benefit from services. Cities and counties that have invested in their outcomes information systems may be justifying it on technical grounds, but they are also contributing to their ability, if not their willingness, to make ethical decisions.

Some writers, however, do address effectiveness issues. In the debate about a "feminist ethics," several writers have stressed what they believe to be the greater predilection for women to make ethical judgments based on pragmatic factors of who is helped rather than principle-based judgments using rules of ethics.[10]

The ethics of collaboration[11]

The ethics of collaboration itself can be assessed in light of the responsibilities of a client-centered agency. If a worker or agency supervisor knows that the agency cannot provide a child or family with the full range of resources needed to become more self-sufficient, it is a form of *malpractice* to

---

The Ethics of DARE

A classic example of the program effectiveness choices faced by professionals working with children and youth may be presented by the DARE program. DARE—Drug Awareness and Resistance Education—was developed by the Los Angeles Police Department as a means of providing substance abuse prevention education to fifth graders. Nine national studies and one by the California Department of Education have demonstrated conclusively that the program has no positive effects on adolescent use of drugs and alcohol, while having slightly positive effects on attitudes toward police.[8a] More than $1 billion is estimated to be spent annually on the program, which relocates thousands of police officers from patrol duties to classroom assignments, and decreases classroom time on education content. The program remains very popular, and schools welcome the program because it places a uniformed officer on their campus. Should professionals who work in prevention education point out the program's ineffectiveness in achieving its announced goals—or remain silent? Is the mis-allocation of these funds and officers an ethical choice, given other uses for the funds, including a need for counseling services in some of the schools that have a DARE officer—but no school counselor?

---

simply make a referral to another agency or to provide a service that the worker knows to be insufficient. A prime example of this may be the unjustifiable chasm between most child welfare and drug treatment agencies in the nation. With 60-80% of the incoming families in the child welfare system from substance-abusing families, for these two agencies and sets of workers not to be in close collaboration is inexcusable, since it is abused children who are often the victims of this lack of collaboration. Yet the norm for most child welfare workers is to give new clients a list of phone numbers of treatment programs and leave it at that. Knowing what a client needs, and knowing that the resources may be in the community, but defining one's own job so narrowly that the help is not provided—this is not a tenable ethical standard.

This perspective can be extended to pose a standard for collaboration viewed in ethical terms:

- We must collaborate with other agencies if we know they can help our client in ways we cannot, and in ways our clients need.
- We must know enough about other agencies whose services our clients need to make a "good handoff" to them. A referral slip is not a good handoff—it places all the burden of achieving connection with the other agency on our clients.
- We must conduct follow-up services to see if our clients got the services we sent them to get, as a means of supporting our clients and also of holding the other agency accountable for what we sent our client to get from them.
- We must collaborate with other agencies if resources of the other agency could clearly help our client and multiply our own effectiveness.

For local government, these standards could be used to periodically conduct an "ethical audit " of programs that goes beyond conflicts of interest and hiring relatives of campaign contributors to asking deeper questions about programs' effectiveness.

Rationing decisions and children's services

Discussions of "rationing" raise very controversial issues, which are controversial in part because they bring to the surface choices that are often well concealed beneath layers of economic and political factors. But in health care it has become very clear that we ration frequently in making conscious or implicit decisions about which patients shall receive care which is limited and which cannot be funded for all patients. When a liver transplant or some other procedure reaches public visibility, and it becomes clear that a deliberate decision is made about ranking one client over another based on some predetermined factors, the ethical underpinnings of decision-making are exposed. Those medical ethicists who have studied Oregon's unique health rationing system argue that the health care debate in Oregon is a lot more honest and public-educating than in other states where the same amount of rationing goes on but is beneath the surface.[12]

But rationing, defined as the allocation of scarce resources based on some predetermined criteria, happens outside the health care arena, and some of these choices, when made in local governments, directly affect children and youth. We also ration foster care and other forms of out-of-home care, since we lack the resources to pay for homes for all children who need to be temporarily or permanently removed from their biological parents' homes. (It is important to note that there is both a human shortage of foster and adoptive families to provide this care and a fiscal shortage of funds to support it.)

Other services for children are also rationed—we decide how serious a child's learning disability needs to be before they are provided special education services, we decide which children are "at-risk," using risk factors that entitle some children to receive preventive services, and we make decisions about counseling needed by a small number of children based on whether we have allocated available funds to other prevention programs that serve all children in a given grade level. Each of the professionals making these decisions operates as a "gatekeeper," whether or not they work in a formal managed care setting. But compared to local government, the health sector has at least faced these ethical choices more explicitly than the typical city or county as it allocates funds for services to children and families.

So rationing is another example of both our aversion to ethical discussion and the unavoidability of fairness criteria in framing the decisions made every day about children and family services. Even if those criteria are completely implicit—"first come, first served" is an example of a fairness criterion—they operate just as though lengthy debate had reached a consensus on that rule of choice among different clients.

Ethical frameworks and special groups: women, minorities, and intergenerational equity

Framing these issues in terms of children and families raises the question of whether fairness demands considering the great differences among children relating to gender, race, and culture.

Gender matters in ethics, and gender obviously matters in the lives of children. Exactly how it matters is a subject that has been intensely debated in the last two decades. But that it matters is indisputable. As Gilligan and Wiggans (1988) state:

> The overwhelmingly male composition of the prison population and the extent to which women care for young children cannot readily be dismissed as irrelevant to theories of morality or excluded from accounts of moral development. If there are no sex differences in empathy or moral reasoning, why are there sex differences in moral and immoral behavior?[13]

The increasing presence of women in local government does not automatically ensure that these issues will be raised, but the focus on family issues like child support, child care, and work requirements in welfare makes it more likely that local government will use ethical frameworks in debating these increasingly visible issues.

The ethics of multiculturalism also raises very difficult issues of how different groups should be treated: the "starting line" is not the same for all groups, and the issue is what advantages should be given to those for whom disproportionate outcomes reveal their disadvantaged status. For some children and youth, fairness becomes defined as a deliberate effort to erase or reduce the potential consequences of luck and discrimination from their lives.

Ethical issues include, of course, the inequities of racial and other forms of discrimination. Insisting that social indicators are always disaggregated by race, gender, and other relevant categories is a tool of analysis, but documenting disproportionate outcomes is not enough if those outcomes do not then become the targets of clear policy that monitors improvement. Ethical analysis needs to go beyond better counting to better policy—and then tracking the effects of that policy to see if conditions get better over time.

There are also important issues affecting children and families that are intensifying because of the age cohorts in American society, in which older Americans increasingly have greater political and economic power than younger ones. With elderly poverty reduced by half since 1960 and poverty among children increasing significantly during that period, intergenerational equity issues are already becoming far more visible in the early 21st century than they have been in the late 20th century. In local government, building more senior centers contrasted with funding for child care is one form of the debate, with a win-win solution emerging in some cities with new construction funds used for "24/7 schools" that are designed to be used around the clock by seniors and other community groups, as well as children of pre-school age. California's pending $25 billion school construction bond underscores how significant the scale of this debate may become in view of outdated school buildings all over the nation.

The future of ethics in local government

Local government is unlikely any time soon to hire its own ethicists, as hospitals do. But its budget officials, its planners, and its elected leaders could use existing tools of ethical analysis more readily than they do at present. In doing so, they might consider the following broad guidelines:

1. Start from an assumption that choices among alternative courses of action have ethical content, rather than weighing only their fiscal, managerial, or psychological impacts.
2. Frame the issue of the motives of the actors involved, not only asking whether we are acting "in the best interests of the child," but also who is interpreting those interests and from what perspective. How disinterested are those interpretations? These "clean hands" issues can be extended to ask what proponents of different policies have done with their own time, talents, and resources about the problem they are addressing, e.g. what local advocates of education vouchers do in enrolling their own children in school, or what local advocates of pro-life policies have done about the adoption gap in child welfare.
3. Ask how children will be affected even if they are "collateral" parties to the decision, e.g., when a parent is enrolled in drug treatment, asking how that parent's children will be affected by the treatment and aftercare.
4. Ask if children have been afforded a full opportunity to act as subjects, instead of being seen and treated only as objects of action that is taken "for" them, e.g., consulting children in custody cases vs. assuming that

courts must act for them prior to the age of majority, or developing active youth participation efforts, as a number of cities have done.

5. Determine what level of effort is required of a worker in making sure that all possible sources of help for a family, even those outside a provider's profession, agency, or cultural competence, have been utilized—this might be called "the collaboration imperative."

6. Determine what efforts have been made to determine whether a given program, practice, or policy is effective in helping the children and families on whom it is targeted—"the effectiveness imperative."

7. Ask what impact the treatment or service provided to one child or family would have if made available to all children and families in a similar position (this is called "horizontal equity" in social policy language, and is a limited version of Kant's categorical imperative—asking what the consequences would be if all persons were treated according to a proposed ethical standard. It may also be a useful corrective to the "pilot project mentality" that treats all new projects as progress).

Conclusion

There is an obvious critique of the effort to apply ethical principles to children's policy. A front-line worker might well say: "We do these things every day, in our gut, intuitively. We do not formulate them as decision rules in most children's agencies, we just decide based on our own reflective practice, experience, and gut. It is thus unrealistic to elevate these to formal principles."

To further burden workers and supervisors who already have barely manageable caseloads with another framework for decision-making must answer a sizable burden of proof: will this make the workers' jobs more difficult or less; will it offer them a chance of getting more resources or becoming more effective in meeting their clients' needs? Those reality tests must govern discussions of ethical decision-making if they are to have an impact on the front lines of work with children and families.

For policy-makers in local government, a different burden of proof must be met. Will this reframing of decisions about children and families clarify the hardest choices they make, or will it simply add a new layer of debate on top of the clash of interests in which they are already immersed? Merely generating a new set of exhortations to "think about the children" will do little to resolve debates among liberals, conservatives, communitarians, and libertarians who are very clear that they know best how to think about the needs of children without doing so in an explicitly ethical framework.

The hope, therefore, is that reframing these issues in ethical terms can meet both these tests and provide language and concepts that are worth using by the workers and policy-makers who affect the lives of the most vulnerable children and families. A basic assumption of this work is that both front-line workers and policymakers would welcome such information, since it may help them make better decisions about policy and practice, as they set about their work of improving the quality of the lives of children.

NOTES

[1] This chapter is drawn in part from a longer paper published for the annual conference of the American Society of Public Administration's Ethics Section in Portland, Oregon in September 1998.

[2] Louis Gawthrop, Public Service and Democracy: Ethical Imperatives for the 21st Century. (Chappaqua, N.Y.: Chatham House Publishers, 1998). Quoted in Donald Menzel, "Discovering the Lost World of Public Service Ethics: Do We Need New Ethics for Public Administrators?" Public Administration Review, (Vol. 59, No. 5, September/ October 1999.).

[3] It may be important to note, however, that local governments seen likely to be drawn into the debates about biotechnology, since locational and zoning powers give them some oversight affecting what kinds of research can be done within city and county limits. These are obviously children and family issues of the near-future, in part because they are about what kinds of children will become members of families.

[4] John W. Glaser, and Ronald P. Hamel. Three Realms of Managed Care. (Kansas City, Mo.: Sheed and Ward, 1997).

[5] Gerald P. Koocher and Patricia Keith-Spiegel. Children, Ethics, and the Law. (Lincoln, Neb.: University of Nebraska Press, 1993).

[6] FY99 State Resources and Services Related to Alcohol and Other Drug Problems: An Analysis of State Alcohol and Drug Abuse Profiles for Fiscal Years 1998 and 1999. (Washington, D.C. National Association of State Alcohol and Drug Abuse Directors, 2001).

[7] Schorr, Common Purpose, 136.

[8] Ethical Currents, (Orange, Ca.: Center for Health Care Ethics, St. Joseph Health System, Spring 1998, No. 53.).

[8a] "How Effective is DARE?" American Journal of Public Health September 1994, 1399. "The DARE program's limited effect on adolescent drug use contrasts with the program's popularity and prevalence. An important implication is that DARE could be taking the place of other, more beneficial drug education programs that kids could be receiving." See also Erin Texeira, "Study Assails School-based Drug Programs," Los Angeles Times, October 21, 1995. Cost estimates are from Edward M. Shepard. "The Economic Costs of D.A.R.E." (Institute of Industrial Relations, 2001); downloaded October 20, 2003 from http://www.reconsider.org/

[9] Peter A. Ubel and Robert M. Arnold, "The Unbearable Rightness of Bedside Rationing," in Glaser and Hamel, Three Realms, 179.

[10] Nel Noddings, Caring: A Feminine Approach to Ethics and Moral Education. (Berkeley, Ca.: University of California Press, 1984). Margaret Urban Walker, Moral Understandings: a Feminist Study in Ethics. (New York: Routledge, 1998).

[11] This section is drawn from an earlier work, Beyond Collaboration to Results.

[12] Daniel Callahan, "Symbols, Rationality, and Justice: Rationing Health Care," in Glaser and Hamel, Three Realms, 3-12.

[13] Carol Gilligan and Grant Wiggins, "The Origins of Morality in Early Childhood Relationships," in Mapping the Moral Domain, Carol Gilligan, Janie Victoria Ward, and Jill McLean Taylor, (eds), (Cambridge, Mass.: Harvard University Press, 1988).

Chapter 6: The Budget Is the Policy

Premises

- Budgets are very complicated—both deliberately and inadvertently
- Budgets for children and family issues are often buried in other categories
- Budget-making is political as well as analytical, and the two processes become entangled with each other at times
- Policy-makers are often frustrated in their efforts to change budgets by unexamined claims that staff and policy leaders cannot make changes due to a lack of discretion
- In fiscal climates where cuts are needed, smart cuts are harder to make than dumb cuts—and dumb, across-the-board cuts often harm children and families
- Annual budgets for innovative projects are usually developed at program and agency levels without an adequate "theory of resources" that makes clear where future funds are supposed to come from—and why they should be granted.

Budgeting is an intensely political process. But the politics are often concealed behind arcane processes, complex funding streams, and off-budget items. For children and family providers and advocates, these layers of complexity and secrecy can be daunting. But if the policy of local government is carried out through its budgeting—and it often is—getting into the budget process is unavoidable.

For those inside the government who want to use the budget process to raise children and family policy to new visibility, some dues must be paid to play the game. Those dues include mastering enough of the process to understand what is happening, as well as what isn't happening.

Watching a budget hearing in which elected leaders are "briefed" on the budget can be a painful exercise. A common event is hearing city or county staff explain how little of their budget is really subject to their discretion, blaming state and federal rigidities for their inability to allocate funds to a favorite project of local legislators. It is undoubtedly true that mandated expenditures make up a significant part of local budgets. But the truth of that statement is at times extended far beyond its verifiable limits, as numerous studies have proven.[1] These studies have taken a constraint cited by local administrative staff as created by state or federal mandates and tracked it back from local funds to its state or federal source, asking at each step "Why is this not possible? Where is the law or regulation that prohibits it?" In a majority of cases, the "prohibition" turned out to be a barrier created by local interpretations, rather than actual state or federal legislation or regulations.

But part-time elected officials—and even those who are full-time—are rarely able to devote their time or their staff's time to such verification efforts. It is not only the mandates game that complicates the process; it can also be the empty coffers game. I recently listened to a senior local administrative official explain to an interested audience why it was not possible to provide substance abuse treatment programs for women and children, citing the lack of funding. This was in a jurisdiction that had spent only 3% of its available state funding for treatment of welfare recipients—a fact that was unknown to the entire audience. And so the official got away with it.[2] The time costs of monitoring such issues is substantial, but children and family advocates—both inside and outside the government—who choose to invest their time elsewhere place their clients at risk.

Budgets are irreversibly political, and it would be naive to expect them to be technical or to be based solely on rational analysis. Long ago, in describing the analysis of federal expenditures, Charles Schultze set forth a continuum of decision-making which ranged from pure politics on one end to pure analysis and rational planning on the other.[3] The point of the continuum is that the only real room for movement is along the mid-points, toward consideration of rational options when that is possible, rather than assuming that politics would or should disappear. Rational budgeting, like the pure theory of markets, assumes full information—and no such polity ever existed. In some eras, the action is mostly at the political end of the continuum, while in others, movement is made toward *more* rational, but never fully rational budgeting.

Why children's budgets matter

Children's budgets can help
- Compare costs of a new project with existing spending in the same area
- Compare the benefits of grant pursuit with the returns from redirection of larger existing funding
- Compare investments over time with trends in city-wide indicators over time
- See which programs are growing most rapidly
- Compare prevention with higher-end, remedial services

But the inevitable influence of politics in budgeting cannot justify a sheriff or police chief having no idea how much of his patrol budget is spent on youth-related activities. In making up a children's budget, there is nearly always a point at which someone in an agency says "we don't break it out that way." And that is often the point: when you don't know that two-thirds of the Medicaid budget goes for older residents and only 20% for children, you have missed another signal of priorities. And it is those signals of priorities that providers, advocates and citizens need if they are to understand local politics as they manifest themselves in local budgets.

It is also important for advocates and providers to understand that politics sometimes involves merely asking "the second question." In a budget hearing, it is possible for elected officials and their staffs to ask for written confirmation of a point made by budget staff or agency heads, especially when the first question has led to a "we can't do it" response. "Could you give me the details on what prevents us from doing it?" is a fair question that too few elected officials ever ask. A well-framed question provides direction to staff, especially those within an agency who may have been trying unsuccessfully to make the case the elected official is trying to make.

Hard times and the cost of credibility

When difficult economic conditions bring reductions in programs for children and families, many providers and advocates adopt a defensive posture and argue against all cuts. But in fact, hard times are the best times to eliminate the worst programs.

At least three arguments can be made for the case for using budget cutbacks as an opportunity to reduce scarce spending on ineffective programs:

1. To defend all programs suggests all are equally effective—and we know that is not true. Having to defend a known untruth is a very weak position. To gain credibility with both the general public and affected communities served by weak programs, funders and advocates should withdraw their support for those programs. The general public suspects that some programs don't work—and affected communities know it.

2. In tight budgets, funding for all programs is scarce. If cuts are going to be made anyway, they can be smart cuts, or dumb cuts
   a. Dumb cuts are across the board cuts that assume all programs have equal claims to resources, without regard to their merit
   b. Smart cuts reduce or eliminate funding for programs with weak claims to scarce resources
   What is a smart cut?
     - A smart cut targets an ineffective program.
     - A smart cut targets programs that have little or no leverage on other resources.
     - A smart cut targets programs that that are isolated and not part of an integrated services effort.
     - A smart cut funds services wherever they are provided most effectively, rather than favoring public employees and cutting back grantees and contractors because they are easier to cut.

3. To allocate scarce funds to programs known to be ineffective, when children and families need good programs more than ever, has ethical content, as we noted in the last chapter: it ignores a core principle for helping agencies—that they should ensure that their help is effective with the people it intends to benefit, rather than simply counting those served. Failing to make any effort to determine programs' effectiveness is to be narrowly agency-centered, not client-centered. Being against accountability for results when funding is scarce is bad politics—and bad ethics as well.

Redirection and accountability, not automatic termination

This argument is not that termination of programs should proceed without any due process or any effort to improve weak programs. A multi-year redirection agenda could be developed in a given community in which lowest-performing programs would be identified carefully, given 1-3 years to produce measurable improvements (or evidence of progress in that direction, or an opportunity to use the same funding to redesign a program that builds on the lessons of what has failed and what has worked in other communities). How these various approaches are combined might vary in each community—but in all of them, a redirection process would have begun.

But how do we know which are the worst programs?

There are several methods of beginning a process of identifying weaker programs, if there is not already such an effort under way. Redirection tools already exist and are in use in many communities. These include:

- Begin using a higher standard of funding, based on revised requests for proposals and contract language that includes greater emphasis upon outcomes data;
- Begin requiring client feedback forms;
- Ask a local university or third party evaluator to interview current and past clients for feedback and to determine whether intended changes in their outcomes have happened;
- Use national best practices literature or "blueprints" programs as a template to determine how well local programs fit these models of successful programs;
- Ask local grantees to submit their best evaluations and measures of success;
- Ask for grantees as volunteers to receive technical assistance in program effectiveness improvement—the agencies least likely to apply are often those with the most concern about being able to document their results;
- Develop evaluation guidelines to help grantees and funders to develop sensible evaluation methods, avoiding both the extremes:
  - "gold standard" evaluation with control groups or
  - simplistic head-counting that makes no effort to determine whether clients benefited from the program.

Inadequate attention to redirection

The not-so-good news is that grantees and funders have devoted far less time and energy to redirection and cutback management efforts than they have to launching pilot projects and seeking small, near-token line items for new programs. Redirection is unquestionably harder, and if it didn't include much more money than newly-funded efforts, it would not be worth it. But the numbers are very clear: redirecting the least effective programs that are already in communities almost certainly represents more "new" resources than are likely to be available from state or federal sources.[4]

Separate from the gains from redirecting ineffective programs are the possible returns from refinancing[5] programs as a further approach to redirection, shifting funding from a less reliable grant to a more certain funding source, such as Medicaid or schools' Title I funding, or setting up a timetable for making such a shift if the program produces outcomes that would justify institutionalized funding.

Where to go hunting

There are clusters of programmatic areas where, unfortunately, a great number of weak programs are easily found. These include:

- School-based drug prevention programs, notably DARE-model programs (which have been found ineffective by six national evaluations, but which still receive hundreds of millions of federal and local funding);
- After-school programs, where well-intentioned programs have ignored the lessons of the dosage required to make a difference for youth that need the most help;
- Parent education, where many programs rely upon Saturday-morning parent education that uses shallow curricula that cannot be evaluated for lasting impact;
- Family support programs that emphasize "counseling," ignore the greater need for family income support in hard times (as discussed further in Chapter 14), and cannot document how many families they have helped to enroll in work support programs that can be worth thousands of dollars annually to hard-pressed families.

Again, this is not an argument that such programs should be eliminated. The goals of each of these programs are on target—it's the design and implementation that have been flawed. If the goals remain important, then the program funding should be redirected to a program that will work.

It should also be noted that quality assurance is part of credibility efforts. There *are* Medicaid mills, poor charter schools, and under-monitored child welfare privatization efforts. Saying so does not betray the goals of these programs; it redeems them by noting that the goals are being undermined by bad programs.

It's about credibility

Funders, advocates, and providers will lose critical credibility in the tight budget times that lie ahead in most states and communities if they remain silent on weak programs or allow themselves to be trapped into defending all programs when resources are scarce. With structural deficits built into federal and state budgets for many years to come, the case for a fair share of resources for children and family services and supports needs to be as strong as possible. Weakening that case by allowing ineffective programs to be sheltered, while good ones are being cut, is demonstrably bad for children, families, and communities. Greater priority for a redirection agenda is the best way to free up funding for the most effective programs that desperately need funding to survive and eventually, to expand to serve more children and families. A redirection agenda can result in two gains: more financial resources for the best programs, and more political capital in making the case for those programs.

Budgeting as the development of a "theory of resources"

Budget decision-making in local government involves both the base expenditures—funding that is part of the budget on an annual basis, like salaries for mandated functions—and funding for innovation—new projects that may have a more short-term impact. Decisions about innovative projects may be made simply based on how much new funding may be available in a given year, or it may be based on a more explicit strategy.

The concept of a "theory of change" has received a great deal of attention in the past several years as a tool to assist comprehensive community-based initiatives and local governments in evaluating and redesigning such initiatives and community change efforts.[6] In budgeting, it can be argued that a related "theory of resources" would help in addressing issues of sustainability and the long-range fiscal future of demonstration projects at the citywide and community level.

The "theory of resources" variation on the theory of change

We believe that a separate emphasis upon a "theory of resources" should be included in the design and evaluation of innovative projects for children and family—and for that matter, for all community change efforts—because the decisions about what it will take to launch, operate, sustain, and take a project to scale are often underemphasized or even ignored in developing new initiatives. Developing an explicit theory of resources[7] can help a local government or an initiative's sponsors develop more articulated ideas about two critical ingredients of a project's success:

- the project's outcomes—which are closely linked to the resources it needs to succeed, and
- its long-term sustainability–the resources it needs to sustain itself or move toward scale, which has proven to be a critical issue in many of community-based initiatives.[8]

The work under way in theory of change evaluation has shown that even the best planning efforts often neglect or avoid specifying what interventions lead to what outcomes and what the theorized logical connections are between the interventions and the outcomes.[9] In the same way, planning and implementation efforts often become so caught up in proposal-writing and grant-chasing for external funding that its theory of resources becomes, in effect, a vague hope that grants will lead to more grants. The critical omission here is that there is often far less discussion of the far greater level of resources *already in the community*. This, in itself, becomes an implicit theory of resources in community planning: what comes into the community from outside sources is worth planning for, while what is already here is unavailable or unchangeable.

To summarize, a theory of resources is needed in community-level planning and budgeting because

4. Assumptions should be made explicit about how the resources of the project fit its outcomes;
5. Assumptions should be made explicit about how the project is to sustain its efforts beyond temporary start-up, seed funding;
6. Targeting the most likely future funders helps to ensure that the project delivers the results which these funders would demand as evidence that the project is worth funding; and
7. Targeting non-financial resources and social capital needed for project success requires advance planning just as much as fund-raising, if not more.

A final reason for taking the theory of resources concept seriously is that if community change efforts are to rise above the level of pilot projects and approach the realm of systems change, the resources required to change the system are obviously larger and more strategic than those required to merely launch a project.

A theory of resources process would address an initiative's needs at three critical levels:

- What resources do we need to achieve results? (the *outcomes* question)
- What resources do we need to sustain those results? (the *sustainability* question)
- What resources do we need to take those results to scale? (the *scale* question)

Each of these requires a different process to develop a plan and a budget for the initiative's efforts to mobilize resources. The outcomes question is about the basic theory or logic model of the program: do we have the resources we need to achieve the short-term and longer-range results we seek? The sustainability question is about "pickup:" who will pick up funding when our temporary grant sources are concluded? And the scale question addresses issues of success: if this works, where will we go to get resources to do more of what has worked well—expanding to a wider geographic area or serving more clients?

Types of resources

At the same time, the planning and budgeting process needs to address the multiple types of resources required by an initiative: financial, human, volunteer, social capital, investment capital, information resources, analytical resources, credibility, legitimacy, visibility, and others. Each of these is a different kind of resource, but to plan only for financial resources would overlook the great importance of the other kinds of resources. But most projects focus so heavily upon funding alone that they neglect the importance of the other kinds of resources.

If cash is the only resource that communities pursue, their efforts to be in and of the community will be frustrated, because citizen energy in the forms of volunteers, self-help, and mutual assistance organizations will be ignored. Moreover, in some projects, gathering the right information about the outcomes of the project may be as important a resource as cash to sustain the project itself.

Resources and collaboration

If the outcomes question is taken seriously, a deeper approach to collaboration will be needed than simply requiring the formation of a collaborative as a governance mechanism. Adding more members to a collaborative is the easy work; groups will usually add any new members who are specified by funders as a condition of a grant to a collaborative. But that does not mean that the parties are seriously collaborating.[10] The theory of resources approach to outcomes has the potential to document the insufficiency of an agency's own resources in ways that can cement collaboration. It gets at the "myth of self-sufficiency," which is often one result of an agency getting an outside grant, leading the agency to conclude "now we can do this by ourselves." But when an agency has only been funded to develop a pilot project, the larger issues of the fit between resources and results are still absent from the grant discussion.

Resources already in the community

In an emphasis on the "bottom line" of results, agencies and collaboratives can be helped to see how inadequate their own resources may be to achieve the outcomes they seek, and why they need better agreements with other providers for joint action. But a clear prerequisite to better agreements is *knowing who those providers are and the total level of spending in the community*, which is where our earlier references to children and family budgets in Chapter 4 are relevant.

In asset mapping, some community initiatives have used the excellent work of John McKnight and his colleagues to document the strengths of the community. But many of these efforts have done a cursory or nonexistent job in mapping the multimillion dollar flows of public and other funding into the neighborhoods they seek to change.[11]

A theory of resources is a theory about redirection and leverage, or an unspoken choice *not* to exercise such leverage or seek redirection of existing funding. It is a theory about which existing agencies and funding flows are the ripest for change, the most susceptible to data and evidence, persuasion, embarrassment, political power, advocacy, or other incentives for genuine collaboration.

A theory of resources addresses not only the different kinds and availability of resources, but it also reveals a community initiative's ideas about *who it is* and who are *the asset controllers in the community*. That is, it makes clear whether the organization believes it is capable of influencing decisions and decision makers who are focused on budgeting the larger resources already in the community. At its core, a theory of resources becomes a theory about local politics and power, in that it assumes that "the real money" *can* be influenced over time. If existing resources are not targeted, the theory, in effect, gives up on achieving such influence, assuming that these resources are beyond any initiative's influence. While this may be a rational conclusion in some communities at some times, we would argue that it can relegate community change efforts to marginal status at best.

"We could never get any say over how *that* money is used" is how one group put it, when the full inventory of spending in their community was presented. They were firmly convinced that inventorying those resources in greater depth was not even a useful effort. Setting aside the self-fulfilling prophecy inherent in their view of themselves, this perspective presents a fundamental "Willie Sutton problem." When reporters asked Willie Sutton why he robbed banks, he answered, "Because that's where the money is."

Figure 2: Real Money

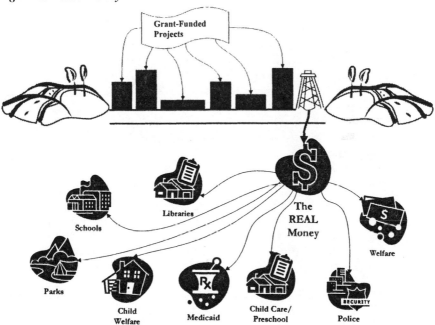

To ignore the funding base that makes up the great bulk of the more than $500 billion spent annually by the public sector on programs for children and families is giving up on any chance of leveraging much greater totals than can ever come to a community through grants. In communities, not knowing where the money is often means having a vague, wishful thinking theory of resources that looks only at the marginal funding that comes in from outside, rather than the institutionalized funds that are already there. Figure 2 depicts this difference, showing projects on top of the surface of the community with the much larger funding "underground" and out of sight of community planners.

Tools for analysis of available resources

As mentioned, McKnight and others have developed excellent frameworks for asset mapping and neighborhood strengths analysis. What are also needed are tools that can track other forms of resources coming into the neighborhoods, including:

- neighborhood budgets, with analysis of the expenditures of all public and private agencies operating in a given area such as an elementary school district;
- estimates of the income benefits flowing to residents of a specific geographic area, using updated census figures made available in 2002; and
- resident surveys on the visibility and effectiveness of public agencies, recognizing that credibility is also a major resource.

Negotiating for resources

To get resources, whether for start-up or sustainability, an agency or community initiative needs to have not only a target for resources, it also needs a strategy for negotiating for resources once it has identified the target. For an after-school prevention program, for example, to suggest in its funding application that it will approach local business groups, the police department, and schools to replace its startup funding is to suggest implicitly that it has a strategy for persuading each of these agencies or groups of three things:

- that the agency or group has resources that could be used for "pickup;"
- that the funding is justified based on the results achieved by the community agency; and
- that the program achieves results that are important to the prospective funder.

In order to negotiate these items, a community program must begin discussions long before the last six months of a three-year grant program. An old saying in politics is relevant: "If you want me in on the landing, you'd better let me in on the takeoff." What this suggests is that opening negotiations as early as possible after grants are received may be the best way to ask a prospective funder the $64,000 question: "what would it take to convince you that this program is worth funding in three years?"

What the question also makes clear is that negotiating funding based on outcomes is often a multi-year process. The first round of negotiations is assessing whether the prospective funder is even interested. A second round, perhaps at the end of the first year, continues the discussion, with further contacts as the results of the program begin to be clearer.

But while this is going on, budgets are changing, the local and state revenue pictures are improving or worsening, and elections are being held. All these may brighten or dim prospects for any one funder, and the program operator will need to track these shifts with care. It may seem easier to simply watch for a new round of grants—but that is where the difference between temporary and institutionalized funding becomes a critical factor. To replace temporary funding with another round of temporary funding is, in effect, to have a very limited theory of resources; to have a game plan for redirecting institutionalized funding may be a much better long-run strategy for getting off the grant-seeking train.

Negotiations II: Where the theory of change and the theory of resources converge

Once a community-based initiative or city agency with an innovative project begins to think seriously about a theory of resources, it is on its way to becoming a serious player in the outcomes business. That is because a central question in thinking about which agencies could pick up future funding is *what it would take to convince them they should.* Resources, in this case, need the closest possible linkage to outcomes.

For example, if a children's hospital is expected to continue funding a grant-initiated medical clinic in the neighborhood, it may be critical to demonstrate that the clinic reduces inappropriate emergency room care. So that indicator—emergency room visits for primary care conditions—becomes an outcome that directly addresses future resources options. Asking potential funders "what do we have to prove to get you aboard?" is a powerful way of raising the issue of a theory of resources, since it begins to surface whether there are *any* outcomes that would be acceptable as proof of effectiveness and of the self-interest of the potential funder. In some cases, there aren't any—there is simply no way the city or county would ever pick up the project. However painful it may be to recognize that fact, it is much better to begin bearing that pain and doing something about it in the first year of a project than in its last six months.

Another way of framing the "pickup question" is in terms of *information strategies*—what data and analysis do we need—and *political strategies*—what allies and approaches do we need? Again, resources consist of more than direct funding, and include both information and political credits or credibility.

A theory of resources also raises and struggles with the same issues raised by the labels of sustainability, durability, institutionalization of demonstration projects, and going to scale. If the theory of change includes clarity about the logical connections between goals-interventions-outcomes, addressing the needs of the entire universe of need is one way to take the theory of change seriously enough to raise questions about the adequacy of resources needed to achieve change. Lisbeth Schorr deals with this powerfully in her book *Common Purpose: Working with Families and Neighborhoods to Rebuild America.*[12] She describes the "hidden ceiling" on going to scale, and raises issues of the fit between resources and results.

The special role of local governments

Ira Cutler's paper on the challenges of sustainability quotes informants who felt that sustainability issues sometimes overlooked local government for spurious reasons:

> Skipping over counties and cities and directly funding neighborhoods cuts off the most likely pick-up funders, and largely foundations are leaving them out as a result of biases—neighborhood-good, city-hall-bad—that are self-defeating.[13]

In many cases, the primary targets for a theory of resources will be one or more agencies of local governments, as the most visible actors in the system of institutionalized funding. In Chapter 1, we set forth the multiple roles of local government in addressing the problems of children and youth. What this framework of multiple roles makes clear is that funding is only one of the resources that local governments can provide. As discussed in Chapter 1, the framework includes a total of fifteen different roles, *only two of which relate directly to funding*. Community change initiatives need a more sophisticated theory of local governmental resources, both to ensure that funding is available in relevant cases and to ensure that a wider agenda of resources is addressed in negotiations with cities, counties, and school districts. We will return to the expectations of community initiatives of local governments and vice-versa, in Chapter 10.

Funders' responsibilities

In a separate article, we have raised the question of the degree to which funders are part of the problem in moving toward results-based accountability.[14] In part, a theory of resources approach is made more difficult because funders create far greater incentives for focusing upon their own grants than the much larger amounts of funding "beneath the surface" and already in the community. If funders themselves know much more about their grants than they do about local education finance or the intricacies of Medicaid reimbursement or managed care, it is understandable that they would not emphasize the redirection agenda as much. But the failure to address redirection options may mislead grantees into devoting disproportionate efforts to grant funding, while virtually ignoring existing funding.

For grantees, the answer is to think beyond the grant to the larger issues of local funding streams. A question that frames this choice is "are we devoting *proportionate* attention to the real money?" If 80-90% of the grantee's resource-seeking efforts go into chasing 10-20% of the funding, the drain on scarce staff energy may be substantial and the effort may be misplaced.

Future Directions

To advance these ideas further, it may be useful to conduct case studies of different approaches to developing implicit theories of resources, building upon Lisbeth Schorr's work on going to scale in *Common Purpose*. Funders and grantees alike need to spend more time reconstructing what happens when elected officials do take things to scale. Hawaii's Healthy Start program represents a commitment through some severe budget crises to sustain a program that serves a large percentage of the most at-risk families. In this and similar areas we need to look for the ingredients that spell success in going to scale in the political environment, as well as the programmatic environment. The resources strategies used by those community initiatives with the most highly developed theories of change could also be mapped.

Pollster and political analyst John Deardourff and several colleagues examined some of these issues in an assessment of state-level advocacy issued by the State Legislative Leaders Foundation in 1995, which remains one of the few works in the field that explicitly addresses political strategies.[15] The constituency-building grants of some foundations have approached these issues, but they focused more often on community mobilization than leveraging elected officials' commitments and examining the rewards and risks of such behavior in support of systems change.

The checklist which follows raises several of the questions addressed in this chapter.

A checklist for developing a theory of resources:

    Questions about effectiveness and resources:

1. What funding and other resources now support the initiative?
2. Are these resources sufficient to achieve the outcomes intended? What assistance from other agencies or community groups will you need to succeed in achieving the outcomes you seek? Are your resources sufficient by themselves, or will you need help from other agencies' resources to have a clear impact? Is the "dosage" your program provides enough to reasonably expect that you will achieve the outcomes you have targeted?
3. Have you inventoried the resources that other agencies are spending in your community to achieve outcomes similar to yours for clients similar to yours?
4. What other agencies in the community may share these outcomes? Are their resources able to be combined with the CCI's to achieve greater impact?
5. Questions about sustainability and resources
6. If the initiative succeeds at its current scale, what are the most likely sources of funding to replace its grant sources when they expire?
7. Why would those new funders agree to support the initiative? What outcomes would convince them that the project was worth sustaining? Why would that source of funding or that agency be selected as a possible target for redirected funding? What cost offsets in future years can you prove—or commit to trying to prove over time?
8. If the initiative succeeds enough to move to the next appropriate scale of operation, and to begin the process of replication, what funding would be used? Will it take more grants or will internal resources be used?
9. What is the likely pace of replication, i.e., how long will it take to make decisions about moving to new sites or expansions that would provide effective services to more of the population that needs those services?

NOTES

[1] Margaret Dunkle of Georgetown University, who has reviewed federal policy as it complicates local decision-making, summarizes as follows: "careful review of federal laws and rules reveals that it is very often state or local policy, or state or local practices,

that pose barriers, NOT federal laws and regulations." Personal communication, May 27, 2002. In one recent federal waiver experiment that encouraged state and local governments to seek waivers of restrictive federal policies, 31% of the waiver requests were withdrawn because federal law already permitted the change. Margaret Dunkle, Understanding Flexibility in Federal Education Programs 2000. (Washington, D.C.: Institute for Educational Leadership, 2000), 59.

[2] Actually, she didn't, because at the end of the session, she was asked by an outsider about the unspent funds, which she said she was unaware of herself.

[3] Charles Schultze, The Politics and Economics of Spending. (Washington, D.C.: The Brookings Institution, 1968).

[4] A thought experiment may make this clearer: States and local governments spend approximately $250 billion a year (of their own money, and a good deal more of federal matching funds) on programs aimed at children and families. Re-allocating the least effective 10% of that funding would have the same effect as a "new" $25 billion—a level of funding inconceivable in any foreseeable federal budget.

[5] Cheryl Hayes, Thinking Broadly: Financing Strategies for Comprehensive Child and Family Initiatives, (Washington, D.C.: The Finance Project, 2002).

[6] Carol Weiss. "Nothing as Practical as Good Theory: Exploring Theory-based Evaluation for Comprehensive Community Initiatives for Children and Families," in New Approaches to Evaluating Community Initiatives, James Connell et al., (eds) (Washington D.C.: The Aspen Institute, 1995).

[7] By "resources," we mean grant funding; redirected funding already in the community through in-kind staff contributions, e.g., staff assigned to work in a family resource center as part of a team; redirected funding through allocation of local funding or nonprofit funding; voluntary staffing by community organizations or mutual assistance groups; voluntary staffing or in-kind contributions by individuals, e.g., donated furniture or mentoring; and any of the other non-financial resources discussed in the article.

[8] Kubish, et al. Voices from the Field II.

[9] Connell, et al. New Approaches.

[10] These ideas are developed further in Sid Gardner, Beyond Collaboration to Results. (Phoenix, Az.: Arizona Prevention Resource Center, 1998).

[11] John P. Kretzmann, John L. McKnight, and Deborah Puntenney. A Guide to Mapping and Mobilizing the Economic Capacities of Local Residents. (Chicago, Ill.: Institute for Policy Research, Northwestern University, 1996).

[12] Schorr. Common Purpose.

[13] Ira Cutler. The Challenge of Sustainability. (Baltimore: The Annie E. Casey Foundation, 2002), 21.

[14] Sid Gardner. "Results-based Accountability: Funders are Part of the Problem— and Can be Part of the Solution." (Fullerton, Ca.: The Center for Collaboration for Children, 1996).

[15] State Legislative Leaders: Keys to Effective Legislation for Children and Families, (Centerville, Mass.: State Legislative Leaders Foundation, 1995).

CHAPTER 7: THE INTERGOVERNMENTAL STEW: CITIES AND COUNTIES; STATES AND THE FEDS

Cities and counties are not the same. Using the label "local government," as this book does, to encompass both of them obscures as much as it reveals, since their roles vis-à-vis each other vary so widely in different parts of the country. In those states where counties have a major role in children and family services, cities may have much lesser roles, but often do less than they could, even with reduced powers. In those states where counties are restricted to law enforcement and judicial roles, cities' roles may be more significant, but counties may still fail to exercise leadership in issues like child support and child welfare, which are linked to counties' legal roles.

Because of these differences, this book at times discusses the two kinds of governments separately. But they have been combined in a single book out of a conviction that the differences should not allow either type of local government to duck its responsibility—and out of a further conviction that in many states, it will be a new level of cooperation and shared purposes between cities and counties that can achieve better results for children and families.

Yet it remains dangerous to generalize about cities and counties, whether taken together as local governments or separated into their distinct roles. American cities range from Greenwich to East St. Louis, from those with annual surpluses and few responsibilities to poor and near-poor families to those that barely survive on state allocations and bail-outs required by their weak revenue base and growing responsibilities for concentrations of lower-income residents. And American counties are just as diverse, from South Texas and Mississippi counties with rural, poor families dominating their demography to largely suburban counties that are self-supporting for most of their local governmental functions.

So what are the common denominators? In looking at their roles concerning children and family policy, it is possible to set forth at least four common functions:

- Cities and counties all have the power of intergovernmental advocacy: they can speak up for their children and families in dealing with states and the federal government.
- Cities and counties all have the capacity, in varying levels, to assess the well-being of their residents: they can gather information, using their own statistics and the state information systems which they sometimes feed, that measure the status of their children and families over time. At times, they are able to convert this information into a form of power or influence in the policy process.
- Cities and counties all deliver some services to children and families, and they can therefore organize and provide those services so that the

services and supports not under their control are better connected to those that they do control.

- Cities and counties, as the level of government "below" the states, are where the state's essential roles in serving children and families are seen in broadest relief and can be evaluated in the greatest depth. Cities and counties are therefore critical monitors of state policy at the local level.

The Unique Role of Cities

Whether they exist in states where counties have major or minor roles in serving children and families, cities at their most limited usually control core functions of law enforcement, parks and recreation, land use control, and some role in youth affairs or youth development. Even in these limited-function cities, nearly all these local governments still possess the four functions described above.

But variations among cities also matter in describing how they can and should address issues of children and youth. Some of those variations are about social, demographic, and economic differences, and include:

- Differences in age makeup—some cities have older populations than the national norms, some have younger populations;
- Differences in income mix;
- Differences in the extent to which they are subdivided into natural communities and neighborhoods;
- Differences in racial, cultural, and linguistic groupings-some are highly diverse, while others are much less reflective of national trends toward diversity.

Other differences affect cities' structure and legal powers, including:

- Differences in form of government: strong-mayor, council-manager and variations on these forms;
- Differences in their relative freedom from state governing powers, based on state constitutions and local charters;
- Differences in legal responsibility for education, as a central policy arena for children and youth.

How do these differences affect cities' ability and willingness to play more strategic roles in developing and carrying out children and family policy? In general, it is obvious that those cities with younger populations will have more pressure to address children and youth issues, while those with more lower-income families will find it both harder to ignore and also harder to meet the needs of those families. Those with more coherent and identifiable neighborhoods tend to have the assets of a focal point closer to the families they seek to help, along with more pressures from those geographic areas to address their needs rather than those of the city as a whole. And those with a diverse population tend to raise and respond to children and family issues in terms of race and culture, although this is affected directly by the relative incomes of the different ethnic groups.

Structurally, cities have more power to respond to children and family issues when they have more freedom from state oversight and control, although this is mitigated by their economic position. A weak-powers city may nevertheless have more active and coherent policy than its legally stronger counterparts who may lack the resources to respond. Mayor or council-manager cities do not appear to divide in any significant way on their capacity or willingness to address children and youth issues, although mayors with greater powers may find themselves more often the targets of groups pressing for family-friendly or pro-children policies. They may also be held accountable for responding to youth delinquency and other problems perceived as the fault of young people involved in risky or anti-social behavior.

Size is the final variable that matters in assessing cities' responses to children and families. "Big cities," especially the 29 above the 500,000 mark (as of Census 2000), are more often the focus of state and federal efforts to address children and family policy, and tend more often to develop their own policies as well.

The Unique Role of Counties

Counties, as already noted, have major roles in services for children and families in those states where state programs are county-administered. Some of the most detailed policy statements have been put forth in the larger counties, including Los Angeles, San Francisco, Nashville-Davidson County, and Multnomah County, Oregon. In some cases these are the products of extraordinary leadership, such as Mayor Bill Purcell in Nashville[1] and the several supporters of the Children's Planning Council in Los Angeles County over more than a decade. In other cases, states have created formal legal frameworks, and county leaders have used these frameworks to develop policy statements.

Counties in a critical number of states administer welfare, child welfare including children's shelters for children removed from their families, maternal and child health, food and nutrition programs, and many other programs. Some operate Head Start programs and other early childhood programs; some are the hosts for community action agencies that operate on a regional basis. And a few are the governing bodies for metropolitan school districts as well. (Connecticut and Rhode Island, as the two states that have no county governments as such, are obviously special cases.)

In a growing number of states, counties have developed coordinating councils or other forms of collaborative bodies. In Alabama, for example, County Children's Policy Councils are chaired by the local juvenile judge, with mandated members from the local offices of state agencies such as Human Resources, Mental Health, Youth Services, and ABC, along with representatives of the local school systems, local child advocates, parents, and citizens. These councils are charged with doing a countywide needs assessment, using a model borrowed from Georgia that cuts across a wide array of children and family services. The Georgia model has eight distinct areas: Child Development (Prenatal through Pre-K), Youth Development (Kindergarten through 12th grade), Family Development, Academic Development (Children & Youth), and Physical Health Development. In California, a network of collaborative councils has grown up without direct state support in more than forty of the state's fifty-eight counties.[2]

Conflict between cities and counties

In counties where major cities also operate programs for children and families, the relations between the two kinds of local governments can become complex and strained, driven by fiscal problems and political finger-pointing. These conflicts arise from several underlying tensions:

- Cities and counties may compete for favorable treatment from state legislatures as they make up—or cut—state budgets;
- Cities and counties may have fundamentally different political bases; with larger geographic areas, counties are more likely to represent suburban and rural voters, while cities may represent lower-income and more diverse voters and residents, especially in those sections of the country where annexation is not possible or more difficult;
- Where counties have major service delivery roles, cities can at times adopt a NIMBY attitude. In one suburban county in California, city governments that had never previously been involved in substance abuse issues banded together in opposition to county policies that allowed halfway houses to locate in cities without adequate review by city staff and elected officials, who were blamed when recovering addicts were perceived as committing antisocial acts;
- When counties do represent more suburban voters, many of the "outer ring" issues affecting children and families (see Chapter 1) such as fair housing, transportation, and environmental impact are fought out in regional forums in which the county may have much more effective power than central cities.

In those few cities that *are* counties or that have effectively merged with their counties in joint city/county governments, such as San Francisco, Boston/Suffolk County, Denver/Denver County, Indianapolis/Marion County, Jacksonville/Duval   County,   Louisville/Jefferson   County,   and Philadelphia/Philadelphia County, the distinction between the two is not relevant, and the capacity of these jurisdictions to represent both central cities and (where their geography permits) suburbs is a net plus in addressing children and family issues without the strains that occur when the governments are separate. In addition, in regions where there are strong regional councils of government, such as Portland, Seattle, and Atlanta, these bodies can sometimes address family issues such as affordable housing or economic development.

But a strained relationship—or none, where children and family issues are concerned—is often the norm between cities and counties. Regional bodies remain more effective in dealing with transportation issues, where their role is formally built into the allocation of more than $200 billion in federal transportation funding, than in the children and family issues that are the focus of this book.

A further distinction needs to be made between cities and counties that are primarily urban and those that are suburban. In the 1992 Presidential race, for the first time, a majority of votes in the general election were cast in suburban districts, and there are more suburban congressional districts than urban and rural districts combined.[3] This growing dominance, in some states, means that cities and their suburbs do not always see human services issues similarly. City-suburb relations are more often about economic development issues than children and family issues, but suburbs are far less likely to have the same urgency about lower-income working families' income or the lack of affordable child care for children with high risk factors. Ferguson notes, however, that suburban taxpayers may be more supportive of aid for inner cities if they feel that funds are being used effectively.[4]

This underscores the importance of accountability for results in programs for children and families, and reminds us that suburban voters in California, North Carolina, Georgia and other states have supported increased spending and taxation for early childhood programs that tend to have a better reputation for effectiveness than other programs for children and families. There may be significant constituency-building benefits to be gained from better documentation by local governments of their programs for children, rather than arguing for them simply based on need. This may also call for greater demonstration of local governments' willingness to eliminate ineffective programs such as DARE, many parent education programs, and other low-dosage prevention programs that have not shown impact.

We will review some of these issues of regionalism and its impact on the children and family agenda in Chapter 11.

Special districts and public authorities: Quasi-local governments

The United States has another set of "local governments" that also have significant impact on children and families in some parts of the nation: special districts and public authorities. Of the 87,849 local governments counted in the 2002 Census of Governments, 35,356 were special districts. Of these 91% were single-purpose districts, with natural resources (water, air pollution, etc.) and transportation as the primary functions. Special districts are the fastest growing type of local government, in contrast to a slight trend toward consolidation of other local governments. This is a result, according to the Census Bureau and others familiar with special district trends, of the greater fiscal capacity of single- and limited purpose governments to raise funding, especially compared with debt and fiscal caps affecting city and county governments. California, Illinois, and Texas account for nearly one-quarter of all the special districts. Public authorities overlap somewhat with special districts, with the "authority" label used by some air pollution, transportation, and other districts.

What are the implications of these forms of local government for children and families? Some children and family innovators have seen new public authorities with state authorization as a way of raising these issues above the strife of local politics, while others have argued that governance reforms seeking wider participation of residents might be enhanced by wider use of such governmental arrangements across city and county lines. The Chatham-Savannah's Youth Futures Authority is perhaps the best-known example of a state-authorized local government entity that addresses these issues through a different governmental structure, although its operations are closely linked to the city, county, and school districts in its region.[5] Special districts have also been formed by regional councils of governments to take control of open space and preserve parklands. In rural areas special districts govern healthcare and hospitals.

Lisbeth Schorr and others, borrowing a label from the British, have referenced the label "QANGOs" to signify quasi-autonomous non-governmental organizations (the term government enterprises is also used) such as the BBC or the Federal National Mortgage Association (Fannie Mae). These national entities also have their local counterparts. Regional entities sometimes operate as semi-autonomous units, although they are made up of local governments in a loose confederation with rotating chairs, The staff of these organizations, especially in the transportation and affordable housing fields, can at times become quite separate from local governments in their operations.

The downside of special districts and authorities as they affect children and family issues can be their lack of direct accountability. A growing literature has examined the accountability issues in public authorities, and has called for closer oversight of both financial and programmatic operations of some of the larger ones. To quote from a publication on Colorado special districts,

> Opposition to special district governments seems to be voiced primarily by county and municipal leaders that have no control over them. Only 20% of voters responded to mail-ballot, district board elections in the year 2000....The benefit of these districts is personalized self-government, managed by locally elected neighbors, at relatively low cost. The disadvantage is potential corruption or incompetence caused by a lack of scrutiny by citizens and the news media. Citizens attend board meetings only to discuss perceived problems.[6]

Similarly, an assessment of special districts in 2002 by the California Senate noted that

> Special districts can decrease accountability....The multiplicity of limited purpose special districts can make it harder for citizens to gather information. Separate special districts may provide water, sewer, parks, library, and fire protection services to the same unincorporated community. Residents have a hard time finding out who's in charge.[7]

In 1994 in Orange County, California, the nation's largest local bankruptcy led to several water districts (and school districts) losing millions of dollars because they had invested their reserves in the County's pooled funding, which ran extraordinary losses due to stock market downturns. In Florida, the Division of Housing and Community Development exercises oversight for special districts and enforces the provisions of the state's special district accountability legislation. In California, after statewide publicity in 2000 about $19 billion held in special districts' reserve funds, legislation was passed requiring larger special districts to report their expenditures to the State Controller.

States and local government: Constraints and enabling roles

The good news about state roles, which are a major force in what local governments can and can't do, is that in some states local governments have been provided new flexibility and some resources for local children and family policy. In other states, state legislation has used cities and counties as the vehicles for carrying out local implementation of statewide children and family policy.

In Georgia, Vermont, North Carolina, Oregon, and other states, state legislation has promoted state-local linkages around children's programs in which cites and counties are encouraged to develop local comprehensive plans. Typically, the meaning of "comprehensive" does not yet extend to all children and youth programs, but only a selected number of those programs that are channeled through the state. In California, a legislative initiative that included only state funding invited six counties to submit comprehensive plans based on locally determined outcomes, in return for negotiated flexibility in state funding. None of these experiments have yet achieved institutionalized, sustained connections between states and their localities across the full range of children and family programs.

A thorough framework for state-local enabling legislation has been developed by Lynn De Lapp, a former staff member of the California legislature, in work published by The Finance Project.[8] This framework is designed to assist state and local leaders in developing legislative strategies to create state/community partnerships in support of comprehensive community initiatives. A related resource reviews selected examples of state legislation.[9]

These state innovations and options for a framework are part of the reason that intergovernmental advocacy is listed as one of the fifteen categories on the matrix of local roles. Cities and counties can be effective lobbyists, but if all they lobby for is new funding for old programs, they will miss the opportunity to put the pieces together in more effective combinations of linked funding streams. In the states that have gone furthest in developing new state-local links, local governments have been given the opportunity to go beyond advocacy for a few new, token-funded categorical programs to a larger, more significant role aimed at coordinating the resources that are already there.

In some states, a large challenge is identifying the flow of state resources into cities and counties–which the state has never done. Often, local governments have never even asked the state to give them such data. Imagine a state legislator who has been told by the state bureaucracy, in response to a formal request from a city or county, that the state cannot really identify the millions of dollars of state funding flowing into her district. That could be a remarkable opportunity to educate state and local legislators about the fragmentation and non-accountability of state-local funding flows. Arizona has an eleven-year old exemplary model of such an inventory for its substance abuse grants, which uses GIS software to locate grants down to the community level. But most states cannot answer a local official's fair—but all too rare—question: "how much state money comes into my district, and from what funding sources in the state budget I approved?"

State-local fiscal inequity is fundamental—but not an adequate excuse

A discussion of state-local relations should never overlook the very real fiscal inequities that exist in many states between urban and rural areas, with suburban legislators often holding the balance of power. In some states this remains one of the most fundamental sources of *de facto* children and youth policy, resulting in education funding imbalances, seriously excessive caseloads in child protective services, mental health services shortages, and other programs that are chronically underfunded. As we saw in Chapter 6, the budget is the policy, and the policy inherent in fiscal inequity constrains cities and counties in many states. Local governments' advocacy roles become all the more important in these cases, and a major issue in children and family policymaking becomes whether the city or county gives priority among its advocacy targets to funding inequities affecting children and families, or simply seeks revenues for its general purpose functions.

Fiscal inequity matters, and it is fundamental in its impact on children and family policy. But at the same time, citing fiscal inequity is too often used as a buffer to divert accountability for use of resources *that are already in the city*— or for efforts to secure additional resources from federal, private, or other sources. Those local governments with clear strategies and a track record of performance may have a stronger case for their advocacy than those that are simply trying to fill budget holes. A redirection agenda that seeks capture of resources from ineffective programs leaves cities and counties with much to do before they can justifiably shift the bulk of their children and family policy burden to the states. Again, many of the roles set forth in Chapter 1 are non-financial roles, and the fiscal equity issues should not obscure those other critical roles.

The missing 400-pound gorilla: The feds

Because this is a book on local government, the role of the federal government is not featured. For several reasons, what once seemed an 800-pound gorilla is now much reduced in size—while remaining the largest animal around. The resumption of federal deficits, the current administration's tilt away from new federal programs that are not related to national security and the continuing fragmentation of the federal program mix—all reinforce the local focus of this book.

But just as it is wrong to ignore the local level, ignoring the national level is also a mistake. That is because

- As noted in discussing family economic success, federal programs can best provide working families with the supports they need to live decent lives;

- As Theda Skocpol and others have made clear, federal action will be required to address those family income supports that are missing from the mix now in place;[10]
- Federal efforts to expand voluntary or mandated use of information tools can reinforce local attempts to move toward results-based accountability;
- Federal support for regional solutions can empower multi-city and multi-county approaches to children and family problems, using the precedent of federal support for regionalism in transportation and environmental issues.

Nonetheless, until federal policy deliberately and over a sustained period seeks to weave together the principles of federalism and efforts to develop children and family policy, it is unlikely that local government will get much direct federal support for children and family policy aside from existing programmatic funding streams. Local officials can hope for it, but for the time being, they should not wait for it before they decide what roles they are going to play using their own resources and authority. Reviewing recent history of federal roles and a prognosis for the near future may make this point clearer.

The federal role

From the Aid for Dependent Children program of the late 1930's (the precursor of Temporary Assistance to Needy Families) through the juvenile delinquency prevention programs of the early 1960's and on to the 2000's, the federal government has launched hundreds of children or family programs or programs aimed at city or county government. But very rarely are all these combined these separate programs and policies. Welfare reform in the late 1990's affected children and families, obviously, but its effects on cities and counties were incidental.

Like local government, the federal government plays multiple roles in developing and implementing children and family policy. These include:

- Funding programs through individual entitlements, state formula grants, and discretionary projects funding
- Funding research and demonstration programs intended to develop and disseminate new knowledge about "what works"
- Training and providing technical assistance to state and local service providers and governmental officials on-site and in national conferences and websites (usually through its funded intermediaries, such as the national resource centers funded by the Children's Bureau)
- Efforts to make it easier to use federal funding streams, through waivers of provisions of federal legislation and efforts to coordinate different programs

Very recent history: The Gore and Bush initiatives

In the Clinton administration, a cluster of intergovernmental projects was consolidated under the Vice-President's office into a set of "communities of practice."[11] This was an attempt to package and connect three separate initiatives:

- *Boost4Kids*: This was a 13-site model of federal efforts to streamline application procedures, using a model developed in San Diego. The initial thirteen "performance partners" were designated in 1999 and matched with a federal "champion" charged with helping the local coalition to leverage federal resources and cut red tape as needed.[12] Eventually sixty other sites were chosen.

- *SafeCities*: This initiative built on Department of Justice after-school programs as a crime prevention initiative, responding to a local plan developed by a coalition led by law enforcement officials, and backed up by a closely linked team of federal officials. A local summit was a central feature in the development of the local plan, with the lesson being the power of the White House to convene and spotlight local efforts to resolve difficult interagency negotiations. An active federal clearinghouse role became a high-credibility support effort provided to local police chiefs and sheriffs.

- *The Skills Network*: This initiative was aimed at workforce improvement under the theme of "lifelong learning," with local coalitions that included labor, business, education, and government. Again, federal interagency working groups provided backup for their local counterparts. Twenty communities participated in this effort.

The Gore initiatives came at the end of a tumultuous administration, but enlisted active support and cooperation from an impressive range of federal, state, and local partners. They included the ingredients that effective federal-local efforts demand: federal interagency backup, high-level sponsorship, and goals that were linked directly to measurable outcomes.

The Bush administration has launched several major cross-cutting initiatives affecting local government: the Office of Faith-Based and Community Initiatives (OFBCI), its "Leave No Child Behind" legislation aimed at education reform, a homelessness initiative that revived the dormant Interagency Council on Homelessness, and a "Brownfields" initiative aimed at restoration of blighted urban areas. The Administration's tax policy affecting families, however, is estimated to include far greater economic impact on lower-income and working poor families (some of which the Bush administration reluctantly included as the price of support from key legislators) than allocations for Bush-initiated grant programs. And of course, homeland security is a final major federal-local "program" with both revenue support and major new staffing by federal employees of metropolitan-owned and operated airports and other facilities.

Earlier history

In two earlier efforts at community-building—the community action programs of the 1960's (and beyond) and the Model Cities programs of the

1960's and 1970's—an initial emphasis upon strategic local planning fell victim to federal and local politics, and was set aside in favor of different strategies that emphasized services over coordination. It is instructive to examine why this happened, and what it may suggest for a renewed emphasis upon strategic planning in local governments.[13]

In the initial formulation of community action as a key component of the war on poverty run by the Office of Economic Opportunity (OEO), the emphasis upon coordination was strong. One review of the history of community action summarized the change that took place as moving "From service coordination to citizen participation."[14]

But the coordination theme and strategic planning of community-based initiatives were far from universally accepted as goals. As an observer of the early community action programs (CAPs) in the mid-1960's noted, the dual themes of citizen involvement and strategic coordination, set forth as the original goals of community action (and later of Model Cities), were more often seen as competitive than reinforcing.

> Too frequently, both critics and supporters of community action have treated the effort to coordinate services and mobilize resources as the established institutions' means of eliminating poverty and resident participation as the device relied upon by the opponents of the status quo. Without resident participation, the charge that there is nothing new in the poverty program will be completely justified. Without a large-scale mobilization and coordination of resources, even the most active resident organizations and leaders will prove ineffective in their efforts to secure change in established institutions. The comments of some regional CAP personnel and a number of CAP directors, as well as the mayors and mayors' representatives with whom I talked would indicate that OEO has not always seen this inter-relationship as clearly as it should have. In part, OEO's preoccupation with resident participation requirements during this first year have to be explained by the fact that it was much easier to evaluate resident participation than mobilization of resources during this time....It is my firm belief based on the cities which I visited and my perceptions of local politics that the active support of the mayor is essential for the success of a CAP...He is the only individual who has the prestige to mobilize both public and private resources in a common effort[15]

But as neat as the bipolar framing of the choices is, a centrist's innate (though later) suspicion is that bipolar explanations often miss the middle. And what this framing misses most is the difference between the coordination agenda, the resident participation agenda, and *the services agenda*, which agencies revert to whenever they can and usually prefer to either of the other two.

A choice to provide direct services was as much the basis for the diversion away from coordination as was the drive for wider participation of neighborhood residents. Peterson and Greenstone describe Sargent Shriver's critical crossroads decision on this point in his role as the first Director of the Office of Economic Opportunity in the mid-1960's:

> While Shriver welcomed the establishment of OEO as an independent
> agency...he saw little political appeal, little prospect for obtaining
> durable popular and congressional support, if he merely coordinated
> various federal departments and agencies....by adding operating
> programs that clearly lacked any coordinating functions, Shriver
> decisively turned community action away from rationalizing the activities
> of existing agencies.[16]

Two years after the Economic Opportunity Act of 1964, the Model Cities
program was enacted into law in 1966, in significant measure as a response to
congressional hearings that documented the fragmentation already visible—
nearly forty years ago—in the host of new categorical programs pouring out at
the floodtide of the Great Society. But Model Cities, like community action, was
about much more than coordination; urban riots and the civil rights movement
were also critical parts of the immediate political environment of Model Cities,
and these tensions were evident throughout the program.

In the archetype of federal coordinative efforts, "CDA 4"[17]—an issuance
from the Department of Housing and Urban Development where Model Cities
was based—set forth the criteria for planning a Model Cities program. This
HUD issuance describes the steps a city should undertake in doing its Model
Cities planning.

In contrast is the summation written two decades later by another who was
there—Marshall Kaplan, who advised and staffed HUD in the Model Cities
effort and evaluated numerous local efforts. He wrote in 1986

> *We have moved away from the holistic to the strategic.* Gone is the
> optimism of the sixties, the belief that we could mount integrated or
> multidisciplinary programs that would cure multiple urban ills....we now
> realize that exogenous, often unpredictable events or nonurban policy
> actions often swamp relatively miniscule public initiatives regarding
> urban areas.[18]

It seems unlikely that urban areas or communities are substantially more
complicated than they already were in the mid-sixties, so it's a fair question to
ask whether strategic approaches to the role of local government are less likely
now that then were during these two earlier efforts. The contrasts are useful to
review:

- Tools for strategic planning, as we saw in Chapter 4, have at least kept
  pace with the complexity of the settings, with local governments having
  access to analytical software, GIS mapping, neighborhood indicators
  and children's report cards, and numerous other more sophisticated
  tools.
- The impact of race and poverty is compounded by a less concentrated
  form of poverty in urban areas and a far more diverse racial and ethnic
  landscape than the predominantly black and white picture of the mid-
  1960's.[19]
- The federal inventory of programs is neither significantly more nor less
  complex than its counterparts in the 1960's. While the 60's saw the
  floodtide of Great Society legislation, often in the form of categorical

initiatives, those that have been consolidated into block grants or eliminated have been succeeded by new grant programs—some providing as few as five or six grants from totals in the $5-10 million range. Keeping track of these has become an industry that includes subscribing to notification services, software, use of the Catalogue of Federal Domestic Assistance, and frequent perusal of multiple federal websites.[20]

None of these make the case that strategic policy is less necessary or harder to develop than it was in the 1960's. The continuing complexity of the federal program mix and the greater diversity in the racial and economic makeup of the children and family population are better arguments in support of developing strategic policy than for giving up on the effort.

The federal prospect

I would sum up forty years of working with and watching federal efforts to create improved local planning and outcomes with the following conclusions:

1. Federal efforts can make a difference, if the right conditions are in place.
2. Those conditions include
   a. Leadership above the level of the federal agencies—no one federal agency can "coordinate" its peers; the Office of Management and Budget can do it with the power of the budget and management oversight, the President or Vice-President can do it, a sub-cabinet unit such as the Domestic Policy Council can do it, if its staff is speaking for the President or has White House clout from another source.
   b. Either new resources or the power to redirect existing resources.
   c. An emphasis on broadly defined goals that cut across more than one federal agency's functions.
   d. Sufficient clarity of purpose to resist a diversion into services programs as the definition of strategic planning.
   e. Local leaders on the other side of the relationship who also want to put the pieces together, rather than simply pursue isolated grants.

Yet the great majority of federal coordination efforts have been directed by a single federal agency seeking to coordinate its peers, or an overhead agency developing a mission-driven reform in which the mission is narrowly defined or process-defined, rather than focused on achieving specific goals and outcomes. For example, the Clinton administration's Comprehensive Communities Program in the Justice Department focused on crime prevention—a clear overall goal—but sought rhetorically to coordinate all the pieces that might logically fit into that, without addressing fatherlessness or early childhood-targeted reduction of child abuse. The Department of Transportation has developed a Transportation Coordination Toolkit, emphasizing transportation issues, but with only passing references to job and economic development priorities.

An exception to this, perhaps, are the extraordinary efforts since 9/11 to coordinate homeland security. But this is clearly an overarching priority, directed with strong White House support, and accompanied by significant resources—though not as much as local governments have sought. As summarized by the executive director of the National Association of Counties in mid-2003, "This is an administration that has a clear interest in reducing federal participation in domestic policy."[21]

So can these conditions ever be met, short of extraordinary national emergency? I believe they can, with rare federal leadership. It *is* rare, in the same way that local leadership of the kind this book calls for can be sometimes rare.

> **Where is the evidence?**
>
> The evidence for the argument that federal leadership is possible lies in part in federal land use and environmental decision-making. In the disposal of military bases in concert with intense local political pressures, the federal government has shown that it can weigh the national interest and local planning and economic demands with considerable care. And in environmental processes that have used sophisticated consensus-building techniques of the kind described briefly in Chapter 4, agreements have been achieved. I would also argue that the Gore initiatives described in this section also provide evidence that smaller-scale coordination efforts can enhance local strategic planning and implementation.

The final chapter of this book is about leadership for a very good reason: without it, the workings of our politics and the short attention span of our current intergovernmental relations will overcome efforts to be strategic, leaving us surrounded with the residue of merely tactical programs. The task of reconciling that residue should be intergovernmentally shared; but it is more likely in the near-term future to be locally led.

NOTES

[1] Prior to his election as Mayor, Purcell served as Director of the Child and Family Policy Center at the Vanderbilt Institute of Public Policy Studies.

[2] For an assessment of these councils' functions and effectiveness, see Sid Gardner. Changing the Rules? County Collaboratives' Roles in Improving Outcomes for Children and Families. (Sacramento, Ca.: The Foundation Consortium, 2000).

[3] Karl Stauber, "Looking at the Big Picture" (2002) downloaded October 22, 2003 from http://www.leopold.iastate.edu/newsletter/2000-3leoletter/agfuture.html. Al From, "Building A New Progressive Majority" (2001). Downloaded October 22, 2003 from http://www.ndol.org/blueprint/winter2001_special/from.html

[4] Ronald Ferguson and Sara Schottland, "Reconceiving the Community Development Field," in Urban Problems and Community Development. Ronald Ferguson and William Dickens [eds.] (Washington: The Brookings Institution, 1999).

[5] Downloaded October 15, 2003, from
http://www.youthfutures.com/youthfutures/partners.asp
[6] http://www.citymtnviews.com/special_districts.asp
[7] Kimia Mizany and April Manatt, "What's So Special about Special Districts?"
(Sacramento, Ca.: State Senate Local Government Committee, 2002).
[8] Lynn DeLapp, Building Strong Communities: Crafting a Legislative Foundation.
(Washington, D.C. The Finance Project, 1996).
[9] Thomas Woods, Building Comprehensive, Community-based Support Systems
for Children & Families: A Review of Legislative Examples. (Washington, D.C. The
Finance Project, 1996).
[10] Theda Skocpol, The Missing Middle. (New York: W.W. Norton and Co., 2000).
[11] Lynn S. Kahn, Results at the Edge: The Ten Rules of Government Reform
(Lanham, Md.: University Press of America, 2003). This section also benefited from
conversations with Morley Winograd, who served as Senior Domestic Policy Advisor to
Vice-President Gore and head of the reinvention effort.
[12] This position was a fascinating echo of the initial Model Cities legislation, which
included a "metropolitan expediter," a federal employee who would have worked with
each Model City in a similar role. The position was excised from the final version of the
Model Cities law out of congressional concerns that the position would supplant
congressional influence within the bureaucracy on behalf of cities in the congressional
districts.
[13] A personal acknowledgement: I had a role in both of these efforts, at local and
federal levels of government. My first assignment in government after leaving graduate
school was to conduct an assessment of new community action agencies in the summer of
1965. Later, I worked in the Model Cities agency in New York City and then became
Director of the Center for Community Planning in the U.S. Department of Health,
Education, and Welfare, which was HEW's response to the Model Cities program.
[14] Paul Peterson and J. David Greenstone, "The Mobilization of Low-Income
Communities through Community Action," in A Decade of Federal Antipoverty
Programs, Robert Haveman, (ed.) (New York: Academic Press, 1977).
[15] I plead guilty to having written this in the summer of 1965 after site visits to ten
CAAs. These conclusions and the concepts in this book at least have the virtue of
consistency over nearly forty years. It should be emphasized that this was a perspective
from the vantage point of the Bureau of the Budget examiner staff (now the Office of
Management and Budget) at a time when service coordination and efficiency were their
priorities, driven by congressional critiques of fragmentation, an overview of the full
inventory of existing federal programs, and budget concerns about the costs of large
income redistribution plans. I agreed then and still agree now with greater emphasis on
efforts to coordinate (and increase the effectiveness of) existing programs and funding
streams in contrast with citizen participation for its own sake. Both are essential, in my
view, but the second received far more emphasis in the 1960's and afterward.
[16] Peterson and Greenstone, A Decade, 245.
[17] CDA stood for City Demonstration Agency.
[18] arshall Kaplan, "Revitalizing the Cities: From Great Expectations to a New
Realism," in Marshall Kaplan and Peggy Cuciti, eds. The Great Society and Its Legacy,
(Durham, N.C.: Duke University Press, 1986).
[19] Robert Pear, "Study Shows Poverty in U.S. Less Concentrated." The New York
Times, May 17, 2003.
[20] At one point in HEW in the late 1960's, we produced the first-ever totals of major
formula grants that flow to the states in a form that was usable by cities participating in

the Model Cities program, so that they could use their Model Cities funding to seek leveraging of funds that "belonged" to the states. The document was never updated, but it summarized the far greater funding available through formula grants in a way that some Model Cities found useful in thinking about how to target their own funds. The Federal Catalogue now includes programs indexed by age group, functional area, and eligible grantee, with more than 112 separate programs indexed for children and youth—exclusive of those for education.

[21] Jonathan Walters, "Block That Grant," Governing, September 2003, 12.

Introduction to Section 3: The Four Forces

A part of making good policy is to see the connectedness of things and not to be paralyzed by them. The chapters of this book illustrate how much children and family policy overlaps the categories we devise to try to contain it:

- Cities and counties are creatures of their neighborhoods and communities, but are also affected profoundly by their economic and political regions.
- Education is a separable issue in governance, given school districts, but it is inescapably about race and culture in this nation, and that means it has wide implications for regional relations between cities and their suburbs—who have shown in many parts of the nation that they do not want inner-city, lower-income children attending "their" schools, whether based on vouchers, voluntary desegregation, regional magnet schools or other policy proposals.

The next four chapters could have been one very long one, because it is in the section that follows that these connections are perhaps closest. Families live their lives embedded in their race and culture, which affects the communities and neighborhoods where families live, and the regions in which their economic and social life takes place. The challenge of this section is to review how each of these four primary forces further complicates the tasks of local government as it tries to move toward strategic policy, rather than token projects.

These four forces come together in powerful ways that differ from city to city, but matter in all cities and counties. The first two—families and generations, and race and culture—are drivers of policy that flow from the demographics of the *people* in a locality, while the second two—communities and neighborhoods, and regional factors—are drivers that flow from the geography, the economics, and the politics of *places*. In some localities, the demographic mix may be the most important driver, as in a city with a high percentage of elderly or children. In others, a high percentage of minority residents may be highly significant to children and family policy. In still others, the strong identity of neighborhoods may matter greatly, while a city with heavy recent out-migration or strong regional transportation systems may be more affected by regional factors.

The four chapters that follow are also connected in time, through the life cycles of children and generations of families—and in space, though the places that families live, work, and raise their children. They address the realities of race, language, and culture that divide communities, while providing social capital on which communities can also build shared values.

Local governments can accept all of these forces as given, or they can choose from among the multiple roles and tools described in prior chapters to give strategic direction to these powerful forces. In each of these four areas, local government can play a leadership role, a reactive role, a target for change, or become a passive bystander. The questions raised by these choices include:

1. *Families and generations*: how will local government support families across the life cycle of their children, in ways that recognize the social capital created by a healthy family?
2. *Race and culture*: how will local government respond to the realities of race, language, and culture as they create both (a) barriers to opportunity, and (b) opportunities for families to build on their shared history?
3. *Communities and neighborhoods*: how will local government help create and support the growth of healthy communities that are good places for families to raise their children and contribute to their community?
4. *Regional realities*: how will local governments who are potential winners and losers in regional economics share the benefits of regional growth patterns and respond to inequitable distribution of those benefits?

While it is easier, and in some written works more conventional, to treat these as separate topics, the connections among them are more important than their separable elements. To discuss family, race, and community without looking at the regional realities of growth is simplistic. To try to understand family dynamics without recognizing the impact of race on millions of families makes no sense, and to look at children and families' future without regard for the places they live is ludicrous.

For a given locality, determining which of these forces are the drivers is the critical task. This demands reviewing all four forces and assessing which ones matter most in developing strategic children and family policy. Which ones most affect the power balance and imbalance among families and communities, which ones command the most resources over time to affect growth and economic outcomes, and which ones appear to underlie disparate social outcomes for children and families?

Nearly forty years ago a superb college professor, Michael Danielson of Princeton's Woodrow Wilson School, framed the issues of urban America as being inescapably about "race, growth, and power," and with the exception of adding the word *poverty,* I have found that framing useful ever since.

CHAPTER 8: FAMILIES AND GENERATIONS: THE CONNECTIONS ACROSS POLICIES

As discussed in Chapter 1, policymaking for children and youth does not automatically include the parents of these children and youth. When families are included, it is usually as the object of specific programs, rather than across the full array of policies that affect families. In reviewing the strategic plans developed by the cities and counties that have taken these ideas furthest, there are some limited references to families and parenting, but rarely in a way that addresses the full range of family issues. What are mentioned are family *projects*:

- The need for parent education
- The need for teen pregnancy prevention and support programs for teen parents
- The need for family reunification or foster family services for children in the child welfare system
- Maternal and child health services, and perinatal support programs that include home visiting
- Generalized family support services, as discussed in Chapter 14
- (In fewer cases, but increasingly) the need for family income supports for lower-income working parents.

None of these represents family policy that weaves together the different ways that government affects families and uses programs to improve families' life chances. Why is family *policy* harder to develop than family projects?

The barriers to family policy

The barriers to city and county leadership roles in family policy include several powerful forces:

- Federal and state government are seen as taking the lead, with little room for local governments to do more than carry out projects funded by outside sources;
- Family policy is often invisible, inherent in "outer ring" issues that are not labeled family issues, such as transportation policy, housing programs, or personnel policies;
- Family policy is perceived as an alternative or competing approach to children's policy, because systems are set up to do one or the other;
- The tension between making policy for all families and targeting resources on the most at-risk families is often resolved by doing some projects in each area without funding either at scale;

- Family issues can be very hot politically, touching on "family values," as well as the difficulty of defining what a family is, and some local officials prefer to leave these issues alone.

The invisibility problem

Family policy is affected in many obvious ways by federal and state governments' actions, as well as their inaction. Federal grant funding for child care, family support programs for parents of special education students, federal tax credits for children and child care, state tax benefits for development of affordable housing, and state policies governing family leave are all examples of governmental policy that originate in Washington and state capitals.

Local governmental policy affecting families is often less visible than state or federal policy, but no less significant. Cities and counties make family policy all the time, but often without explicitly intending to affect families:

- Decisions about where to locate major business expansions, schools, and new housing;
- Decisions about their own personnel policies that model family-friendly practices (or its opposite), such as encouraging parents in lower-income jobs to take paid time off to attend their children's parent-teacher conferences and to serve in community leadership or youth sports-oriented positions;
- Decisions about which issues to add to their legislative program at the state legislature.

Making family policy more visible requires reviewing the three realms of family policy introduced in Chapter 1:

- *Direct impact*—such as child care funding or family resource centers;
- *Indirect impact*—such as economic development and child care accreditation;
- *"Outer ring" impact* on families—such as environmental disparities in lower-income neighborhoods, the impact of housing codes and tax policies on affordability of housing, or issues involving civil liberties or privacy rights.

While cities may spend more of their time on family policies with direct impact, the second and third of these may have more profound and lasting impact, and family policy-making needs to address all three.

Another framework occurs in Kathleen Sylvester's recent monograph, in which she suggests that families can be seen as the innermost core of community life, with neighborhoods as the next layer and communities as the third, outer layer.[1] To the extent that local government encompasses more than one community, as it does in most counties, local government then becomes the fourth layer, with a clear responsibility: to support and remove barriers to the effective functioning of the other three.

Not-so-good practices—fragmenting the family

In some cases, family policy is the result of a clear understanding of the clinical and programmatic details of good practice. But good practice is often ignored, in half-efforts to work on children *or* family issues, as when:

- Treatment agencies don't count a client's children or accept any responsibility for their well-being;
- Child welfare agencies don't assess parents for substance abuse;
- Child welfare agencies identify substance-abusing parents but don't assess their children for its effects—either prenatally or postnatally;
- Children's mental health agencies and schools' special education units don't include the issues of parents' substance abuse in their assessments of seriously emotionally disturbed students;
- Preschool providers who include parents as active participants in their programs but fail to share information with schools about parents' strengths and needs;
- Schools never ask early care providers for information about parents in the first place.

Each of these is a program area where serving children well requires serving families, and vice-versa. But when the agencies are set up—as they so often are—to serve one or the other, good practice is irrelevant because "that is not what we do here." One remembers Lisbeth Schorr's powerful quotation from Sister Mary Paul at Sunset Park in Brooklyn:

> "No one ever says, this may be what you need, but it's not part of my job to get it." That simple statement of a flexible, unbureaucratic approach characterized what I had observed in dozens of effective programs.[2]

It *is* flexible, and it is also family-strengthening in ways that many programs are not. But converting good practice—or common sense, that says if you serve the kids, you ought to also serve the parents—into policy requires the ability to do two things that both challenge the status quo of children and family services:

- To document current practices as they isolate children's services from family services, and
- To develop ways to link the two more closely.

For all the rhetoric of "family-friendly" agencies and "family-centered practice," the typical city and county agencies operate either children's programs or family programs, and the rules of each are barriers to collaborating with the other.

Political risks

The political heat of family issues arises from multiple sources:

- "Family values" has come to connote a particular aggressiveness of conservative groups in patrolling the boundaries between government and the family, with these groups on alert to what they regard as invasions of families' privacy and the rights of parents to decide what is best for their children. As a result, political leaders are very cautious about setting off these groups by addressing family issues;

- Family issues include issues of race and culture, in which, for example, what is culturally acceptable as parental punishment in one culture may be seen as child abuse by the dominant culture and the laws of the state;
- Family issues include centuries-old notions of who are the deserving and the undeserving poor, whether parents are responsible for their economic conditions, and how much government, employers, and families themselves should be held accountable for what families earn and how they spend it. These include values deep in the political culture of voters, which were carefully negotiated and evoked in the 1996 compromise over welfare reform. Local officials may not want to unnecessarily re-enter the debates over parents' personal responsibility for their poverty if they can avoid it—or pass it upward to state and federal levels;
- Family policies may also require debate over the definition of what is a family—another hot issue for groups all along the political spectrum, from those that believe "alternative families" should receive equal treatment to those for whom only the nuclear, one-man, one-woman family is acceptable.

More than two decades ago, Gilbert Steiner set forth his view of the futility of even trying to make family policy at the national level.[3] He points out that definitions of what is good for families differ greatly among feminists, fundamentalists, child development specialists, and different ethnic and cultural groups. He further notes that the interventionist bent of many proposals for family services support—child care, child welfare intervention, home visiting— is fundamentally at odds with the widespread attitude that children are their parents' responsibility, and that the state should leave parents alone unless they are egregiously violating community norms.

Writing twenty-two years ago, Steiner could not fully anticipate the expansion of child care under legislation that ended welfare entitlements in the name of personal responsibility. But his general point is a powerful warning to would-be family policy-makers. In pressing local governments to "make family policy," we should not lose sight of the continued resistance to crossing the line into what is perceived as family territory. Politically active national organizations remain vigilant in patrolling what they believe to be the proper boundaries between government and family. While the reality may be a large middle ground between the poles of families that are left alone and governments intervening on many fronts, local officials should not ignore Steiner's cautions.

Some of these issues have far more symbolic importance than their actual effect on daily operations. In the area of defining who is a family, for example, in some counties recent increases in adoption in response to the adoption initiative of the Clinton administration have come substantially in response to a relaxation of barriers to adoption by single, gay, and lesbian parents. In fact, in some areas of the nation, a substantial percentage of new adoptive parents fall into these categories.[4] Understandably, child welfare officials have not trumpeted this achievement.

Overall, however, it is important for local policy leaders and staff to understand that family issues *do* have political content and will require political constituencies to support any decisions made that are more than token allocations. While some constituencies may be troubled by family policy made by local government, others will recognize the critical connection between family policy and community building and may prove a balancing force to opposing elements.

Frameworks for family policy

Approaching family policy issues in local government can be done through a logical process of planning, through responding to specific crises or events in the recent life of the community, or through using a consensus issue as the entry point for a wider discussion of the problems affecting families. Whichever approach is used, the tendency to be diverted to the smallest possible element of policy will often overcome the need for a wide-lens view. The risk remains that without a framework for policy, we will simply launch projects, rather than making policy.

To correct for this bias toward projects, some cities and counties have developed coalitions, collaboratives, or internal coordinating bodies that attempt to work across multiple program areas to address children and family issues. Only a few of these have developed full strategic plans, however; in most of these bodies, the latest state or federal deadline for proposals for new funding or renewals drives discussion of what passes for policy. In a few of these coalitions, major state initiatives such as early care and education/school readiness initiatives or youth prevention initiatives have been the focus of the discussion about family programs and policy.

One way of framing the attempt to address family policy is to use a life cycle approach to different categories of families, distinguishing between all families and those with special needs, as illustrated in this chart:

Table 3: Life Cycle Approach to Categories of Families

Target Group	All Families	Families with special needs
Working parents	Income supports [EITC, nutrition programs, child support, etc.]	Family support programs
Non-working parents	Family leave policies	Job training
Pre-school aged children	Child development information, immunizations, well-baby care	Home visiting, school readiness through quality child development programs or Head Start
School-aged children	School mechanisms for parent involvement	Dropout prevention
Children with disabilities	Adoption assistance	Early intervention support services for parents

Using this approach, family policy would involve assessing the scale of the community's problems in each of these overlapping areas and deciding where a concentration of resources might achieve sustainable impact that rises above the project level. The universe of need approach set forth as a planning tool in Chapter 4 can help set boundaries for this process.

In Hawaii, Multnomah County, Oregon, and other sites, for example, a strategic decision has been made to focus home visiting resources on a critical percentage of the first-time births to mothers whose risk factors are unusually high. These families are then followed home, helped to connect with medical homes, and supported during on a 6-year school readiness effort that requires tracking these parents and children over time until they enroll in school. In such policy initiatives, the major challenge is designing and implementing the appropriate "handoffs" from one agency—early care—to the next institution that serves children—the K-12 school system. We discuss this handoff in more detail in Chapter 12. Developing and staffing these bridges between agencies can become critical means of responding more fully to the life cycle of children than is possible under the current fragmented pattern of agency operations.

Moving into decisions about content

Cities and counties that are serious about addressing family policy need to adopt an orderly process that is more than a one-shot planning workshop or conference. But whatever process and framework is used must ultimately move into the *content* of the planning—to decisions about which families to help, how to get the help to them, and what it will cost.

The life cycle approach suggested above offers a broad framework for moving into those decisions, for local staff who are willing to do more than grant-chasing and project-launching. Critical elements of that framework include:

- The demographics: What families live here, what trends can we see in who goes and who stays?
- The income mix: what economic realities affect our families?
- The budget and effectiveness choices: which programs work and which are worth what they cost?

Demographic realities

Using the tools described in Chapter 4, local staff can review the Census and newer data to develop detailed profiles of their families. But it will require a second or even a third level of analysis that goes beyond merely counting families, or even counting how many of them are single parents trying to do what President Bush has called the hardest job of all—raising kids alone. Beyond that level, we need to know more if we are going to develop a serious family policy by asking:

- How many of them are raising their grandchildren—and why? We know that the number is in the millions, (the 2000 Census says 2.4 million) but we need to know much more about why they are taking on a job that can be harder than single parenting.
- How many of them are responsible for both their children and their parents—what does the demography of *three-generation* programs look like? What can cities do with bus passes or a different kind of family leave or rebuilding schools so that child care and elder care are in the same wing, instead of building facilities and neighborhoods increasingly marked by a new segregation by age?
- What caretaking roles are being played by extended family members, both informally and formally through kinship care, and what help and recognition do these caretakers need from their local governments?[5]
- How many of our families are homeless or need to live in shelters temporarily in order to be safe? The annual U.S. Conference of Mayors survey of homelessness in American cities in December 2001 found that requests for emergency food assistance rose an average of 23 percent and requests for emergency shelter assistance increased an average of 13 percent in the 27 cities surveyed.[6]
- What do ethnic, racial, and age trends indicate about the different kinds of families in our community and how separately children may be living their daily lives, despite being schooled together? Are there adequate norms of behavior to enable a community to develop youth standards that can be applied to all of the youth in a community, or will parents who desire their children to be raised separately from a secular culture increasingly seek a voluntary segregation of their children from others so that their own value systems can be conveyed and enforced?

Income realities

The income mix in a city or county makes up a fundamental part of its families' reality. Families that earn enough can do things for their children that the public sector won't have to; families that are nearer the margin find it more difficult, and may need more help, at least for a time. So city and county staff need to know:

- Which of the more than a dozen income benefit and work support programs that provide cash or in-kind assistance are not fully utilized by lower-income working families in their communities, and how do those enrollment figures compare with national figures which make clear that many of these programs fail to enroll sizable numbers of eligible lower-income working families?[7]

- How has the new array of programs for fathers affected the income support they bring to their children, both voluntarily and through mandated child support? What can local government do to provide father-oriented programs through using their contractors, their parks and other facilities, and their personnel policies (e.g. allowing non-custodial working fathers time off to attend their children's school activities)?

- How do geography and income intersect; what happens to families in working class neighborhoods when their income improves? Can upwardly mobile families be held in the neighborhoods they could potentially anchor, or are they likely to move out into safer neighborhoods with better schools? We will revisit these issues in Chapter 10 when we address neighborhoods and communities as part of policymaking, and again in Chapter 14, which discusses local governments' support for family resource centers.

Spending and effectiveness realities

Well-intentioned programs that try to help families are not enough; local officials who are serious about this agenda will need to ask harder questions at budget time about:

- Which home visiting programs work and which are just new fads without the resources or professional training to make a difference? In one county that recently assessed all of its existing home visiting programs, nine programs were operating with separate eligibility, targeting, funding, and professional staffing; another county documented work by sixteen programs—and in neither county were there any operational links among the programs, each with its own overhead and administrative structure, but none reaching a significant percentage of the children at risk.

- Which early child education programs are really developmental in their impact on children and which are merely custodial—in view of the fact that some studies have found that 12-15% of all child care is not merely inadequate, but actually harmful to children?[8]

- What kinds of parent support and education make a difference? In one California community of 300,000 in 1995, there were 63 separate parent education programs, none of which devoted resources to assessing whether parents were actually behaving differently toward their children or whether their children were benefiting from the ten Saturday mornings of instruction that make up the typical dosage.[9]

* What information systems are missing that are needed to document the effectiveness of family-serving programs that have previously only counted their clients, and how much time and money will it take to build this needed infrastructure for accountability?

The special role of two-generation programs

"Two-generation programs" have been documented to be more effective than parent-only or child-only programs in home visiting, in child development and school readiness, in substance abuse treatment and prevention, and in several other fields.[10] They are invariably more expensive, but more effective than single-focus programs for some families when applied in sufficient dosage to have a lasting impact. A single-focus drug treatment program, for example, simply sends mothers to drug treatment while keeping their children in inadequate child care. Such a program does nothing for the child's development or the parent's ability to parent better, compared with programs that include support for parent education for recovering mothers.

Here, again, the challenge to local government is simply to ask better questions:

* Why have we left the parents out of the design of this program?
* How will children be affected by the services we are providing to their parents?
* How much would the increased cost of serving children and parents in the same program be offset by larger savings? What have other localities learned about the impact of such programs?

The special role of three-generation programs

For an increasing number of families, family policy demands a multi-generational perspective that goes beyond serving parent and child to recognition that some parents are concerned about caretaking for their parents, while others are able to tap their parents and other members of their extended families as resources. Both dependency and interdependency are relevant in considering multi-generational caretaking.

Ira Cutler and his colleagues at Cornerstone Consulting have pointed out that some extended families provide a wide range of *de facto* subsidies to health and human services systems—many of which are most visible at the local level. They note, for example, that

> The evidence suggests that an under-funded federal childcare system is subsidized in large part by the grandmothers, aunts, and other relatives who provide *unsubsidized* childcare to the children of low-income mothers and two wage earner families.[11]

At the same time that these relatives are providing a supply of services in many families, a growing elderly population also creates a demand for extended family care, especially in immigrant families and single-parent families where extended care is either a cultural value or an economic imperative.

This increase in the importance of the extended family occurs, as Cutler points out, due to several changes:

- changes in immigration patterns,
- a continuing increased reliance on extended families in African American and other minority communities,
- changes in state child welfare systems that emphasize kinship care,
- increased numbers of grandparent-headed households,
- increased numbers of single parent households, and
- the overall aging of the population.

But governments—at local and other levels—have not responded to these changes with openness to either the resources of or the need for extended care. Vague and inconsistent public agency rules and practices about eligibility and relative responsibility have caused low-income extended families to stay in the background for fear of complicating their situation and threatening the continued receipt of benefits. Thus, in many cases extended families are taught that it is wise to hide their contributions.

So local governments need to do two things at a minimum to respond to these changes:

- In their demographic analyses, they need to determine how large the resources and needs are among extended family members, including families with three generations of need, and
- They need to make sure that local rules do no harm to families relying upon these resources or meeting these needs—and to eliminate the barriers if they find that they are doing harm.

The growing importance of three-generation policy arises in part from demographic changes, with the bulge of baby boomers born after World War II reaching retirement age and projected to swell the population of "early elderly," from 55 to 65, at the same time that life expectancy due to medical advances is increasing the number of "middle elderly" from 65 to 85 and the "oldest old" above 85. Family policy is being profoundly affected at all three levels of the federal system by the medical costs and the housing resources owned by and required by these three groups.

An intense debate is emerging between those who regard the entitlements of this growing group of "elderly" residents of cities and counties as the leading fiscal threat to all levels of government, and those who regard the growth in the number and percentage of older Americans as a net resource for the nation. Theodore Roszak is an articulate spokesman for the latter perspective in his 2001 book *Longevity Revolution*, in which he argues that longevity "is inevitable and it is good."[12] On the other side of the debate, numerous groups have called for limits on entitlements, viewing Social Security and Medicare as the primary "budget-breakers."

Local governments have long been active in implementing the Older Americans Act, operating senior centers and other programs for seniors. Local policy leaders are acutely aware of the political activism of this sizable and growing group—which votes in far greater proportions than their actual percentages of population (due significantly to the non-voting of the youngest voters). Often this political power is contrasted with the lesser political strength of children and families, as though the interests of these two groups were diametrically opposed. But Roszak and others have amassed several arguments and much evidence that older residents, like racial and ethnic groups, are more diverse in their politics than they are sometimes perceived to be.

Efforts have been made at local and national levels to develop intergenerational coalitions, but they have proven difficult to construct beyond the level of generalities. One important example is the dependent care tax credit which provides support to eligible "sandwich generation" parents who are caring for their own children and/or their own parents. A contrasting issue, demonstrating the difficulty of achieving intergenerational equity, is the fact that indexing benefits to inflation is public policy far more often for benefit programs for the elderly than it is for benefits for children and families.

> **Another Modest Proposal**
>
> If one third of the over-65 population in a California city of 140,000 worked 10 hours a week in some form of community service, it would represent the equivalent of 900 full-time workers. If 10% of the property taxes of these residents (or equivalent rent reductions) were eliminated, it would represent a total cost of approximately $500,000 or $555 per full-time position—for a benefit that most geriatric specialists would view as a clear health benefit to the workers, and that many in the community would see as a major contribution to the community.

Rather than viewing the elderly as a monolithic bloc, local governments need a better sense of the distinctions among their elderly, including:

- How many have independent incomes compared with those who are dependent on their children?
- How many are able to cover their medical costs with their own coverage compared with those that require subsidies from local government?
- How many are caring for their grandchildren?
- How many volunteer for some form of community service?

The size of this group—or these groups, if the distinctions suggested are made—make clear that local officials will need to understand the family impact of the oldest family members in their cities and counties. In some localities, this interest has led in recent years to development of "senior report cards" or annual reports on the conditions of the elderly that parallel children's report cards.

Mistakes made in family policy-making

Family policy in local government can take several mistaken paths:

- Confusing single projects with policy, in which a pilot project for a few families is spotlighted as though it represented real policy change
- Developing policy statements that are really only lists of "motherhood and apple pie" goals that make no choices among competing priorities
- Spreading resources so thinly that lessons of "what works" are ignored, and low-dosage programs are launched rather than concentrating of resources on real priorities
- Funding new programs without redirecting resources from ineffective old programs, with inadequate efforts in place to improve accountability for results
- Allowing external grant funding to determine local priorities, rather than local needs or community strengths, and devoting disproportionate time and energy to grant pursuit, rather than efforts to make better use of much larger resources already in the community
- Responding only to symptoms, such as housing shortages, rather than causes, such as low-wage jobs and regional economic conditions
- Ignoring the geography of family income and mobility, and assuming that programs that help families will automatically help the places where they live now
- Making policy for children *or* families—failing to recognize that the two focal points of local policy need to be connected.

What can cities and counties do? Family policy as choice of roles

The frameworks laid out in this chapter could help local governments move toward more reflective choices in making family policy. Cities and counties can address family policy using multiple roles. The matrix of roles introduced in Chapter 1 can again be useful in laying out fifteen different choices about how local governments seek to influence the lives of families and their children. In choosing among these options, a city or county would review each of these roles in responding to data about family needs at the local level.

Table 4: Examples of Family Policy or Programs

Role	Examples of Family Policy or Program
Participation in coalitions	Involvement in sponsorship of Healthy Families outreach coalitions
Convening stakeholders	Regional forums on impact of commuting time of family life
Endorse grants	Support local community-based organizations' efforts to fund family literacy
Seek funds from private sources	Proposals to community foundations for family support programs

Collect/provide information	Annual family indicators report; biennial survey of random sample of parents and youth on their attitudes toward government services
Provide residents with information	Use of software or checklists developed to provide working parents with information about potential eligibility for work support benefits
Training	Parent leadership courses in how to change education policy
Intergovernmental advocacy	Joining other cities and counties in supporting proposals for family-friendly state legislation and issuing annual reviews of local delegation members' support for these legislative packages
Use local regulatory powers	Requiring set-asides of affordable housing in new developments for residents, for local teachers, public safety workers, or other families; providing zoning waivers for "in-law" apartments or detached units that could house extended family members involved in dependent care
Use local economic role	Construction of family centers as part of city-school district joint use agreements
Model employer policies	Child care and dependent care benefits; released time for parent-teacher meetings and school advisory committees
Taxing powers	Tax incentives for senior voluntary service
Use local police powers	Holding parents accountable for adolescent vandalism or truancy; rewarding parents for neighborhood patrols performed with local youth
Direct funding, non-local government staff	Line items for local community organizations serving children and families; allocations of city- and county-channeled block grants
Direct Funding, Own Staff	Out-stationed staff in FRCs

At the local level, advocates within and outside local government could use this matrix of roles to do their own annual review of progress made across the government on family policy agendas. But that impact must be aimed at more than launching new programs; it must address family policy in light of other realities, to which we now turn.

NOTES

[1] Kate Sylvester, *Listening to Families: The Role of Values in Shaping Effective Social Policy:* (Washington, D.C.: Social Policy Action Network, 2001).
[2] Schorr, *Common Purpose*, 5

[3] Gilbert Steiner, The Futility of Family Policy. (Washington, D.C.: The Brookings Institution, 1981)

[4] Personal communications, June 2002, county and adoption agency officials.

[5] Ira Cutler, The Ties That Bind: a Look at the Extended Family. Unpublished report. (Port Chester, N.Y.: Cornerstone Consulting, 2001).

[6] "Hunger and Homelessness Up Sharply in Major U.S. Cities," U.S. Conference of Mayors. (Washington, D.C. December 12, 2001).

[7] Materials compiled for a February 2002 Casey Foundation conference on Family Economic Success describe several examples of state and local policy aimed at addressing these issues of under-enrollment and family economic self-sufficiency. See www.aecf.org.

[8] Cost, Quality & Child Outcomes Study Team, Cost, Quality, and Child Outcomes in Child Care Center, Public Report, second edition. (Denver, Colo.: Economics Department, University of Colorado at Denver, 1995)

[9] N.Dickon Reppucci, Preston A. Britner, and Jennifer L. Woolard, Preventing Child Abuse and Neglect through Parent Education. (Baltimore, Md.: Paul H. Brookes, 1997)

[10] Robert G. St.Pierre, Jean I. Layzer, and Helen V. Barnes, Regenerating Two-generation Programs. (Cambridge. Mass.: Abt Associates, 1996). Anne Brady and Julia Coffman, "Parenting Programs and Poverty: What's Our Evidence?" The Evaluation Exchange, (Cambridge. Mass.: Harvard Family Research Project, 1996). Benefits of Residential Substance Abuse Treatment for Pregnant and Parenting Women: Highlights from a study of 50 demonstration programs of the Center for Substance Abuse Treatment. Caliber Associates. Rockville. Md.: Substance Abuse and Mental Health Administration, Center for Substance Treatment, 2001).

[11] Ira Cutler, The Ties That Bind.

[12] Theodore Roszak, Longevity Revolution: As Boomers Become Elders. (Berkeley, CA.: Berkeley Hills Books, 2001).

CHAPTER 9: RACE, CULTURE, AND RELIGION AS CHILDREN AND FAMILY ISSUES

Values based on race, culture, and religion are fundamental to many families as they socialize their children. They are also central to local government, where many racial and cultural issues are most visible in geographic and political conflict. As we have seen in the earlier chapters, the issues of race and culture are inextricably connected with the tasks of making coherent policy for children and youth in local government, for five reasons:

1. How parents raise their children is significantly defined by their culture, which is itself defined as the ways we pass on customs and practices from one generation to another.

2. Children in the U.S. are more diverse than the total U.S. population; the percentage of minority population in school in 2000 was 39%; in the total U.S. population it is only 28.6%. The minority youth population, which is now 34% of the total youth population, will more than double from 1995 to 2050, while the "non-minority" youth population will decline. Minority children 0-5 will exceed the non-minority children in this age group by 2030. At current trends, racial and ethnic minority populations will account for nearly 90% of the total growth in the U.S. population from 1995 to 2050.

3. In increasing numbers of local governments, the issues of immigration and undocumented parents form a substantial portion of the continuing debates involving issues of race and culture.

4. Race has been a major challenge to American local governments as long as there have been local governments in this country. The challenge of responding to the realities of race and culture is visible through a long list of the issues that have faced those governments: local and regionalized armed conflict with the original inhabitants of the nation, slavery, secession, segregation, desegregation, housing discrimination, ethnic politics, patronage, policing, crime and delinquency. Because it is closer to the people, local government is closer to the tensions of race as a deep legacy of American history—and its effects are far from fading.

5. The operations of local government are never neutral on issues of race and culture—the literature on administrative evil and structural racism both make clear that not to have policy on issues of discrimination and bias is itself a policy. [1]

So race, culture, and sometimes language matter to local government because they are about who lives in a city or county, where they live, and what cultural and other values affect families who are raising their children in a

specific race and culture and community. We will deal with religion later in this
chapter.

Structural racism: a new lens[2]

An emerging set of tools for assessment of structural racism provides an
important lens through which to view local government and children and family
policy. Structural racism is defined by Lawrence as

> the enduring characteristics of American political, economic, and civic
> life—tangible and psychological—that create, re-create, and maintain
> white privilege.[3]

If the lens of structural racism is used in developing and assessing policy for
children and families, a set of further questions must be addressed:

- What disparate outcomes for minority children and families can be
  traced to differences in treatment by the courts, by education and other
  systems, and by the exclusion of these families from social benefits
  available to members of the dominant race and culture? (e.g. different
  sentences in juvenile courts for similar crimes, test scores highly
  correlated with teacher training and qualifications which are in turn
  correlated with race and income of schools and school districts, college
  admissions affected by access to information about advanced placement
  courses);

- What existing biases in favor of children and families of the dominant
  race and culture are evident in current policy? (e.g. housing affordability
  due to lending practices);

- What existing biases blocking opportunity and access for children and
  families of minority races and cultures are evident? (e.g. reduction of
  resources for English as a second language programs).

Yet as important as structural racism can be as a lens, it is not the only lens
for understanding power and the lack of power. An important debate is under
way about how important this lens is in contrast to others: class and income,
education, gender, and the lens of structural fiscal deficits built into the federal
system of governing. Undeniably, many of these other lenses are affected
profoundly by race and culture. It is impossible to surgically separate race and
class or race and the origins of the federal system—to pick only two of the other
lenses. To blame local outcomes on federalism or an anti-tax political outlook
ignores the degree to which both our constitutional history and our recent
political firestorms have had major racial ingredients.

Lawrence points out the ease with which discussions of community
building and, less often, discussions of children and family problems, slip into a
race-avoidant posture. Tracing the history of urban reform, and using Alice
O'Connor's thoughtful review of urban remedial efforts, Lawrence sees the
empowerment movement that had the potential to challenge systemic privilege
being transformed into an emphasis on enhanced personal capacity, and
"stripped of its progressive community-level connotations for the framing of
social policy during the 1980s." Lawrence and his colleagues see

comprehensiveness replacing empowerment in the 1990's and linked to building social capital in place-based initiatives.[4] As Lawrence summarizes:

> Interest in comprehensive community initiatives arose from several legitimate concerns, but racial equity was not one of them.[5]

The reference to place-based initiatives suggests another facet of the issue of race as it affects children and families: the extent to which policy is about *the intersection of place and race in the lives of children.* Place and race affect many of the dimensions of children's lives:

- where they will go to school,
- where they can play safely,
- whether their parents choose to remain in a stabilizing neighborhood or move further out into the suburbs where the twin factors of better schools and increased safety beckon.

In Chapter 2, we first reviewed the perspectives of Ferguson and others that schools and safety were the anchors of community development. As we brighten the spotlight on race, we see that these are factors that matter across races and cultures and throughout the entire metropolitan area. Whenever they can, parents will move to where their children have better schools and safer areas to play— that is a fundamental driving force in children and family policy. Race is not the only factor in those decisions, but it can be a decisive factor, and policy makers ignore it at their peril.

Race and multi-cultural communities

In some national discussions of race and community building, there often comes what some of us have termed "the California moment." By that we mean the point at which someone, typically but not always from California, makes the point that a standard black-white paradigm of the effects of race is not adequate to explain several phenomena visible in other states (especially Hawai'i and New Mexico), but clearest in California:

- communities in which a majority may be both "of color" and middle/upper income;
- communities in which the primary racial tension is between African-Americans displaced by Latinos or Asians;
- communities in which economic oppression takes the form of minority garment workers who are working illegally for minority small business owners; and
- deep nationalistic tensions within groups inappropriately placed under a single label: "Asian" or "Latino/Hispanic."

Obviously, more is going on here than black-white racial relations. Angela Blackwell, Stewart Kwoh, and Manuel Pastor have made a major contribution in their jointly authored work *Searching for the Uncommon Common Ground,* which is not only written by three Californians, but draws upon a wide array of materials to explain how multi-racial and multi-cultural communities must recognize race and its complicated history in the United States. They write

> A black-white lens is not going to capture the nuances of the struggle of immigrants.[6]

Yet, they caution,

> In a time of increasing diversity, it might be tempting to look beyond the black-white framework that structures race relations and social and economic opportunity. To the contrary, as other racial minorities grow, it becomes increasingly important to address the fundamental question of fairness for African Americans, *which affects the fortunes of the other groups…*
>
> The fact is that the inferiority attributed to blacks has defined policy discussions as well as the way that other racial minorities are viewed.[7]

If planning for children and family policy is to be strategic, it must begin with the question we have stated at several points in this book: who lives here? Once that question is answered, race and culture are on the table in all but a small percentage of the cities and counties in the nation. Rural areas that were once largely separate from these discussions are finding themselves newly impacted by the immigration of lower-income workers to their regions. Yet the data collection cannot stop with mere counting of the racial and cultural attributes of the population—it must continue on to ask the critical, second question: what are the conditions affecting those children and families and what are the underlying causes of those conditions?

That is the question that begins to examine the tragic correlations between race and income and poor outcomes. That question then leads on to analysis of the disparate outcomes that underscore what Lawrence and his colleagues stress: to be race-avoidant is to miss something very important that is happening in communities to children and families, including the ways that public institutions, private markets, and personal choices made by the majority (or a powerful white minority) become barriers to opportunity for racial minorities.

One of the best diagnostic warnings of shallow strategic thinking is when disparate outcomes are left out of or minimized in planning and policy development. Several examples are evident in recent city and state policy:

- To announce a drop in the dropout rate, without assessing what is happening to poor Latino youth;
- To track the arrest rate without determining how sentencing differences among racial and linguistic groups may affect incarceration of youth;
- To note the higher rates of kinship care among racial minorities in the child welfare system, without recognizing both the strength of the pattern of kin support and the burden this places on older relatives who often lack adequate public and community support for the caretaking role they are playing;
- To assess the quality of day care chosen by parents without assessing the differences in the quality and quantity of information about child development given to different groups of parents.

These are unmistakably bad practices in children and family policy development. Yet they are common in many of the "report cards" heralded as signs of concern for children and youth. The trend line may be noted, the disparate outcomes may even be counted, but the causes and effects of the outcomes are not assessed in enough depth to create the public policy changes and community support they need to be changed.

In part, this flows from the issue of who is at the table doing the assessment and who is helping to interpret it. This can be another result of what Hedy Chang and her colleagues at California Tomorrow have called "the legacy of token governance."[8] This legacy arises from the long history in many communities of grass-roots groups and community members being added to a wider coalition, but in a way that is not inclusive. As we discuss in the next chapter in looking at "ladders of participation," the bottom rungs of these ladders are often where token forms of participation stop, rather than raising community involvement to higher and more genuine levels of decision-making and participation.

Race, culture, elections, and power

To take racially disparate outcomes seriously in strategic planning also requires rising above the individualistic and group analysis that focuses only on the question "why is this group not doing well?" As Blackwell and her colleagues note, it demands taking geography, economics, and politics seriously. Each of these raises fundamental questions about power.

We will look further at the regional geography of "smart and equitable growth" in Chapter 11. Economic power affects family opportunities in obvious ways, based on decisions about hiring, locating businesses, and businesses' own family-friendly (or family-harming) practices. Racial divides can affect all of these, as firms implement or avoid affirmative action and make locational decisions that often seek to avoid concentrations of minority neighborhoods and poverty. And local government can document and confront these disparities in economics, or remain silent and allow market forces to reinforce racial disparities.

Political realities lead local policy makers to modify the first question: who lives here, to ask *who votes here?* If the answer is that increasingly racial minorities are voting or not voting, it can matter a great deal. And the generational non-voting phenomena noted in Chapter 8, with fewer younger voters participating in elections than their older counterparts, can worsen the impact of racial divides in a community when a larger group of young residents does not vote. If racial minorities vote less, and younger voters vote less, the arithmetic is unavoidable: despite a disproportionately large group of young minority residents, these non-voters will matter less to political outcomes.

As we will see in the following chapter, it may require community-level and neighborhood strategies to reverse this electoral non-participation. Winning at the level of governance closest to a voter—getting a health clinic for a school, replacing an unresponsive principal—may increase the sense of political efficacy of racial minorities in lower-income communities enough to make them feel that participation in citywide and countywide elections is worth it. When we examine two different "ladders of citizen involvement" in the next chapter, we will find that as groups move up the ladder and are offered—or seize on their own—new avenues for participation, more political action is possible.

Immigration as an unavoidable issue for local governments

Race and culture intersect with national policy on immigration in increasingly powerful ways, even outside the Western and Southwestern states where these issues have been traditionally part of the political landscape. One of every five children under age 18 living in the United States—a total of 14 million—is an immigrant or has immigrant parents. Budget debates in cities and counties have included explicit charges and counter-charges about how much undocumented residents and workers cost local budgets. No conclusive figures have yet emerged, with an array of estimates that range from a net positive effect on the public sector to a major drain in some areas.

With immigrant populations made up of a substantial portion of children and youth, strategic policy at the local level may encounter several issues concerning immigrant children and families:

- The extent to which uninsured children are from undocumented families in which the children, having been born in the U.S., are legally entitled to benefits, but their parents are not and are thus reluctant to register their children for Medicaid and other health coverage;
- The difficulty of parent education and parent involvement efforts by schools and other agencies when parents are reluctant to engage with public agencies;
- Uncertainty about which benefits immigrant families may be eligible to receive, or under which circumstances they may be eligible to receive them.

A painful reality that most local governments ignore is an important fact that repeated studies have documented: the longer an immigrant group stays in the U.S., the worse its youth indicators become. First generation adolescents have far fewer pregnancies, arrests, and drug involvement than their more assimilated counterparts. The gradual undermining of families' cultural foundations by residence in a different culture have the effect, documented in numerous studies, of creating a split in generations between youth who seek assimilation and parents and older generations who cling to tradition.[9] And, as we will see in Chapter 11 on regionalism, immigration also intersects with the effects of regional growth on children and family policy, since there has been a definite concentration of immigrant poor families in the cities of the Southwest.

Religion: declining or rising variable?

While it may not seem to fit in a chapter on race and culture, the growing importance of religion at several levels in children and family policy fits readily into a broadened focus on multiple forms of diversity, including class and housing type (such as "trailer/mobile home children" and "motel children"), the documented status of families of immigrants, and religious diversity.

Local governments should neither ignore religious issues in children and family policy nor treat it as falling on the far side of the church-state barrier and thus separate from the local policy debate. It is not, as several trends make clear:

- expansion of home schooling for religious reasons, by parents who do not want their children exposed to what they see as a secular, profane society in the schools;
- the tensions created by the 9/11 terrorist attacks, with their consequences for an increasingly visible Muslim religious minority whose children tend to attend public schools in their communities;
- the strong resistance of fundamentalist religious families to any interventions in the school that treat sex, gender, or other taboo subjects that are seen by these groups as the exclusive province of the family;
- combined religious and cultural practices that result in teen pregnancies and younger marriages as a valued tradition in conflict with American adolescent patterns, which creates inter-family tensions heightened by student friendships and peer pressures;
- schools and youth development agencies' increased sensitivity to teasing and bullying, which can be aimed at members of religious minorities.

In an era when faith-based services programs are gaining new funding and new federal support, it is impossible to ignore the resurgence of religion as a factor in local governments' response to the problems of children and families. The growing evidence that some faith-based programs have had results as good or better than secular programs, and that spiritually based programs possess strengths that produce statistically robust findings, cannot be ignored by local governments in seeking to do strategic planning for children and families.[10]

Once a strategic plan moves to the vital issues of resources, it is necessarily in search of what works, because resources are scarce and because non-cash, community-based resources are invaluable. But faith-based resources have become more than one more item on the checklist. They represent more than simply asking "Are churches in the coalition? Great, move on." They represent both an option for increased resources and an option for increased effectiveness in children and family services, despite the difficulties of assuring that their services are provided in an inclusive way that preserves their religious dimension without limiting parent choice. Glenn and others who have examined the faith-based options have concluded that preserving that special dimension is possible, citing use of outcomes standards, peer review, and informed choice by parents as the appropriate safeguards.[11]

Local government and faith-based organizations

The issue of the appropriate role of faith-based organizations (FBOs) will work itself out in coming years far more at the local level than in state and federal policy arenas, since it is local service delivery that is often at issue in state and federal debates about FBOs. As Dionne and Chen state in their excellent Brookings compilation on faith-based programs,

> In principle, Americans want the government to help faith-based organizations. In practice, they worry about what that help might mean.[12]

Working out the practicalities of this new-old idea is happening already in local governments, as hundreds of examples make clear. In education, child care, substance abuse treatment, pregnancy prevention, and youth development, multiple models of faith-based organizational innovation are expanding, in response to local leadership, the availability of federal funding, and new federal encouragement from policy leaders.

The substantial differences in intent among different proponents of faith-based organizations will also play out in local contests. Those who seek religious conversion of those using FBO services are very different from those who see the role of FBOs as "speaking truth to power," in the Old Testament prophetic tradition of remaining separate from the sources of public power and free to criticize both its means and ends. As Dionne and Chen note, "Faith-based groups, after all, are often the most powerful advocates for those who are left out and among the only institutions over which the poor have control."[13]

But seeing the causes of poverty and discrimination as socially and economically determined is a very different world view than seeing poverty primarily as the responsibility of the poor themselves. Local governments have become immersed in the responding to exclusionary policies of some organizations, as United Way funders decide in some parts of the country to end their support for organizations such as the Boy Scouts and others that refuse to allow homosexuals or women to participate in their programs. And then there is also the important difference (echoing our discussion of family resource centers in Chapter 14) between those who see FBOs as replacing government-funded public agencies and those who see them as important supplements to existing secular agencies, able to expand outreach to harder-to-serve populations that currently funded agencies have trouble serving.

This issue also intersects with the growing role of local governments in education, since the fastest growing sector in non-public schools is schools sponsored by evangelical congregations and organizations.[14] If we are right in predicting that the middle ground of charter schools (and not vouchers) is the most likely growth area in education choice, it will be in this arena of religiously organized schools (as well as the growth in some states of home schooling for religious reasons) where a sizable segment of the debate about use of public funds for faith-based purposes will take place.

Local government will at times play a referee's role in the debates over the future of FBOs, and at times it will need to be a more active convener of FBOs and other nonprofits to work with governments. In many cities and some counties, the topics most often bringing these groups together have been the problems of the homeless population and the operation of shelters for homeless families and victims of family violence. Local government can also play a critical information-providing role, in educating both congregations and the larger community about which families among their neighbors are having difficulty making ends meet. Local congregations have proven to be a highly receptive audience for children's report cards, which can serve as educational devices for some more insulated congregations, laying out basic facts about haves and have-nots in their own communities.

The value attached to social capital cannot be divorced from the debate about local roles of FBOs, since thousands of volunteer hours, a deep sense of intentional community, and a concern for the larger society are inherent in the work of many FBOs. A city or county seeking to build social capital as a foundation for new social capital creation will ignore congregations and their social programs at its peril, since they make up a sizable portion of the organizational base for many social capital-building efforts.

Summary: Local government as laboratory of diversity

As the populations of American cities and counties become more diverse, the challenges to their governments in responding to that diversity will become greater. Few arenas will have more impact on the daily lives of children and families, regardless of where in the diversity continuum they fall: growing "minorities," shrinking "majorities," or religious enclaves seeking to preserve a different culture apart from the mainstream of American life. Being strategic in this setting may requiring being flexible above all, seeking to tap all the strengths of diversity while handling all its tensions at the same time.

But it will require familiarity with the tools of racial disparity analysis, and willingness to use those tools in addressing causes, not just a willingness to include the disparities in annual reports. These issues are not dealt with in much depth in most of the products developed by national organizations that represent local governments. Problems affecting children and families are still approached in categorical frames, without discussion of the underlying power dynamics that affect disparate outcomes.

Yet with affordable housing, attention to disparate outcomes in juvenile justice, dropouts, and early childhood programs, cities and counties have worked with their partners in local communities to address disparity as the downside of diversity. These issues need to stay visible as an integral part of strategic planning at the local level, as diversity increases while resources remain constrained.

NOTES

[1] Guy B. Adams and Danny L. Balfour, Unmasking Administrative Evil, (Thousand Oaks, Ca.: Sage Publications, 1998).

[2] This section draws upon work by the Aspen Roundtable for Comprehensive Community Initiatives, especially publications developed by Keith Lawrence and Stacy Sutton. It also draws upon a discussion of structural racism and community building held in Washington under the auspices of the Aspen Institute on July 19, 2002 as well as a discussion of structural racism held at the Aspen Institute in Colorado in July 2003.

[3] Keith Lawrence, "Expanding Comprehensiveness: Structural Racism and Community Building in the United States," in Rebuilding Community: Policy and

Practice In Urban Regeneration. John Pierson and Joan Smith, eds. (New York: Palgrave, 2001), 45.
    [4] Alice O'Connor, "Swimming Against the Tide: a Brief History of Federal Policy in Poor Communities, in R. Ferguson and W. Dickens (eds.) Urban Problems and Community Development. (Washington D.C.: The Brookings Institution, 1999). Lawrence, "Expanding Comprehensiveness," 41
    [5] Lawrence, "Expanding Comprehensiveness," 42.
    [6] Angela Blackwell, Stewart Kwoh, and Manuel Pastor, Searching for the Uncommon Common Ground, .(W.W. Norton and Co, 2002), 70
    [7] Blackwell, et al., Searching, 70. [emphasis added]
    [8] Hedy Nai-Lin Chang, Denise De La Rosa, Cecilia Leong. 1994) Drawing Strength from Diversity: Effective Services for Children, Youth, and Families. (San Francisco, CA.: California Tomorrow. 1994). Hedy Chang, et al. Walking the Walk: Principles for Building Community Capacity for Equity and Diversity. (San Francisco, Ca.: California Tomorrow. 2000).
    [9] "A Matter of Choice: Forks in the Road for Juvenile Justice." Advocasey, (Baltimore, Md. The Annie E. Casey Foundation. Spring 2001).
    [10] Donald J. Hernandez and Evan Charney, editors The Health and Well-Being of Children in Immigrant Families. Committee on the Health and Adjustment of Immigrant Children and Families, National Research Council. (Washington, D.C.: National Academy Press, 1998). Donald J. Hernandez and Katherine Darke, Trends In The Wellbeing Of America's Children And Youth, Part Two. The Well-Being Of Immigrant Children, Native-Born Children With Immigrant Parents, And Native-Born Children With Native-Born Parents. (Washington D.C.: National Academy of Sciences, 1998), 427.
    [11] Ibid. p. 275-286.
    [12] E.J. Dionne and Ming Hsu Chen [eds.] Sacred Places, Civic Purposes. (Washington, D.C.: The Brookings Institution, 2001), 2.
    [13] Ibid.
    [14] Frederick Hess. Revolution at the Margins: The Impact of Competition on Urban School Systems. (Washington, D.C.: The Brookings Institution, 2001)

CHAPTER 10: COMMUNITY AND NEIGHBORHOOD ROLES IN CHILDREN AND FAMILY POLICY

In this chapter, two overlapping challenges are assessed:
- The effort to work at the level of neighborhoods to build communities that work for their residents, especially their children and families; and
- The effort to develop positive roles for local governments in that process of community building.

An extensive literature and practice has emerged, receded, and re-emerged in the past four decades, since the Great Society programs of the mid-60's, reviewing the activities and potential benefits of a neighborhood- or community-based approach to dealing with the problems of residents of lower-income areas of cities and counties.[1] It is not the central purpose of this book to review this literature, but to underscore how much these efforts make up a significant part of local policy affecting children and families.

At the same time, two sizable gaps must be recognized:
- some of these community building efforts and initiatives do not address children and family issues directly, and
- some local governments are not actively involved in these community-building efforts.

In Chapter 2 we sought to explain why local government has been so often omitted from the theory and practice of children and family policy and from community building. Here our focus is upon what local government *can* do and the risks of omitting a significant role for local governments.

Why should community-level initiatives connect with children and family policy?

Community building and children and family policy overlap so much that they should be connected at every possible point.
- Communities and neighborhoods are closest to where children and youth live their lives. In fact, the community context is even more "local" than local government in many cities and counties. The community that families live in is obviously part of the answer to how and where children and youth achieve or fail to achieve their potential.
- Children are embedded in families, which are themselves influenced by their community. At the same time, families affect the community.[2]
- Social capital grows or declines at neighborhood and community levels, and local governmental policy can enhance social capital-building to achieve better outcomes for children and youth.[3]

- Community building initiatives that are silent on children and families are as flawed as those that are silent on race and culture, or those that are silent on income differences among the residents of the community. To try to build communities without attention to their families is, in Old Testament terms, to try to make bricks without straw—trying to build a strong foundation without the materials needed to hold the foundation together. Family life gives a community its character, carrying its message of hope that young people will grow up here and that older people will stay here to watch them grow.

The most obvious intersection of children and family agendas and the community development field comes in the antipoverty orientation of some community development initiatives. This focus has led to a concern for lower-income working families in many of these initiatives, especially in the aftermath of welfare reform that has moved millions of families from dependency on AFDC to a post-TANF near-poverty status in lower-income communities. Other links arise in the inherent tension between "people-based" and "place-based" initiatives, which must both cope with the question of the extent to which geographically defined initiatives can address the needs of highly mobile families.

Why do some community-level initiatives seek change in children and family policy?

These connections have been obvious to some funders and local leaders, who have placed families at the center of their community building initiatives.

- Several foundations, including the Annie E. Casey Foundation, have placed their bets on comprehensive community initiatives as the best path to changing children and family policy at the local level. The omission in some of these initiatives, as discussed in Chapter 2, of an explicit link to a leadership role for local government takes nothing away from the connection that *has* been attempted between community building and the children and family agenda.
- Some community initiatives have taken children and youth issues to be their central focus, such as the Caring Communities in Missouri, the broadest Healthy Starts (school-linked services models) in California, and other efforts. Some community-building efforts have evolved into education reform, as in Hartford's Ford-funded Neighborhood and Family Initiative. Others, like Santa Ana's Latino Health Access, have moved from a health agenda to a wider concern with community building defined more broadly. Blackwell, in describing the gains achieved by community building approaches, cites two primary examples: the reduction of infant mortality in Oakland and the reduction of youth homicide in Boston.[4]

But not all students and practitioners of community building would make so direct a link.

Why do some community-level initiatives largely ignore children and family policy?

- In many cases, these models and initiatives operate deliberately or inadvertently separate from city and county government, see themselves as an alternative to politics, and ignore the Willie Sutton problem—the fact that local governments still control most of the public resources available at the local level. The $966 billion in local government spending remains largely invisible to these initiatives.

- Some community initiatives, to the extent that they move beyond physical development, housing, and economic development, focus on jobs, but do so in a way that is often isolated from children and youth issues.[5]

- Research has made clear that family-level variables such as income and education are usually more powerful in their impact on children's outcomes than community variables, and some advocates for children and family policy have over-simplified this to essentially ignore community factors as they affect parenting and children.[6]

The factors that underlie this neglect of local government are those that were discussed in greater depth in Chapter 2: a suspicion of local politics and strong memories of historical roles for city governments that justify those suspicions, a belief that the federal and state levels matter much more to children and family politics, and a one-dimensional, budget-constrained view of what local government could do to be helpful.

Leaving local government out of community building

For many community initiatives and community building efforts, local government is at best an after-thought, perceived as a potential barrier rather than a partner, or at best, an entity that can run interference with other sources of power and resources. But if cities and counties are largely left out of efforts to address community problems at the community level, then those governments will be less accountable for solutions at the community level. Clearly, local governments exercise a greater percentage of influence over community initiatives' success than many of those initiatives have recognized. That influence arises both in what those governments do and what they do not do.

The problem may be framed as the answer to a broad question: what percentage of the outcomes of community-based efforts could be affected by local government? Obviously, it cannot be answered with precision, and it depends upon what a given community coalition is trying to do, but if it is trying to work in arenas where local government is a major force, a significant percentage of that agenda is affected by local government. Yet community coalitions act as if local government influenced only 5-10% of the outcomes of community initiatives, when the actual percentages seem more like 30-40% in many areas—and as much as 50-60% in others. The point, again, is not that these figures can be calculated with precision: it is that many community coalitions have not spent much time even asking what the percentage really is, or reviewing the multiple roles which local governments could play in support of their efforts.

This ignoring of local government recalls the phrase coined by Paul Hill which we have cited before: the tendency for reformers to sometimes operate in a "zone of wishful thinking," in which hoped-for changes are assumed likely, even though they are outside the control of the reformers. Assuming that local government will become active in community-building without sustained negotiations may be operating in such a zone of wishful thinking.

In some communities, the bridge between community building and local government has been spanned by advocacy efforts, rather than positive initiatives from local governments. Community building, as Blackwell and others note, shares some of its goals and methods with earlier approaches, including community action programs of the 1960's.[7] Without the same active federal sponsorship that community action had in the 60's, the current version seeks the same empowerment of local residents. Because it *is* local, it necessarily encounters local government, whether it seeks its involvement in partnership, targets it as a focus of advocacy, or attempts middle ground strategies.

In a brief, but thoughtful discussion of the role of government in the Sandtown Neighborhood Initiative, Pru Brown and her colleagues summarized the neighborhood-city government interaction in a few pithy quotes:

> When you take on government, you also take on some of the baggage...The city represents a very powerful force [but] there...need to be some checks and balances.

They conclude by recommending that community initiatives

> Retain adequate autonomy in the community. Don't invite the public sector to participate in the neighborhood's internal affairs.[8]

But this seems very short-sighted advice, given that the city (and often the county as well) *is* involved in "internal affairs," unavoidably and inextricably: The public sector decides when the trash will be picked up, when the police will patrol, which youth will be arrested, and what child care and liquor licenses will be granted. And in some circumstances, it can also influence whether the children of the neighborhood will learn in school. If these are not "internal affairs" of the neighborhood, it is hard to imagine what issues are more important or more internal.

What could local governments do in support of community building?

As suggested by the matrix of local government roles in Chapter 1, the resources of local governments extend well beyond their own budgets and locally controlled revenues. Those resources include:

- the convening power of local government
- the advocacy power of local government vis-a-vis state and federal governments in support of community initiatives
- the legal powers of local government—to regulate, to sue, to license

- the publicity powers of local government—the "bully pulpit" function of public education and persuasion
- the outreach and referral powers of local governmental agencies to connect residents with the full array of income benefits local residents are entitled to receive for working
- information strategies—collecting and using services data, geographic information systems data
- access to grants—what local governments can endorse as no-cost, credible support for community coalitions' funding proposals

The argument is not that local government leadership is essential or likely in all cases. A separate community-building entity with a genuine governance role *is* essential, in order to concentrate on issues that will not be as central to a citywide or to a countywide government as they would be to a more neighborhood- or community-focused entity. But the fact remains that the full array of roles that local government can play is usually under-emphasized in implementing a community-level governance entity. In some cases, this may be because the community initiatives do not know what to ask for from local government.

Do community initiatives know what to ask for?

At times, it appears as though community groups do not understand local government in sufficient depth to know what to ask for or how to negotiate with them. But in part this is because these groups lack a clear idea about what are plausible local responses to their requests.

We may need better categories of plausible local action in support of community building. We need to be able to rate local governments' leadership roles in response to community building initiatives. In the same way that municipal finance ratings gauge a local government's practices in handling money, community advocates across the nation may need a "red circles" approach to gauging local government's practices toward community building.[9] A scorecard of support for community-building could give local groups the ability to advocate for their own local governments to step up to wider and deeper commitments, based on the areas where the city or county is weakest.

Such a scorecard of support might include such criteria as rating local government on a "poor, fair, good, better, best" scale for their governmental functions, including:

- purchasing practices—do cities and counties buy from or contract with local community-based manufacturers and service providers?
- hiring policies—do they hire people from the neighborhood to work in the neighborhood, or do the people who work in the neighborhood get trained and promoted based on their responsiveness to the neighborhood?
- leadership/advocacy roles in negotiating regional agreements for jobs and transportation
- outreach to enroll local residents in income benefit programs

- low-interest loan programs for affordable housing
- legislative proposals to the state legislature in support of expanded and more flexible funding streams for community building efforts
- allowing community organizations' and coalitions' staff to participate in local government training programs
- support for community coalitions' efforts to enlist wider involvement of local businesses
- redistricting service areas to ensure that city/county service districts correspond to natural communities of shared geographic identity
- encouraging annual ratings of city and county agencies' performance on a district basis, based on citizen surveys or other forms of neighborhood and community-level feedback.

Support in the form of line items in local budgets should not be excluded, but it seems clear that wide involvement of a local government in most of the above activities could be worth much more to a community organization or coalition than a $100,000 line item for core budgets.

It is also important to assess the barriers created or reduced by local governments. At times, it is what local government do *not* do that matters most to community building. If they do not

- formally oppose organizing efforts, even if some of the targets are local governments,
- block state or federal grants that fund community initiatives, or
- use local regulatory powers to delay or block proposed economic development efforts,

then their roles may be somewhat passive, but they will not be negative. In some cases, if local government simply *did less harm*, it would represent real progress, if the city or country has been a major barrier to moving ahead.

The balanced argument

In view of these arguments for a more carefully differentiated roles for local government, the case can be made for a more nuanced approach to the role of local government in community building. Such an approach would avoid both the extremes of ignoring local government almost entirely or, on the other hand, assuming that local government must always be a leading player in community building strategies. A middle ground role is often what is needed and what is most appropriate, working out the role of local government in a way that reflects local realities and peculiarities, but in all cases assuming that that role is too important to be relegated to becoming "just one more partner in the collaboration."

Some evidence is available to show how this nuanced role might operate. Chaskin reviewed seven community-based initiatives as they relate to local government, finding great variations among them. These range from the formal sponsorship of the Baltimore initiative to three of the seven that do not even have local government representation on the governing boards. All seven sought some form of generally described "partnership" with the neighborhood initiatives, which was seen as including:

- Feedback on city planning for the area
- Ideas on what the city should do and what was most needed in the area
- Expertise and technical assistance needed by the neighborhood
- Access to city decision-making processes (as a reciprocal of city access to neighborhood leaders and residents)
- Ensure accountability for results viewed from outside the neighborhood (as the reciprocal, according to some, of the city's accountability to the neighborhoods for results within the initiative areas).[10]

What local government was felt to be uniquely able to provide, at least in some sites, were resources in response to neighborhood requests or demands, information about city operations, and balancing neighborhood interests in the initiative area with citywide priorities and those of other neighborhoods not part of the initiative. Neighborhood respondents also recognized the unique legal mandates of local government to provide certain services and to be accountable for use of state and federal funds that are channeled to neighborhoods through the city.

At the same time, public officials in the seven cities had some concerns about the limitations of neighborhood-based governance entities in

- Making city policy, (which was seen as inappropriate) rather than informing its development;
- Ensuring accountability for results in achieving their mission;
- Balancing needs across citywide areas.

Chaskin acknowledges that the relatively small scale of these initiatives means that local governments may have been able to treat them merely as one more geographically organized interest group, not large enough to represent a threat.

A further limitation of neighborhood governance initiatives may result from the possibility that city-initiated neighborhood efforts may claim much wider loyalties and accountability than those initiated outside city government. In a review of the historical background of current efforts, Chaskin notes that during the 1970s and beyond,

> A broad focus on decentralization led many municipalities to seek to incorporate neighborhoods into the structure of local government through the creation (or recognition) of various forms of neighborhood councils, associations and other local mechanisms.[11]

This is an important difference. These city-endorsed *neighborhood governments* or adjuncts to government were not neighborhood *governance* as the term is currently understood—they were formally city-sponsored efforts to extend city government itself into the neighborhoods and make it both more effective and more responsive. Some of these efforts distinguished between *administrative decentralization* aimed at more effective city operations and *political decentralization* aimed at wider inclusiveness. In some, notably New York in the 1970s, it was believed that the administrative form was needed as a prerequisite to the credibility needed to achieve the political variation.[12] Where such efforts were citywide, as they were in New York and Portland, they have had far greater breadth than neighborhood-specific entities that may have only addressed certain program areas.

How could a more active local government role in community building reinforce children, youth, and family policy?

With respect to the more explicit children and family agenda, several problems are ignored or treated lightly in these sources that focus on community building. These include:

- The mobility of families, as a social force which cities might want to increase to achieve local purposes, such as neighborhood renewal or family improvement (it should also be noted that there are still some counties that regularly use one-way bus tickets to other parts of the country as means of exporting their lower-income families—in some cases to known jobs, in others to reduce the numbers of dependent residents).[13]

- Some family initiatives seek to preserve families in or near their original neighborhoods, seeing proximity as a value in achieving better child welfare outcomes. In contrast, some initiatives recognize the value of removing adults with substance abuse and other problems from the neighborhoods where they originally had problems and where there may be many "triggers" for relapse as well as few opportunities for transitional, "sober living" housing for reunified families.

- The out-stationing of city and county staff in decentralized agency offices, in schools, or in family resource centers as a means of working at community levels, but with services fully controlled by city or county governments.

- As major service providers, health clinics and hospitals represent a significant part of the local governmental service delivery network, whether directly operated or subsidized through private or nonprofit contractors.

It may be useful to contrast the different, but overlapping approaches taken in local government to community building and children and family policy:

Table 5: Children, Youth,, and Family Policy vs. Community-building Policy

CYF Policy	Community-building policy
Focuses (to varying degrees) on where children and families live, but may seek out-migration for family reasons	Focuses on who lives in the neighborhood and seeks to stabilize or reduce out-migration
Seeks to address child and family life cycles at key transition points, e.g., birth, school readiness, adolescence, high school graduation	Seeks to address neighborhood dynamics over time; assesses current neighborhood assets and develops a vision of what neighborhood can become as a result of community-building
Views schools and safety as critical issues	Views schools and safety (in varying degrees) as critical issues
Focuses on major children- and family-serving institutions—early care, schools, hospitals	Focuses on building neighborhood-specific institutions
Tends to emphasize positive youth development options	May emphasize youth development but has concern about anti-social youth behavior affecting quality of neighborhood life
Strong emphasis on parent involvement	Strong emphasis on resident involvement

Resisting the romanticizing of neighborhoods

At the same time that local governments address community building efforts in greater depth, they should do so based on close familiarity with the shortcomings of community organizations and coalitions:

- Their predictable focus on the immediate, rather than the long-term;
- A tendency to seek additional projects, rather than focusing on wider policy reforms;
- The tendency of "community forums" to be dominated by provider groups who have staff able to participate in such forums, while working residents with children find it difficult (and of questionable value) to take time away from work and family to participate in local government processes;
- Low voter turnouts in some lower-income neighborhoods;
- A NIMBY resistance to locating treatment programs and social services agencies in neighborhoods, especially those that have historically been dumping grounds for such programs;
- An orientation to the categorical, rather than seeing the value of comprehensive, integrated programs.

These are all understandable inclinations, given the fragmenting approach of typical programs; why should anyone expect that neighborhoods would react to a categorical, project-oriented social services system with a vision of integrated services, when no such reality exists?

Without romanticizing the community, local governments could respond to the realities of their communities with more genuine efforts to build participation. The question then arises as to what forms of participation are serious and which are token.

When is participation serious? The Arnstein-Epstein ladders

In 1969 Sherry Arnstein wrote a book called *Citizen Participation*, which set forth what she called a "ladder of citizen participation," which has really not been improved upon in the last thirty-plus years.[14]   And Joyce Epstein, addressing similar issues in the education world, has described a set of six stages of parent involvement in education that move from the token to the genuine.[15] In the early 21st century, we may need to know more about inclusive governance than what Arnstein and Epstein have given us—but they have provided a great foundation for what we need to learn that may be new.

The point that both of these frameworks make is a simple, powerful one, and one that we keep forgetting. It is that we can easily do citizen involvement in a shallow, pro forma way, or, with more effort, we can get serious about it. We go up the ladder from the shallow to the serious, and as we rise, we involve more people, tap more citizen energy, build more social capital, work harder and make more connections with resources at scale—which inevitably leads us back to local government.

If we try to adapt these two older frameworks to the specifics of community initiatives, we end up with a ladder of citizen involvement that makes the Arnstein-Epstein ladders concrete:

1. Involvement in one-time hearings
2. Involvement in needs assessment on a continuing basis: setting priorities, going beyond listing needs
3. Involvement in developing criteria for funding allocations and priority-setting
4. Involvement in actually making decisions on funding: a representative committee as part of the final process of choice
5. Training/capacity-building for citizen leadership roles: what are we spending now for children and family programs? What do we know now about what works? How can we affect the outcomes of the discussion? How can we monitor what happens in implementation?
6. Involvement in evaluating programs' progress and success through selecting and monitoring the outcomes and indicators used to track progress.

These are only suggestive. Each city and county (or advocates seeking to assess their local governments) could come up with its own ladder, applying these concepts to its own setting in determining what involvement is possible and necessary. And then, as described above, ratings of the level of local government citizen involvement would enable a regular, public review of the authenticity of participation efforts.

The civic engagement or civic renewal movement and local government roles

In Chapter 3, in discussing tools for strategic planning, we reviewed the efforts of the deliberative democracy movement, which is sometimes labeled "civic renewal" or "civic engagement." The civic engagement movement is an important part of the context of local policymaking. It is our view, in fact, that cities and counties with active citizen involvement through multiple mechanisms will produce better policy, through an engagement process that extends well outside the boundaries of the government. Local government leaders should seek to widen participation as a means of assuring more legitimate policy that reflects a wider set of attitudes and ideas than exist within government alone.

But civic engagement cannot substitute for elected officials' engagement. It is a critical supplement to it, it can legitimate and validate it, and it can assure that implementation, once policy is clearly set, will proceed with active citizen, provider, and client support, rather than being imposed in a top-down, autocratic way. Civic engagement is greatly needed in many cities and counties where the policy process is dominated by a small group of stakeholders.

Yet at times, civic engagement can degenerate into token allocations of symbolic resources, in which a consultation process goes on or pilot efforts are begun while access to benefits is restricted for many families. In fact, some communities have used the "participation game" as the process equivalent of pilot projects—using involvement in program planning as a substitute for serious policy roles. Peter Benson adds a second critique of process-heavy civic engagement:

> An emphasis [on civic engagement] should not overshadow the need for people to reconnect with their fellow citizens in relationships of mutual support, care, and shared responsibility.[16]

Here it is very important to be clear what I am trying to say, and what I am not trying to say. I am not deprecating the entire civic engagement effort, or saying that politics is everything, or that only elected officials and their local agencies in the public sector can make a difference. I have lived and worked in too many communities where the leadership was temporarily moribund, hopelessly committed to the status quo, incurably reactionary—or worse—to believe that local government is the salvation of children or the only way to make things happen. I am critical of local government in this book not because I believe the civic engagement effort is irrelevant, but because I think it is insufficient to make things happen for children at scale—for *enough* children.

Local government is not the only way to make things happen for children. But it must always be one of the key *targets* for local action.

Community organizations and coalitions as advocates

In a remarkable understatement, one student of local politics asserts

> Established local politicians and leaders in the private sector do not generally welcome the mobilization of new groups unless they are potential allies.[17]

Because of this reluctance to rely upon new groups if they are not allies, advocacy groups adopt tactics along a continuum from *becoming* allies with local government, to trying to *seem like* allies on some issues, to being very clear that they are not allies but that they will respond positively if local officials respond positively to their ideas on children and youth policy, and finally on to a stance that is based on unrelenting, adversarial relationships.

In a discussion of community organizations which is relevant to children and youth-serving organizations and advocates, Weir distinguishes among three broad categories of government-community relationships:

1. "Elite-dominated systems" with weak connections between community groups and economic and political power centers;
2. "Patronage-permeated" systems in which politics, often partisan, organizes the transactions among community groups and power-holders; and
3. A more inclusionary political setting in which the doors are more open to expanded participation, for political reasons that are driven in part by local demographics and voting statistics and partly by the enlightenment of local politicians—who have, in some cities and counties, arisen from community groups themselves.

In a book which is trying to capture what local government can do at its best to address children and youth issues, our preference is obviously for the third, most inclusive possible approach to these issues. At the same time, we should not be naive in assuming that this approach will prevail or ever become the norm in local government. But by proposing standards by which local governments can be judged in their performance on these issues, we are also suggesting how outside groups can increase the pressure for higher norms.

At times, these recommendations and concepts will be most relevant to the political outsider, who may have access to local government as a senior official, but who may not be in the majority. As "champions" of issues concerning children and youth, local elected officials can play many important roles short of being able to control resources or command a majority. For example, if the city doesn't have its own report card on community progress, a council member can develop her own, with the help of local community coalitions and universities.

Neighborhood action alone is insufficient: the wider lens

Finally, a broad answer is essential to a question that has too rarely been framed in community-building work: what percentage of the changes sought by community-building in community outcomes can be achieved by actions focused primarily within the community itself?

A variety of analysts have concluded that the neighborhood approach cannot be treated as if it were self-sufficient. What is under-emphasized, in this view, is not only the local government within which the community initiative takes place—it is also *all of the other local governments* in the region.

> Although issues of fair housing, discrimination, and diversity sometimes
> focus on the problems of a particular neighborhood, the overall problems

> associated with these issues cannot be solved solely, if at all, at the
> neighborhood level...it will not be possible to solve the problems of
> neighborhood inequalities without also addressing issues of regional
> inequalities...other issues of critical importance to neighborhoods but
> best addressed regionally include the deconcentration of public housing
> and poverty, welfare reform, public transportation, and environmental
> quality.[18]

In this sense, neighborhood reform by itself cannot succeed without local government. The fatal flaw in bottom-up strategies that fail to aim at local government is the need for responsive city and county agencies in order for neighborhood reforms to operate at scale in an institutionalized structure and process. Unless the neighborhood has extraordinary economic assets that enable it to adopt what amounts to a self-sufficiency strategy, neighborhood reform isolated by itself is doomed to marginality.

The Aspen Roundtable has come to similar conclusions, based on a decade of work with comprehensive community initiatives (CCIs) and a highly sensitive awareness of what community initiatives can do well and what they find difficult, for very understandable reasons. In *Voices from the Field II*, Anne Kubisch and her colleagues write

> It is at the level of engaging the policies and practices of external
> resources that CCIs have fallen most short. It is possible that their
> emphasis on "localism" steered them away from this type of work from
> the outset, but other factors also came into play. For the most part, poor
> communities are not well-situated to take the lead in building coalitions
> across neighborhoods and constituencies...Without sophisticated
> strategies for using structural, institutional, policy, and social levers for
> change, the work of CCIs will be merely palliative, rather than
> transformative.[19]

The neighborhood in the region

An increasing number of analysts and political leaders have pointed out new connections between urban neighborhoods and regional sprawl. Some of these have suggested the prospect of new coalitions of inner-ring suburbs, business leaders, and both in- and out-commuters affected by their long commutes.[20] Race remains central to these issues, as newer regional solutions run into older attitudes about racial minorities and their outward mobility.[21] And tensions remain between efforts to strengthen the economic appeal of central cities and their neighborhoods and efforts to expand out-commuting of central city residents to suburban and exurban jobs.

The city in which a community-based initiative operates is not always the local government most relevant to its goals; in many parts of the country, the county government or a regional governance mechanism may be the entity that is trying hardest to cope with housing, transportation, and jobs in the regional economy. And community change may depend as much on this supra-local policy environment as on what the city itself does. City-suburban tensions (and increasingly, old-suburb vs. new-suburb tensions) play out in a regional context, and looking at city policy alone misses a good deal of the structure of influence that affects community outcomes. The classic example is the economic development arena—the intersection of geographic, political, and economic power where decisions are made about where jobs are located, which affects the length of parents' commutes, which in turn affects parents' time with their children.

This leads us to the concern of our next chapter—the force of regionalism in community change and in a children and family agenda.

NOTES

[1] As noted in chapter 2, these concepts and practice predate the Great Society in some cases, going back more than a century to settlement houses and even earlier charitable institutions that included both community operations and a comprehensiveness that was appropriate for their time.

[2] Jeanne Brooks-Gunn, "Big-City Kids and Their Families: Integration of Research and Practice," in Children and Their Families in Big Cities, Albert Kahn and Sheila Kammerman, (eds) (New York: Columbia University, 1996), 265.

[3] Building Community: Exploring the Role of Social Capital and Local Government (Washington, D.C.: The National Civic League, 1998).

[4] Blackwell et al. Searching, 132.

[5] Brooks-Gunn, "Big-City Kids," 264.

[6] Brooks-Gunn, "Big-City Kids."

[7] Blackwell et al. Searching.

[8] Prudence Brown, Benjamin Butler, Ralph Hamilton, The Sandtown-Winchester Neighborhood Transformation Initiative: Lessons learned about Community Building and Implementation. (Baltimore. Md.: The Annie E. Casey Foundation and Enterprise Foundation, 2001).

[9] This refers to the Consumers Reports practice of using red and black circles to represent the quality of different elements of an automobile's performance and repair ratings.

[10] Robert Chaskin and Ali Abunimah, A View From The City: Local Government Perspectives On Neighborhood-based Governance In Community-building Initiatives. (Chicago: Chapin Hall, 1997).

[11] Chaskin and Abunimah, A View, 19

[12] John Mudd, Neighborhood Services. (New Haven, Ct.: Yale University Press, 1984).

[13] Discussions with county staff in California Central Valley counties and informal communications from staff at The Finance Project's site at www.welfareinfo.org

[14] Sherry Arnstein. "A Ladder of Citizen Participation," Journal of the American Planning Association, (Vol. 35, No. 4, July 1969), 216-224.

[15] Joan Epstein, School and family partnerships: Preparing educators and improving schools. (Boulder, Co.: Westview Press, 2001).

[16] Peter Benson, All Kids Are Our Kids. (San Francisco, Ca.: Jossey-Bass, 1997).

[17] Margaret Weir, "Power, Money, and Politics," in Urban Problems and Community Development, Ronald Ferguson and William Dickens, (eds.) (Washington, D.C.: Brookings Institution, 1999).

[18] William Peterman, Neighborhood Planning and Community-based Development. (Thousand Oaks, Ca.: Sage Publications, 2000), 170-171.

[19] Kubisch et al., Voices II, 103.

[20] Blackwell, et al. Searching, 156-7.

[21] David Rusk. Inside Game, Outside Game. (Washington, D.C. The Brookings Institution/The Century Foundation, 1998).

CHAPTER 11: REGIONALISM AND A FAMILY AGENDA

As we saw in looking at the links between cities and counties in Chapter 7, the regional setting is an increasingly important arena for local government. Families live much of their lives in regional settings:

- Many parents work in one city and live in another; some commute across two or more counties to get from their home to their work because they cannot afford housing in the city or suburb where they work; others out-commute from lower-cost city housing to jobs in the suburbs;
- Older children and families often find their preferred forms of entertainment and recreation in another region.

As these examples make clear, jobs, housing, transportation, and family income are all interwoven in a regional network of political, geographic, and economic issues.

Some of the good news is that regional issues are in a brighter spotlight than they have been in some time. In his introduction to Myron Orfield's 2002 Brookings Institution assessment, *American Metropolitics*, Bruce Katz states,

> After years of academic neglect, corporate indifference, and political hostility, metropolitan thinking has reemerged as a potent force in the United States....The new metropolitan thinking contends that the shape and quality of metropolitan growth in America are no longer desirable or sustainable... [they] exacerbate deep racial, ethnic, and class divisions in our society.[1]

While this literature discusses education as a major feature, most other children and family issues are not addressed, although jobs and family income do receive some attention, primarily in economic, rather than family terms.[2]

But the other, not-so-good news is that urban policy (meaning both metropolitan and central city issues) has all but disappeared from the federal agenda, as noted in Chapter 7. Janet Pack summarizes: "Urban policy has become largely a state and local preoccupation."[3]

One of the few works on regional issues that addresses children and family issues, though again, not very directly, is David Rusk's *Inside Game, Outside Game*. Rusk describes the regional agenda without much explicit attention to children and families, with two important exceptions:

- His attention to fair housing, as one of the three core strategies he recommends for addressing the problems of older cities that cannot annex land, and
- His references to concentrated poverty as a natural outgrowth of fiscal disparities between cities and suburbs. His chapter on what he calls "the poverty machine" discusses the impact of family structure on poverty,

citing the data of Paul Jargowsky, W.J. Wilson, and others on single parent families and concentrated poverty in urban neighborhoods. [4]

And Rusk cites with great approval Portland's summary version of its vision statement: "everyone can see Mt. Hood and every child can walk to a library."[5] He points out that the latter goal is about safety and about the availability of libraries, but also about the concentration of resources in family-friendly areas of cities. And he blends Clinton and Dole rhetoric (from the 1996 presidential election) to state that in his view "it takes a family, a neighborhood, and a school to raise a child."[6]

But his references to transportation as a regional issue are exclusively spatial. He notes that as a mayor (of Albuquerque from 1977 to 1981), he was not actively involved in regional governing bodies, which only had responsibility for allocating transportation funding. But this overlooks the fact that in many regions the transportation issue has powerful negative impact on family life in thousands of hours lost annually to out-commuting from expensive (or unsafe) central cities to farther, more affordable suburbs.

Jargowsky, Wilson, and others have written about the causes and effects of concentration of poverty in inner city neighborhoods. Their analysis makes clear it is not possible to explain these trends by events solely within city boundaries; regional patterns, notably the "push" out of cities and the "pull" into suburbs, have affected these changes.[7] But there is little discussion in most of these works of the impact on children and families.

Fortunately, the work of a number of commentators and policy leaders has begun to fill the gap in addressing local government roles in regional bodies on behalf of children and families. Notable among these is the work of PolicyLink, the Oakland-based organization headed by Angela Blackwell. In their discussions of a smart growth agenda, Blackwell and her colleagues have blended a concern with social justice and environmental concerns about urban sprawl in more depth than any other organization in the nation.

Several of the observations in Blackwell's recent book, co-authored with Stewart Kwoh and Manuel Pastor, reflect this concern, and their conviction that "Those concerned about equity, environment, and economy may be able to find common ground…" Blackwell and her colleagues note that federal transportation funding is paying new attention to reverse commuters and that Maryland, Oregon, and other states have begun to pressure developers to pay for the full costs of the infrastructure which their housing developments require.[8]

Other writers have also recognized that spatial and structural changes exacerbate a number of social problems that have long plagued urban communities.[9] The spatial layout of many metropolitan areas mirrors the income equality of its families. Lower-income families find it harder to afford houses near the fastest growing job markets. Spires points out that "uneven economic, spatial, and social development are all inter-related pieces of the metropolitan puzzle." Tax policies of local governments reinforce these patterns, as cities and counties (and their states) compete for new business that represent new revenue

sources, and large-lot residential zoning policies add further pressure to lower-
and middle-income families' search for housing nearer their jobs.

But the response to these interwoven causes is often one-dimensional,
focusing on housing as the major family-related remedy. In a list of eight policy
changes that respond to sprawl and uneven development, Spires mentions only
affordable housing as an explicitly family-related issue.

In the same compilation, however, Amy Helling addresses the impact on
poor children and families of transportation imbalance, stating

> If urban sprawl imposes social costs on metropolitan area residents, some
> of these costs fall particularly heavily on low-income families and their
> children.[10]

Helling notes that poor children are affected not only by the lack of mobility
compared with suburban children in a car-oriented community, but also the
increased risks of walking in urban areas and a lack of safe recreation space. But
she neglects to point out the serious loss of family time for working class parents
in both suburbs and inner cities when parents have to rise early for a one hour-
plus commute (whether it is an out-commute or an in-commute) and when they
come home late.

In a paper assessing the impact of welfare reform's work requirements on
New York City parents' ability to monitor their children's homework in an
environment of high-stakes testing, an end to social promotion, and mandated
summer school for children who are behind grade level, Margaret Chin and
Katherine Newman coin the phrase "time poverty" to refer to the cross-pressures
created by these policy trends.[11] The phrase also seems apt for those parents
whose out-commute or in-commute from affordable housing to work comes at
the expense of time with their children.

In fact, it is not difficult to define commuting time as a barrier to literacy,
since a key variable in acquiring reading skills has been documented in
numerous studies to be the time a child is read to by her parents.[12] Parents who
are in their cars for 3-4 hours a day are not only not available for reading or
homework supervision   they are also considerably more fatigued and irritable
when they arrive home. And if their pre-school or school-age children have been
in sub-standard, but affordable child care during that time, the whole family
loses some of what it sought to gain by "moving out."

Housing as a family income issue

There is no question that housing affordability is both a regional and an
urban issue of major importance to families. The cost barriers to lower-cost
construction, both zoning restrictions and labor costs, are important obstacles to
accommodating families in better housing, as are discriminatory lending policies
affecting lower-income and minority families.

Housing issues are usually framed as connected with family income, but the
remedy is far more often seen as housing subsidies than addressing low family
income. Housing affordability is not often linked to either livable wage
campaigns or local governments' efforts to connect their residents (and non-
resident workers) to the full range of family income supports to which they are

entitled as lower-income workers. Addressing the issues discussed in Chapter 8 and ensuring that workers receive the full array of income benefits to which they are entitled could make the difference, for some families, between renting and being able to buy a home. It is possible to argue that housing affordability is at least as much about under-utilized family income supports as it is about the need for new subsidies.[13] If a city does not provide its own workers, its contract workers, its residents, or its in-commuting non-resident workers with any information about family income supports—which is certainly the norm in most cities—it is obviously unknown how much family income supports could contribute to greater affordability of housing for any of these groups.[14]

Health issues and sprawl

PolicyLink and other organizations have also begun to define the connections between regional equity, sprawl, and health disparities. The poor environmental conditions in inner cities have been documented before, but what PolicyLink has added is a compilation of sources that have addressed environmental and public health problems linked to commuting in and out of inner cities, and of newer suburbs as well. These studies emphasize several intersections of sprawl and effects on children and families:

- Childhood asthma rates more than doubled from 1980 to 1995, as ozone and other automobile-related pollutants increased along with metropolitan sprawl.[15]
- The prevalence of adults who were overweight or obese rose from 1976 to 1999 from 47% to 61%, with a lack of physical activity and sedentary living habits contributing significantly to these increases.
- Long commutes and the cul-de-sac structure of suburban neighborhoods discourage walking and biking as transportation.[16]
- Certain aspects of sprawl, such as commuting, may exact a mental health toll. For some time automobile commuting has been of interest to psychologists as a source of stress, stress-related health problems, and even physical ailments. Evidence links commuting to back pain, cardiovascular disease, and self-reported stress. It seems reasonable to hypothesize that anger and frustration among drivers is not restricted to their cars. When angry people arrive at work or at home, what are the implications for work and family relations? If the phenomenon known as "commuting stress" affects well-being and social relationships both on the roads and off, and if this set of problems is aggravated by increasingly long and difficult commutes on crowded roads, then sprawl may in this manner threaten mental health.[17]
- As Robert Putnam argues in *Bowling Alone*, the simple fact of more driving time means less time with family or friends, and less time to devote to community activities, from neighborhood barbecues to P.T.A. meetings. Putnam estimates that each additional ten minutes of driving time predicts a ten per cent decline in civic involvement.

Here is where geography and climate can worsen the effects of housing affordability: when moving away from urban centers, many middle and lower-income working parents seek lower-priced housing. This increases the length of their commute, but it may also place their family in the middle of prevailing air currents that bring them the worst of urban pollution—as well as the pollution resulting from their own commutes. For residents of the Bay Area and Southern California, the equation is simple: cheaper housing is where dirtier air piles up. The prevailing winds blow from the ocean inland, and the cheaper housing is further inland.

Sprawl is a family issue. Regional solutions to family dilemmas—dealing *across* governments with the issues of cheaper housing vs. dirtier air and longer commutes—are the only solutions that make sense economically and geographically. But the politics are far more difficult. The alternative to politics is sometimes to seek legal forerunners of political consensus, and to litigate. The evidence of the equity issues is building up, as epidemiological studies, land use and housing studies, and the emergency room visits of children with asthma all increase. Legal action seems increasingly likely in the decades ahead if political action does not respond to the growing body of evidence that sprawl affects families differentially, based on their incomes.

Local governments and their regions

As we discussed in Chapter 7 in reviewing the relations between cities and counties, local government leaders are critical leaders and mediators in these discussions about the patterns of growth—both central city leaders of minority coalitions and suburban leaders. Even with state leadership as in Maryland and Oregon around "smart growth" regional efforts, it is local governments that will need to negotiate new arrangements that are enabled, but not assured by state legislation.

Myron Orfield is optimistic about a new politics of metropolitan growth, seeing the swing districts in the 25 largest U.S. metro regions that are in fiscally or socially stressed areas as the "true pivot points of American politics."[18] He believes that at-risk suburbs share enough in common with central cities that they will make common cause with those cities on some regional issues. With nearly a third of the nation's poor living in what are officially classified as suburbs, the dichotomy between poor cities and wealthy suburbs is blurring, creating new opportunities for coalition-building.

Using detailed analysis of seventy-four metropolitan economies, Manuel Pastor and his colleagues have analyzed the relationship between growth and poverty.[19] Their conclusion is stark and instructive for local officials:

> eventually poverty and inequality will drag you down. In a new economy
> in which collaboration maters, you are only as strong as the team to
> which you belong.

They assess three "regions that work" which have combined rapid economic growth and relative improvements in equity: greater Boston, the San Jose-Silicon Valley region, and the Charlotte area in North Carolina. In another context, Pastor has described the regional economics of Silicon Valley as it is made up of different levels of workers:

> ...behind every software engineer is a nanny or a food-service worker. There's a tremendous amount of economic energy there. The question is how do you harness it.[20]

Like Orfield, Pastor and his colleagues see the potential for urban mayors and inner-ring suburbs to find common cause, but they also point out that the regional issues that most directly affect poverty and inequality—schools and housing—are "among the biggest obstacles to regional cooperation."[21] They point out that in addition to urban mayors, there are three other potential constituencies for a regional equity agenda: residents of the inner-ring suburbs as they see their communities declining, leaders of community-based organizations and community development corporations who see the region passing by their place-based initiatives, and metropolitan labor councils who see their workers tied to regional, not city- or suburb-specific economies.[22] But they return to the critical role of local government, citing "the willingness of local governments to use public policy creatively" as a key element in successful metropolitan areas that have addressed growth and poverty together.

Further evidence for this thesis of city-older suburb convergence in some areas comes from analysis of the concentration of poverty which Jargowsky has recently updated. Jargowsky and his colleagues at the Brookings Institution used Census 2000 data to review his earlier findings about concentration of poverty, and found that the number of people living in high-poverty neighborhoods declined by 2.5 million, or 24 percent, to 7.9 million in 2000 from 10.4 million in 1990. In 1990, 15 percent of all poor people lived in high-poverty neighborhoods. By 2000, the proportion had declined to 10 percent.[23]

Geographically, Jargowsky found "a bull's-eye pattern: improvements in the central city and increasing poverty in the inner ring of suburbs." A number of older, inner-ring suburbs around major metropolitan areas actually experienced increases in poverty over the decade, though poverty rates in these areas generally remain well below 40 percent. Poverty increased in the older suburbs of Detroit, Chicago, Cleveland and Dallas, he said, while California also showed a large increase in the *population* of high-poverty neighborhoods. One reason, Jargowsky suggested, was the influx of low-income Latin Americans. Such poverty, though cause for concern, may be different from poverty elsewhere, he said. "Western inner-city barrios may be more of a gateway than inner-city ghettos in other areas of the country," Jargowsky said. "Immigrants are moving into the barrios for opportunity, as part of an assimilation process that may channel many of them into jobs."

Can elected leaders see the future?

It asks a great deal of a local elected official to see her constituency as made up of five different levels of workers:

- Residents who work in the city and elsewhere
- Residents who work for the city

- Non-residents who work for the city
- Non-residents who work under contract to city vendors
- Non-residents who work for private firms in the city.

Obviously, only the first two are local voters. But all five groups spend some of their money locally, and all five contribute to the well-being of the city as earners and workers. Can we expect that local leaders will see the benefits of at least providing information about family income support programs to all five groups? Can we expect that they would see the benefits of focusing housing affordability efforts on any of the last three groups? In the answer lies a critical signal of the willingness and capacity of local elected officials to think more regionally than they do today.

The grounds for cautious optimism lie in the combined force of the evidence cited in this chapter. The argument from transportation or housing effects alone, as powerful as it has become, may not be enough. But combined with the environmental impacts of sprawl, its racial equity consequences, its public health effects, and its impacts on family support for learning, the case is much stronger that regional policies increasingly matter to local officials. And there is the growing evidence compiled by Pastor and others that business leaders are beginning to recognize the business costs in retention and turnover of employees who would rather live and work in closer proximity, the most mobile of whom will move to regions where that is possible if they must. All of these taken together may convince a hypothetical officeholder that she cannot avoid the worst effects of regional growth, whether she is in the central city, a close-in suburb, or a more exclusive suburb.

Conclusion

While the regional agenda is not often framed as choices about children and family policy, the effects of regional dynamics have profound impact on families. Local governments throughout regions, whether in inner cities or outer suburbs, will be buffeted by the winds created by regional events and trends. The conclusions reached by the researchers and advocates cited in this chapter— that a regional approach is a precondition for addressing equity and poverty as it affects families—are more and more widely held views, although there is less consensus on the strategies need to create the regional forces needed for greater equity. The tools available to map those dynamics are increasingly available to show the effects on families, for those local governments willing to see the evidence.

NOTES

[1] Myron Orfield, American Metropolitics: The New Suburban Reality. (Washington, D.C.: The Brookings Institution, 2002), xi.

[2] The concern for education is not just one item on a list of issues; Orfield quotes a suburban city manager: "You should see the white homeowners in this city. Whether they have kids or not, they are constantly monitoring the test scores at the school. At the first hint of change, everybody will be out of there." [40]

[3] Janet Pack. Growth and Convergence in Metropolitan America. (Washington, D.C.: The Brookings Institution, 2002), 2.

[4] David Rusk. Inside Game, Outside Game. Washington, D.C. The Brookings Institution/The Century Foundation, 1998).

[5] Rusk, Inside Game, 177. Presumably greater sensitivity to children with disabilities would be reflected in later drafts.

[6] Rusk, Inside Game, 125.

[7] Paul Jargowsky "Sprawl, Concentration of Poverty, and Urban Inequality," in Gregory D. Squires, (ed.) Urban Sprawl: Causes, Consequences, and Policy Responses. (Washington, D.C.: The Urban Institute Press, 2002).

[8] Blackwell, et al. Searching, 157-159.

[9] Gregory Squires, "Urban Sprawl and Uneven Development," in Squires, Urban Sprawl, 4.

[10] Amy Helling, "Transportation, Land Use, and the Impacts of Sprawl on Poor Children" in Squires, Urban Sprawl, 119.

[11] Margaret Chin and Katherine S. Newman, "High Stakes: Time Poverty, Testing, and the Children of the Working Poor." (New York: Foundation for Child Development, 2002).

[12] Nancy Padak, Connie Sapin, and Dianna Baycich, A Decade of Family Literacy: Programs, Outcomes, and Future Prospects. Information Series No. 389 (Ohio Literacy Resource Center, Kent State University, ERIC Clearinghouse on Adult, Career, and Vocational Education, 2002).

[13] Michael A. Stegman, Walter R. Davis, and Roberto Quercia The Earned Income Tax Credit as an Instrument of Housing Policy. (Washington, D.C.: The Brookings Institution, 2003).

[14] In an analysis undertaken as part of a strategic planning effort in one California city of 160,000, Scott Spitzer produced estimates that as much as $7 million a year in one income support program—the Earned Income Tax Credit—was not being claimed by residents, with a substantially larger amount potentially available to workers who worked in that city but did not live there. Obviously, an annual housing affordability subsidy program of $7 million would be perceived as a significant proposal—but in this case the benefits would be entirely federally funded.

[15] Richard J. Jackson and Chris Kochtitzky. Creating a Healthy Environment: the Impact of the Built Environment on Public Health. (Atlanta: Center for Disease Control and Prevention, 2001).

[16] Valerie Gregg "Taming Urban Sprawl," Public Health. (Emory University, Spring 2001).

[17] Howard Frumkin, Urban Sprawl and Public Health. Public Health Reports, (Vol. 117, 2001).

[18] Orfield, American Metropolitics, 4. Orfield goes on to argue that an association of at-risk suburban communities could be built that would bring these particular local governments together in a coalition; his diagnosis relies heavily upon careful demographic analysis of suburbs into three categories: at-risk suburbs, which make up 40% of the population of the 25 largest metro areas, bedroom-developing suburbs, which make up 26%, and affluent job centers, which make up 7%. Central cities make up the remaining 28% of population in these 25 areas. 175-76.

[19] Manuel Pastor, (ed.) Peter Dreier, Eugene Grigsby III, Marta Lopez Garza, Regions That Work: How Cities and Suburbs Can Grow Together. (Minneapolis: University of Minnesota Press, 2000).

[20] Lawrence M. Fisher, "Job-rich Silicon Valley has turned fallow, survey finds," New York Times, January 20, 2003.

[21] Pastor, et al. Regions, 10.

[22] Ibid. 9.

[23] Paul Jargowsky, *Stunning Progress, Hidden Problems: The Dramatic Decline of Concentrated Poverty in the 1990s.* (Washington: The Brookings Institution, 2003).

Introduction to Section 4:

The four chapters that follow are content chapters, focusing upon specific areas of children and family policy. Obviously, there could be a dozen or more other content chapters, addressing child care, child welfare, jobs and economic development, juvenile justice, health, mental health, and other topics.

These four have been selected, however, because they are so deeply fundamental to the roles of local government, and because they are unavoidable if a city or county's leaders are serious about the task of being more strategic about children and family policy. Education remains the largest "children's program," and as such it cannot be dismissed as just one more of a long list of program areas. Substance abuse, as an intergenerational problem with profound impact on communities and neighborhoods, has such powerful family effects that it, too, cannot be ignored or briefly summarized. Its impact is profound on many other systems—those agencies that refer clients to substance abuse programs and those affected by substance abuse.

Family support programs, especially in a time of worsening family income for millions of American families with children, have become an emerging programmatic area for many local governments as they seek to expand the economic success of their families. Finally, youth development is what many cities regard as their primary function in children and youth programs. Youth development has the potential to be an entry point for a wider discussion in many localities that starts with seeing youth as a problem but goes "upstream" to address the problems of younger children that give rise to youth issues, and that also works preventively to try to respond to problems before they worsen.

So this section spotlights these four sets of policy issues that cut across other children and family areas, since they each challenge local governments to become more strategic, rather than treating all program areas as equally important. Being strategic involves recognizing that some issues and problems are more important than others. It is our judgment that these four are much more important.

CHAPTER 12: EDUCATION AND LEARNING—
THE INESCAPABLE PRIORITIES

Developing a children and youth agenda without including education is logically, financially, and at times, politically difficult for cities and counties. Yet until recently, many localities have tried to exclude education from children and family policy, because the system is so large and dominating. In some local policy statements, education is mentioned only in passing, reflecting an obvious decision to pass over those issues not under the direct control of the city or county. But recently, an increasing number of local governments have stepped up to addressing education issues, in particular in those city governments whose mayors are held accountable for education, whether they are in direct control or not.

That is not to say that education is always addressed as part of an *integrated* strategy. In some cities, education has been just one more fragmented issue, held apart from the health, early childhood, and family services programs that are ideally linked with it in an integrated approach. New York's Beacon Schools, as previously noted, remain perhaps the prime example of an integrated approach—and those community-based, school-linked programs are clearly not at the center of the recent effort by Mayor Bloomberg to gain legislative control of the school system. Over the past decade, mayors in other major cities have expanded their roles in school district operations, including Chicago, Cleveland, Detroit, Harrisburg, Pennsylvania, Oakland, Washington, D.C., and Boston.[1]

But whether integrated with the rest of their efforts or not, cities and counties are in the learning business, whether they want to be or not. They cannot avoid education, for several reasons:[2]

- *Because the amount of money involved is so large.* Education dwarfs all other children and youth expenses; once the education tab is settled, there may not be much else left for cities and counties. With local governments often operating at the bottom of the feeding chain of the federal system, paying attention to a very large competitor for scarce funds is obviously advisable. As we saw in Chapter 1, the amounts spent on education at the local level often exceed all city and county spending for other children and youth programs.

- *Because the politics are so visible,* as seen over the past decade in Chicago, Los Angeles, New York, Boston, Baltimore, and other large cities. Mayors in particular can't leave independent systems alone if they are going to be blamed anyway for the perceived failures of urban education. In part, this "blame the mayor" syndrome is a result of the growing cross-pressure on public education by conservative advocates for choice and inner-city advocates for accountability; in part it is a more general disdain of suburban voters and residents for loosely defined "city problems" which disaggregate, as David Rusk and others note, into high crime and poor schools.[3] At the same time, federal Leave No Child Behind legislation has brightened the spotlight on test scores still further (in what some have called the Leave No Child Untested approach). Mayors are obviously affected when some of the schools in their city are formally labeled "low-performing" by the federal government. Whatever its origins, mayors have responded by trying to either change the politics by using their own organizations and prestige to elect supportive candidates, change the state law to achieve greater control, or affect exiting appointees where Boards are not elected. As summarized by the National League of Cities' Audrey Hutchinson,

> ...increasingly mayors are taking direct control over the school system in their cities. Usually such efforts take place where there is "academic bankruptcy" coupled with a strong desire to turn around these low-performing schools.[4]

- *Because the school agenda and the youth crime agenda overlap unavoidably.* A Mayor who has taken an active stance on youth crime cannot help but notice when youth crime takes place—in the hours immediately after middle and high schools let out. So after-school programs become a concern (as discussed in the youth development section of Chapter 15), and city police work closely with school security personnel—or *become* school security personnel through the school resource officer concept. Cities thus find themselves in the after-school segment of the education business, if not in the classroom.

- *Because the effects on the cities' economic development prospects are so profound.* The combination of K-12 education, vocational education, and adult education makes up an important part of any city or county's economic infrastructure. Adults are in the learning business, too. In some cities, the adult education system is a vital part of the economic development system because of the vital functions it plays with adult literacy, English-language instruction, and vocational education. These are municipal functions, not just education functions. They affect the quality of the local workforce and the ability of new immigrants to move into the working and middle classes that can stabilize a city.

- *Because of the competition among localities for economic development.* As the National League of Cities has stressed, "The quality of public schools and the long-term prospects of cities...are closely linked." The connection is based in part on the central role that schools play in building stable communities and shaping residents' perceptions of the quality of community life. Municipal leaders also understand that a strong public education system is a great asset as their cities compete for new jobs and industries. An NLC survey found that local officials view improvements in the quality of elementary and secondary education as one of the three most effective strategies for promoting local economic development and reducing poverty.[5] Federal efforts to strengthen local coordination of economic development links with welfare clients' job training also lead cities back into the K-12 system, since it is such an important provider of these services—whether or not it is perceived as doing a good job.

- Because *preschool children become school children*, and cities and counties' investments made in early childhood development, relying upon growing evidence of the importance of early intervention on long-term outcomes for children and youth, can be erased over time by what some have called "the third grade fade." This refers to the likelihood that early child development programs' effects will begin to disappear in schools which do not continue to provide the same ingredients that characterize Head Start and other quality child development: active parent involvement, health care linkages, and early attention to behavior and social skills.

- *Because the real estate controlled by education is prime in some localities*, and cities and counties have begun to recognize that school buildings are often available for youth and community programs, since schools only use them one-sixth of the time (assuming an 8-hour school day and a 180-day school year). Some cities have recognized this for decades, in states like Michigan where the community schools movement is well-established. At the same time, cities' and counties' own facilities, especially libraries and parks, are available for after-school programs in cooperative ventures that save money for both schools and localities.

- *Because realtors use computers to sell houses.* Realtors have developed a highly sophisticated, and increasingly online capacity to access school test scores for a given residential neighborhood. In some Southern California neighborhoods, there is a highly functioning *international* network that can pinpoint specific schools as the most desirable for incoming higher-income immigrant families from Asia, which affects housing prices in those neighborhoods. This does not always have a wholly positive effect, because along with test scores, family income can also be researched online, with an effect that can add to existing economic segregation.[6]

A caveat

This chapter is not a full discussion of the wide field of education reform; it focuses upon education reform as local governments seek to participate in and lead it, in the context of their efforts to move toward a children and family agenda. It will address several of the boundary issues where the efforts of local government to develop such policy come into closest contact with the K-12 education system. But it may be useful to revisit the distinction made by Paul Hill and Mary Beth Celio in their work *Fixing Urban Schools*, which is specifically aimed at "individuals and institutions outside the educational system [who] are being asked to create rescue strategies for the public schools."[7]

Hill and Celio use the image (already referenced in Chapter 1) of a set of zones in education reform in which the innermost zone of strategies includes controllable elements in the school that contribute to school achievement, a second zone includes elements in a reform effort that reform may stimulate, and an outer "zone of wishful thinking" that includes events or actions essential to the reform's success but which it cannot cause or control.[8] The importance of this outer zone is that local governments are often key players in this zone, in ways that education systems cannot be, and thus local governments are potentially able to bring to bear resources which reform needs but cannot command on its own. So education reform and the role of local government may be linked, but only if educational leaders seek the resources of local government as a further asset for reform, or if local leaders cross the boundary for their own reasons, including those cited above.

A premise: the 1/3 and 91% factors

Education reform includes many "schools"—pun intended—and someone setting out to discuss even a portion of education reform should declare to which schools they belong. My own experience in local government and other settings has convinced me that education, like all other children-serving systems, cannot reform itself from within. This is an observation very much in keeping with Hill and Celio's notion of the three zones. But very unlike Hill and Celio—and the mainstream of education reform, it should be noted—I also do not believe in the efficacy of educentric reforms that ignore, as their work essentially does, the need for learning supports and school-linked services, sometimes framed as community schools. I join James Comer, Howard Adelman, Martin Blank, and numerous others, who, though often outnumbered in discussions of how to reform education, believe that communities, public and private services agencies, and parents are vital partners in learning. What follows from that conviction is that education reform that relegates them to the sidelines will itself become fixated solely on what happens in the classroom, rather than what is happening in families or communities.[9]

The two numbers that underlie this conviction for me are 1/3 and 9%:

- 1/3 is the percentage of students who come into classrooms with other barriers to learning—not an inability to learn—but family conditions, disabilities, health problems, and other barriers that cannot be addressed solely by classroom based-changes;[10] Among others, john powell cites the effects of family instability on education, noting the higher mobility, poor nutrition, substance abuse, crime, and health crises that affect children's readiness to learn.[11]
- 9% is the amount of a child's life from birth to 18 that she spends in a K-12 classroom, suggesting to me and others that the other 91% matters as much—if not proportionately more—to her potential for learning, and thus should not be ignored in education reform.

This premise leads me to place even more emphasis on the importance of local governments, since their role can be so significant in guiding local agencies and forging school-community ties in the communities they represent and serve. It is unfair to hold school districts responsible for forming partnerships with the dozens—even hundreds—of agencies and organizations that affect children's futures during that 91% of their lives outside schools. But local governments can be held responsible for being at least in on the discussion of how the 91% can be more fully mobilized for better learning outcomes.

What can cities and counties do? What have they tried to do?

The potential role of local governments in affecting education policy and finance, as already noted, is powerfully constrained by the legal environment of those relations. Within those constraints, cities and counties have sought to achieve several different impacts:

1. ***Resources***: Local governments have brought their own resources to help school districts and to leverage changes they want from education. This is more painful for those cities and counties who have no direct, mandated role in education, because the funds they come up with could be used for other local services. Assistance may take the form of large payments from city to school district, or it may be negotiated across dozens of smaller boundaries. For example, in one California city, there is a continuing tension over two school-city financial issues: who pays for the crossing guards and who pays for the DARE police officers who provide drug prevention services in schools. Setting aside (for the moment; see following chapter) the complete

    > Mayor Ron Gonzalez of San Jose has developed "10 Positive Ways A Mayor Can Help Improve Public Education," including housing assistance for teachers, preschool investments, school safety, after-school programs, charter schools, awards for schools' progress, parent involvement, a School/City Collaborative, support for school bonds for facilities, and visibility efforts: "use our influence with civic leaders, other elected officials, businesses and community organizations, and the media to ensure that education stays at the top of the public agenda, to celebrate success, and to achieve results that benefit our students and community."[11a]

    ineffectiveness of the DARE program, these are smaller examples of the breadth of the city-school agenda and the different ways that schools can get help.

2. ***Non-financial resources***: There are important resources that are not cash, and local governments at times provide these in lieu of or cash, in ways that can be as valuable as cash. Public health nurses, for example, have helped provide health services in some schools. Aside from DARE staffing, schools have benefited from changes in police and county sheriff patrol routes, and some counties have out-stationed parole officers at high schools where there is, unfortunately, a large enough caseload to justify the assignments.

3. ***Political support for change***: Another kind of resource is political support, whether with local unions, state legislators, the media, or

business leadership. City officials have been involved in all of these on behalf of education reform agendas that they support. In the case of a school district that is in takeover status or close to it, a city government may be able to restore some credibility that may have been lost by lending its support for resources that state leaders may not be willing to grant the school district if it is acting by itself. Hill and Celio refer to state mandates, from which local officials may be able to win new flexibility in return for their support for change.[12] Intergovernmental advocacy is a local role set forth in the matrix presented in Chapter 1, and it is vital in this area. In some cities, activist leadership is less important as a political role than providing a neutral forum and convening authority for various stakeholders to negotiate agreements that could not be achieved within the confines of the school district itself. Cities have been active conveners and players in some California Healthy Start collaboratives, where state funding is channeled through schools (prior to its elimination in the 2002 budget cuts), but a broad coalition is needed for effective use of the funding.

4. ***Mobilizing parents and the wider community***: In sites where a major effort has been made to develop a coalition around early childhood issues, cities and counties may be able to play a role in mobilizing constituencies that schools cannot do by themselves. In the accounts of efforts made in Chicago and other cities, it appears that such efforts have definitely been made.

5. ***Pressure for accountability***: However unwelcome by school districts, local governments can monitor and publicize basic district-level report card indicators of child and youth well-being, including dropouts (measured by attrition from 9th to 12th grade rather than the artificial measures used by many school districts), kindergarten hold-backs, emergency certification of temporary teachers, reading scores relative to school income levels, and other vital information. Hill and Celio call this role being a "critical friend organization." Cities can also broker independent evaluations of education reform by local universities and other nonprofits that can provide a neutral, expert assessment of reforms' effectiveness. In Indianapolis and a few other cities, mayors have taken the lead in framing middle ground options between the status quo and vouchers with their support for charter schools; Indianapolis' mayor has formal legal authority to set up such schools, and has used it.

6. ***Linking students to public and community services and supports***: Accepting the premises summarized above as "one-third plus 9%" leads to schools seeking help with the non-educational portion of their task of reducing barriers to learning. Local governments have demonstrated in many cities and counties that they can and will play that role, by joining in after-school tutoring and recreational programs, by locating health clinics at or near schools, by paying for and staffing family resource centers at or near schools, and in dozens of other ways. In her book on community schools, Joy Dryfoos includes a rich chapter on the nearly

150 years of history of local efforts to operate what she terms "full-service schools," and the excellent work of Martin Blank and his colleagues at the Coalition of Community Schools Coalition has added a wide inventory of current efforts, including numerous examples of city-school cooperation.[13]

7. *Joint use of facilities*:   The community schools concept can become concrete in the joint use of facilities. In California, as of late 2003, the final segment of a $25 billion state school bonding proposal is pending, with the potential for the largest multi-year school construction program in the state's history. To design those schools so that city child care and elder center programs, county health services, and other services could be housed at new and rehabilitated schools would take large steps in the direction of community-wide connections to schools, and would require major new roles for city and county governments. City recreation departments that staff after-school programs with their own employees can create a revenue stream for schools when school playgrounds and other facilities are used on a fee basis.

8. *Early childhood programs and school readiness*:   As noted above, some cities and counties have developed extensive commitments in support of early childhood and school readiness programs—referred to in some areas as a "P-5 agenda"—prenatal through age 5. In North Carolina, California, and other states, special efforts have been made on a county level to allocate state funding for comprehensive early childhood programs. But all of these efforts rely upon preschool systems and public schools working together more closely on the handoff of preschool "graduates." The literature on the fade-out effects of early childhood programs in primary grades is a painful reminder that one-time investments in early intervention that are not sustained can achieve little lasting impact. These issues are discussed further below.

9. *Youth development and in-school prevention programs*:   Schools are the sites for numerous prevention programs, both those that are built into the curriculum and those that are school-based but part of after-school activities. Some of those include dropout prevention, teen pregnancy prevention, drug and alcohol abuse prevention, and violence prevention. Some city governments have adopted a "positive youth development" approach, using the ideas of the Search Institute, Karen Pittman, and others, as discussed further in Chapter 15 on youth development.

Blackwell and her colleagues point out that it is the *K-14* system, not just the K-12 system that matters to children and families, and suggest that community colleges could play the same role in the 21st century that settlement houses played in the late 19th and early 20th centuries, as institutions that help immigrants adapt to the U.S. economy and society in job, language, and literacy training.[14]

10. *A civic action agenda*: Cities have also played leadership roles with school districts in providing sites and funding for community service options for students, and for senior citizens.[15]

The barriers to connection

For all the breadth of this agenda, the barriers to realizing it through better school-city-county connections are sizable. Four of those barriers deserve special emphasis.

The tangled finances of state and local government, discussed in Chapter 7, make up the largest barrier to strategic local governmental involvement in schools. When the state and its localities are in dispute over their relative shares of state budgets, education may be the most dominant single spending item in those budgets—but that does not make it a subject of wide consensus between school boards and local governments.

The same dynamic that creates token, fragmented programs in local government has led to program proliferation in school districts. A recent catalogue of Los Angeles Unified School District activities counted more than 230 separate at-risk programs for students. In another school district with 45,000 students, more than 60 parent education programs were operating in the school district and the local community in the mid-1990s. For local governments to do more than merely add to the inventory of programs requires a clear vision of what the new programs are intended to achieve, and how progress and success will be measured over time. The fit between intended outcomes and available resources needs to be addressed with care; a pilot project for fifty dropouts may be an excellent demonstration program, but without a plan for sustainability and a concept of how to take the program to scale, the program remains merely another project added to the existing inventory of projects, worsening the challenge of coordinating all the disparate pieces.

Geography can frustrate the best-intentioned partners. In one California city, five different school districts operate within city boundaries; within a given school district, there can be five or more cities. In marked contrast (in contrast with California, at least) are the neatness of Connecticut and those other states where the city boundary *is* the school district boundary.[16]

Culture matters, and not just the kinds of culture that is counted in racial, ethnic, and linguistic categories. Organizational culture is also difficult to overcome, and general purpose governments differ widely from schools in their organizational culture. In a recent review of collaboration among "education and other agencies," as the agenda put it, a school administrator indignantly expressed her disagreement with the topic: "we are *not* an agency!" Different professional education and training, different recruitment patterns, different socialization to a profession, different state regulatory oversight—all of these differences can create obstacles to city-county attempts to work with schools.

Yet for all these barriers, as we have seen, a critical sub-set of local government leaders have taken risks to move toward more controlling roles in education. One arena in which they have done so with special interest in the past few years has been at the front end of the education system, in an arena where they have more control: in the realm of school readiness.

School readiness as part of the local education agenda

If a community or its leaders begin their problem solving with the issues of children, they will quickly find themselves thinking about schools. Some may try hard to stop thinking about schools—because they are so hard to reform. But it is hard to ignore the largest agency that serves children and that is entrusted with preparing them for life and work.

Some communities, however, have pressed their problem-solving efforts harder and asked what it is about schools that is really the problem. Some of these groups find themselves inevitably headed "upstream," concerned about younger children of preschool age and their readiness for schools. Some schools gladly add to this mindset, being quick to blame parents for sending them children not ready to learn, and this can give further urgency to the process.

Thus school readiness is attractive to communities as a place to begin for several reasons:

- It flows logically from a concern with schools and academic achievement;
- It allows paying attention to academic achievement without having to penetrate the entire school structure and reform it (although, as we shall see, the "handoff" function becomes critical);
- It allows a community to attract resources for the most appealing children of all—younger children;
- It allows a community to work with children's first teachers—their parents;
- Above all, from the vantage point of local elected leaders—it doesn't "belong to" the schools—it requires coalitions of parents, other providers, and including, but rarely dominated by schools.

For all these reasons, school readiness beckons to children's policy makers, as well as those who see family policy as including support for parents' roles in preparing their children to learn. Cities and counties have a role in early care and education through their zoning rules, their child care offices, use of their facilities, and their own personnel policies (to the extent they provide support for their own employees who are parents).[17]

The intersection between local government and children is very active around issues of work and child care (increasingly the broader label of *early care and education* (ECE) is being used in this area). Whether a city or county operates within a state-administered health and welfare system or not, local government has had a strong role in job training, or, using an earlier label, "manpower" programs, since the early 1960's. Early care and education program roles are partly local by definition, requiring local licensing and zoning in most parts of the country.

At the same time, these issues of work, child care, and family are also programmatic arenas that are far more subject to national and regional economic tides than some other local government activities. Economic forces at work in the local economy have a great impact on which families can afford to have one parent stay home, which families cannot rise above the poverty level despite full-time work, and which families are forced to use the older brothers and sisters of younger children as unpaid care-takers. Cities and counties can do a great deal to ride the tides of economic change well—they can do little to reverse them.

Yet school readiness, as one of the most important outcomes of quality early care and education, is part of the unavoidable agenda of many local governments. Dennis Campo, of the San Antonio Mayor's Office, has described how local business leaders identified a lack of school readiness as the underlying cause of a lack of job readiness by high school graduates in the San Antonio area. Thus an active agenda including jobs, economic development, and family income leads directly to school readiness as a part of that policy agenda.

A critical role for local government is to regulate the terms of trade between early care and education and the schools that receive the "graduates" of school readiness campaigns who are transitioning to elementary schools from preschools and child care. The depth and seriousness of school readiness campaigns can be determined in part by whether school officials are seen as merely another set of stakeholders who need to be at the table or, in contrast, as the most accountable system needed to make school readiness more than a short-run initiative. If the problem of "third grade fade" is to be addressed, it will take early care providers and schools negotiating in depth, with each side needed to give and get something from the other. Cities and counties can be critical "referees" for these negotiations, providing a neutral forum for bargaining. In doing so, it is important to understand what the content of those negotiations can include.[18]

What do schools need from early care providers?[19]

Schools would benefit if parents with children enrolled in ECE programs learned about schools' rules and expectations before they enroll in the school system. Some schools have developed "bridge programs" that connect children and parents who are getting ready to transition to kindergarten or first grade, including visiting programs, shared readiness testing, and counseling for children whose ages are close to the cutoff points for enrollment. Other schools have provided "summer camps" for pre-kindergartners that expose children who have never attended preschool to the requirements of kindergarten. Once schools and ECE providers are actively exploring these and other options in regularly scheduled meetings, some of the preconditions for systems change will have been met.

The second question is equally important:

What do early care providers need from schools?

As less powerful parties, and much more fragmented providers, in a discussion between ECE providers and schools, ECE providers need to plan carefully for what they will ask school systems to do to help them. Some of the issues that ECE providers can raise in these discussions include:

- the ability of schools to plan new or renovated school buildings with space for child care programs;
- the data which schools can collect on the academic performance of "graduates" of ECE agencies, especially the vital indicators of kindergarten and first-grade holdbacks and holdouts (students whose parents are encouraged not to enroll them), which are an early warning sign of academic and/or behavioral problems to come;
- links to school health providers who may be able to provide health screening services to younger siblings of students;
- links to schools' early intervention resources for students with special needs, in light of the legal responsibilities for schools to identify and serve children with special needs;[20]
- "open doors" to parents who have become used to being active participants in ECE programs but may find schools less inviting;
- K-3 teachers' training and released time to see what ECE providers are doing, what performance measures they may be using, and what portfolios and other information about children are available to teachers when ECE "graduates" enter the school system.

A Modest Proposal

A final example of how cities are "moving into" education without confronting the thorny issues of education reform is the affordable housing programs that have targeted teachers (and, in some areas, law enforcement personnel) who live in the cities where they teach. The unfortunate reality is that many entry-level teachers qualify for affordable housing that is aimed at those below the median income. The opportunity this presents is to allow cities in regions where there are affordable housing agreements to meet those agreements by supplementing teachers' salaries, using low-interest loans, set-asides of affordable housing units in new development as a condition of building permits, using city-owned land to write down housing costs, and other methods that have the net result of lowering teachers' living costs—which amounts to higher salaries.

The advantage is not only increasing the earnings of teachers—it is encouraging new teachers just beginning their careers to see themselves as part of the social capital of their community, becoming Little League and soccer coaches, participating in PTA as both teachers and parents, and learning more about the daily lives of the children they teach.

Cities with an even deeper commitment to children and families might consider adding child care workers to the mix, conditioned upon their staying in the profession (increasingly in California and other teacher-shortage areas, early care teachers are moving out of early care into teaching, attracted by the higher salaries) and continuing their education in child development and related fields.

A further set of indicators that an active school readiness coalition is in place would be the existence of specified characteristics for "a school which is ready," including criteria for institutional changes such as those listed above. Some practitioners in the school readiness arena use the shorthand label SR^2 to indicate that both kinds of school readiness matter, and that greater readiness of children and parents must always be matched by improved readiness of the schools themselves.

Above all, having a regular table around which schools and ECE providers can discuss these issues can be an important systems change itself, since these contacts are usually not systemic, but sporadic. Cities and counties may be able to create that table and facilitate early care-school negotiations, as key players that care about both sets of outcomes.

NOTES

[1] "New, Improved, Mayors Take Over City Schools," by Michael Kirst and Katrina Bulkley, Phi Delta Kappan, March 2000. "Jerry Brown's Next Project: Oakland Schools," by Catherine Gewertz, Education Week, 2/23/00. "Plan to Improve Worst Schools Interests Mayor," by David Herszenhorn, The New York Times, 5/10/99. "Control of Detroit Schools Is Transferred to Mayor and Governor," by Keith Brandsher, The New York Times, 3/26/99. "Takeover Plan for Detroit Shifts Gears," by Bess Keller, Education Week, 3/24/99. "In Cleveland, Mayor White Takes Control," by Kerry A. White, Education Week, 9/16/98 "Mayors: Take Charge! Commentary," Center for Education reform, downloaded October 18, 2003 from http://edreform.com/oped/990306DAD.htm G. Hovenic, "What should be a city's role in our schools?" San Diego Daily Transcript, December 4, 2002. Catherine Gewertz, "N.Y.C. Mayor Gains Control Over Schools" Education Week, June 19, 2002.

[2] In some states the question is irrelevant, because either the boards of education are completely subservient to the cities—appointed by the Mayor or the Council—or they are subject to the local government's decisions on their budgets. While there are exceptions, it is in several of the largest or most visible cities—New York, Baltimore, Richmond, Hartford (and all Connecticut cities) that cities are responsible for the financing, but not directly the governance and policy of the schools. For these mayors, there is no choice about getting involved with education; their budgets are involved, so they are. Some counties are also more involved in school district issues because districts are county-wide; in Maryland, Virginia, North Carolina, and a few other states, the district boundaries and counties are coterminous, so county government finds it harder to avoid education issues than in those counties where there are as many as eighty different separate districts.

[3] David Rusk, Inside Game, Outside Game. (Washington, D.C.: The Century Foundation/The Brookings Institution, 1999), 131.

[4] Audrey M. Hutchinson, "The View from City Hall," in Rethinking Accountablity, Voices in Urban Education No. 1: Spring 2003. (Annenburg Institute for School Reform. Providence, R.I.: Brown University, 2003).

[5] Audrey M. Hutchison, Education as a City Priority. (Washington, D.C.: National League of Cities Institute for Youth, Education, and Families, 2002), 1.

[6] One of the most interesting byproducts of the availability of this data—but one that has thus far been little utilized—is the capacity to develop graphs that depict test scores as they correlate with socio-economic variables, including family income. The correlation is as expected, with higher test scores in high-income neighborhoods. But the most interesting results of such graphs [for examples, see Conditions of Children reports in Orange County at http://www.oc.ca.gov/hca/cscc/report/index.htm], is to see the outliers—schools that have significantly higher or lower academic achievement than schools at the same levels of socio-economic status. The reasons for these variations would seem to be researchable—and very important to understand better.

[7] Paul Hill and Mary Beth Celio, Fixing Urban Schools. (Washington, D.C.: The Brookings Institution, 1998), vii.

[8] Hill and Celio, Fixing, 16-17.

[9] James Comer, Waiting for a Miracle. (New York: Plume, 1998); Howard Adelman and Linda Taylor, Introduction to a Component for Addressing Barriers to Student Learning. (Los Angeles: School Mental Health Program at U.C.L.A., 2001); Martin Blank and Jeanne Jehl, Community Schools: Improving Student Learning/ Strengthening Schools, Families, and Communities (Washington, D.C. Institute for Educational Leadership, 2002)

[10] The estimate of one-third of students is derived from a composite of the data that reveals how many students live in single-parent households, live in poverty or near the poverty level, have learning disabilities, live in some form of out-of-home care, use alcohol and other drugs in ways that affects their academic performance, or simply attend so sporadically that they cannot learn because they are not in the classroom for a substantial portion of the school year. The percentage is much less in higher-income districts, much more in most lower-income, inner-city and rural districts.

[11] j. powell, "Sprawl, Fragmentation, and the Persistence of Racial Inequality," in Urban Sprawl: Causes, Consequences, and Policy Responses, Gregory Squires, (ed). (Washington, D.C.: The Urban Institute Press, 2002), 87-88.

[11a] Ronald Gonzalez," 10 Positive Ways A Mayor Can Help Improve Public Education." (City of San Jose, 2001). http://www.sjmayor.org/education/smartstarttopten.html

[12] Hill and Celio, Fixing, 69.

[13] Joy Dryfoos, Full-Service Schools. (San Francisco, CA.: Jossey-Bass, 1994). CCS is at http://www.communityschools.org/index.html

[14] Blackwell, et al. Searching, 177.

[15] Robert Putnam and Lewis M. Feldstein, Better Together: Restoring the American Community. (New York: Simon and Shuster, 2003).

[16] Neatness is not everything, however. Some of the multi-city districts enable a kind of internal redistribution effect, in including lower-income neighborhoods with more affluent suburban areas of the same school district as it cuts across multiple cities and towns. In states where cities and suburbs have completely separate school districts, the poorer ones have to rely upon the state for redistribution assistance.

[17] Several of these options for support were discussed in a special audioconference on school readiness hosted by the National League of Cities on June 6, 2002.

[18] A separate paper setting forth a framework for negotiations between early care providers and school districts has been developed by Jeanne Jehl and the author for the Casey Foundation and is available at www.cffutures.org.

[19] A portion of this section is taken from a monograph on school readiness and systems change prepared for UCLA's Center for Healthier Children, Families, and Communities in 2002.

[20] This refers to the federal special education legislative responsibility that can be accessed through local SELPAs—Special Education Local Planning Areas, which cover a school district or set of districts.

CHAPTER 13: ABUSE OF ALCOHOL AND OTHER DRUGS AS A CHILDREN AND FAMILY ISSUE

This book includes chapters on four of the programmatic areas that affect children and families: education, substance abuse, family support, and youth development. The importance of education, as the single largest public expenditure on children and youth, is obvious. The importance of substance abuse is judged in this book to be critical to local government for several major reasons:

- As a family disease, addiction and substance abuse affect millions of children and youth in life-changing ways, contributing directly and indirectly to many of the other problems of children and youth; whether it is a direct cause or a contributory factor, the disease has an ongoing effect on the referral of children within the systems devoted to health and mental health, children's services, and education; it both creates and overlaps with part of the caseloads of child welfare, juvenile justice, mental illness, special education, and other systems, as documented in numerous studies;

- The costs of substance abuse—both direct costs of prevention and treatment programs and the costs of its effects in health, law enforcement, education, and other spending—affect local government directly and divert resources that could be used to support other services to children and families;

- The use, sales, and marketing of alcohol and other drugs (AOD) affect a neighborhood's safety and its ability to attract positive economic development;

- The widespread use of AOD in some neighborhoods undermines local residents' faith in the law enforcement authorities in their community and affects their own perceptions of the future of their neighborhood in terms of its safety;

- Local governmental powers include siting decisions about where treatment facilities will be located, as well as where "halfway houses" and other transitional housing for recovering persons can be placed;

- Many cities and some counties operate or fund prevention programs aimed at communitywide and adolescent substance abuse;

- The costs of "shoveling up" the mess created by the consequences of AOD, to use the phrase coined by the Center for Addiction and Substance Abuse, is estimated to be a total of $81 billion in all 50 state budgets—a substantial portion of which is spent by city and county governments.[1]

Why do AOD issues matter to children and family policy?

- Two-thirds of the families entering the child welfare system are affected by substance abuse;
- Substance abuse is a family disease, with both a genetic component and a family environmental component;
- Substance abuse affects 9% of the children in the nation who live in a household with at least one adult who is alcoholic or chemically dependent on other drugs; this equals at least 6 million of the children 0-18 in the U.S.[2] This can be contrasted with the 500,000 children who live in out-of-home care, or the approximately 10-12% of children who have a disability that affects their capacity to learn without accommodations to those disabilities;
- Substance abuse affects many of the 2.4 million children who are being raised by their grandparents (as discussed above in Chapter 8);
- Substance abuse affects the learning abilities of millions of children—some because they have developmental disabilities caused by prenatal substance exposure or other forms of neglect and abuse, others because they lack a caring adult in their lives who will ask about their homework, find a safe, quiet place to do it, and help them with it ;
- Substance abuse affects the estimated half million adolescents who go beyond experimental use of alcohol and other drugs to chemical dependency, but do not receive any treatment for their addiction;[3]
- The great majority of cities and counties that track local births do an inadequate job of working with hospitals and physicians in screening those births for substance abuse, despite the evidence that 7-12% of all births are of substance-exposed infants.[4]

Figure 3 illustrates a summary of the different methods of exposure of children and youth to substance abuse impacts.[5] The implications of the chart are that multiple responses are needed at each of the exposure points, rather than a narrow single-program focus on substance-exposed births, adolescent prevention, or environmental and public education efforts that operate across an entire community. Yet single-program efforts are typical, with only a handful of American cities having developed comprehensive treatment and prevention efforts across all of these points of exposure.

Figure 3: How Are Children Exposed to Alcohol, Tobacco, and Other Drugs?

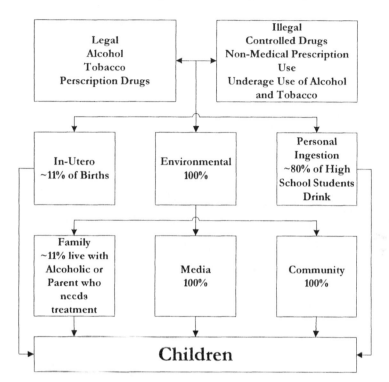

What can local government do about AOD effects and costs? The four tasks

Fortunately, a number of organizations have devoted significant resources over the past two decades to testing different models of community-wide prevention, and the lessons of those investments have been well evaluated. The Center for Substance Abuse Prevention and the Robert Wood Johnson Foundation-supported Join Together network have published a wide array of materials on effective community prevention approaches. Organizations such as Drug Strategies have developed non-clinical versions of these materials that summarize the ingredients of effective prevention programs, which have been used in some states and local sites to shift funds away from ineffective models such as DARE toward those that have proven they can achieve lasting outcomes.[6]

So *digesting and implementing these lessons of what works* is the first task of local government. This will demand shifting resources from well-intentioned but ineffective programs toward the models that have proven effective. The prevention efforts that are focused on individuals also need to be connected with those that operate on a community-wide basis, addressing environmental factors such as a higher percentage of liquor outlets permitted in lower-income minority neighborhoods than in middle-income areas. The implications of these efforts for the zoning and licensing authority of local governments are obvious.

The second task is *linking AOD prevention to the other varieties of prevention programs* that are often fragmented, low-dosage efforts at the local level. In most sizable cities and counties, there are dozens of locally implemented programs aimed at prevention of other risky behavior by adolescents. Typically, pregnancy prevention, violence prevention tobacco prevention, gang prevention, and other youth-targeted programs are each operated separately, with no agreement on common measures of success. This fragmentation ignores the likelihood that many of the youth who are most likely to be involved in one form of risky behavior are also highly at risk for the others. Many of the success ingredients in each of these AOD-specific programs—peer support, refusal skills, "booster" programs that work over more than a single program year—are also factors in the other prevention programs. But if the programs are operated in isolation from each other, they will at worst become competitive for scarce fiscal and volunteer resources, and at best simply ignore each other, missing the opportunity for synergy and economies of scale.

The third task of prevention in local governments is to recognize that one of the most effective forms of prevention for children and youth is *effective treatment for their parents and other caretakers*. A new body of family-centered practice has emerged out of a decade of exemplary programs that provide both residential and out-patient treatment to parents and their children, based on the realization that children's services must be linked to parents' treatment services if the cyclical inter-generational effects of substance abuse are to be ended.[7] Typically, however, the treatment agencies and prevention units—not unlike child welfare and welfare—may be housed in the same overall structure but operate separately from each other.

Finally, local government can address AOD issues comprehensively by using new frameworks for planning, delivering, and evaluating treatment services that emphasize *need, demand,* and *capacity* to provide effective treatment. This three-part framework enables a more refined method of allocating resources from a patchwork of multiple funding streams, rather than lurching from one new grant program to another, doing a "needs assessment" that emphasizes whatever group the new funding is aimed at serving. What this makes more difficult is weaving together multiple funding sources, using an inventory of funding, through a strategic planning process.

In most cities and counties, treatment services are "planned" by allocating the available funding to the mandated groups that must be served according to federal and state law, with a priority given to those that are politically "hottest." As a result, on average, women make up only 30-35% of all publicly supported treatment slots across the nation. As county officials admitted in one state where an assessment of local-level planning was undertaken, allocations are driven by grant funding rather than need or program effectiveness.

To move from grant-driven programs to strategic planning, each of these three elements—need, demand, and capacity—must be used. This requires more than simply saying that a national or statewide prevalence figure should be proportionately allocated to the city or county. The simplistic method would argue that if adolescents are 10% of need—they should get 10% of the funding. A more strategic method would also ask whether current adolescent services are effective, which program models have worked best locally and around the nation, and how better outreach to adolescents least likely to be served might improve enrollment and retention of these clients.

For treatment of substance-abusing parents, using prevalence estimates as a basis for determining need ignores the fact that parents' need for services, as assessed based on the consequences of their use, is not the same thing as parents actually enrolling in services. The definition of need, as we have learned from a decade of women's treatment programs, must be widened to include the need for the services that go beyond drug or alcohol treatment itself to the critical supports needed for many women in treatment: child care, transportation, vocational and literacy services, and mental health and post-trauma services. Increased institutional demand for services is also emerging from the expansion of drug courts and statewide initiatives such as those in Arizona and California that divert some drug arrestees from prison to treatment. Welfare and child welfare systems have also increased their demands on the treatment system for services to parents in both systems, as described in five separate national reports over the last four years.[8] But this increase in institutional demand is not the same thing as the treatment system having the capacity to provide effective treatment or the tools and the will to monitor outcomes of treatment as part of a newly accountable system.

Using this new framework of redefined need, demand, and capacity, local governments can better plan for use of state and federal resources—which flow from more than a dozen different funding streams in some localities—to address family problems that result from substance abuse. Arizona has developed an inventory process with annual reports for twelve years that provides a base for analysis of where funding is going and how effectively it is being used. But few other states or localities have even taken the first step to develop a comprehensive inventory.

The critical intersection: child abuse and substance abuse

At the local level in states where counties have a service delivery role in the child welfare system, AOD problems affect a majority of the cases entering the child welfare system. The federal government in 2002 created the National Center on Substance Abuse and Child Welfare, in recognition of how much these two systems need to work with each other to help families where substance abuse affects child maltreatment.

Although there is a well-documented connection between family violence and substance abuse, the more frequent child welfare report is of a substance-abusing parent who is accused of neglect, not physical abuse. In 2001, approximately 903,000 children were found to be victims of child maltreatment, with more than half of them (57 percent) suffering neglect.[9] Neglect is highly correlated with poverty and substance abuse. While neglect is sometimes treated as less serious than physical abuse, research suggests that neglect can also be dangerous.

> Studies of child fatalities related to child maltreatment indicate that children die from neglect almost as often as from physical abuse. A review of 556 child fatality cases reported to CPS (child protective services) agencies in 1986 indicated that 44.3 percent were related to physical neglect. ...The child typically died because a caregiver was not there at a critical moment. The fatal neglect was most often a preventable accident associated with a single, life-threatening incident. In 39 percent of the cases, the neglectful families were previously known to CPS agencies.[10]

As a result of the close relationship between neglect and substance abuse, child welfare agencies find themselves in the AOD treatment business, while AOD treatment agencies increasingly recognize that the children of parents in treatment can both affect treatment outcomes and are themselves affected by their parents' substance abuse. With "faster clocks" governing both child welfare and welfare decision-making about when to terminate parents' rights and when to terminate parents' welfare payments (as a result of the Adoption and Safe Families Act of 1997 and the Temporary Assistance to Needy Families legislation of 1996), the need to coordinate treatment with these other timetables calls for much closer working relations than has been the norm.

In response, several states and counties have developed model programs to connect their child welfare and treatment agencies in common efforts. Seven of these were profiled in a recent report published by the Center for Substance Abuse Treatment.[11]

As a part of its local inventory of spending and its development of annual indicators, localities should monitor their caseloads of families who overlap the caseloads of welfare, child welfare, and substance abuse treatment to determine how well these agencies are working together to achieve shared outcomes, or if they have developed linkages similar to those of the best practices sites profiled in recent materials.

The issues of adolescent substance abuse

National statistics show that adolescent substance abuse is getting better, getting worse, or about the same—depending on which statistics you use. But at the local level, there are few cities and counties that are able to review annually a set of indicators that allow them to answer the accountability question: how widely do our youth use and abuse alcohol and other illegal drugs, and how well are our programs responding to the problem?

Competing perspectives on the youth drug problem are offered in two recent press releases:

> More kids use marijuana than cocaine, heroin, ecstasy and all other illicit drugs combined. While marijuana use has declined slightly in the last year, the number of 8th graders who used the drug doubled between 1991 and 2001 from one in ten to one in five.

Recent data from the University of Michigan's *Monitoring the Future* survey show the first significant downturn in youth drug use in nearly a decade, with reduced drug use noted among 8th, 10th, and 12th graders.[12]

The White House Office of National Drug Control Policy issued both of these reports in 2003. While both are backed with statistical data, the difference in tone—the far more negative cast of the first, the upbeat outlook of the second—makes clear that there is ample evidence to show both progress and serious remaining problems. And so the challenge remains local: how do cities and counties develop a specific score card in this vital area that enables them to track progress and problems against indicators that they have chosen locally as the best benchmarks to measure themselves against?

It is possible to develop a sub-set of the annual indicators report called for in Chapter 4 that monitors alcohol, tobacco, and other drug use at the city and county levels. Drug Strategies, a national research organization on drug issues based in Washington, has produced a series of state and local profiles, and has developed a methodology for doing a local profile and keeping it current.[13] An annual household survey, youth surveys, surveys of parents' attitudes and community norms, DUI records, review of youth arrest records and police calls to parties where underage drinking is prevalent—all these make up the elements of a comprehensive annual indicators report. But the threshold decision remains whether the local government wants to hold itself and its citizens accountable with an annual overview of the problem.

With respect to adolescent treatment, a new report shows that the number of adolescents aged 12 to 17 admitted to addiction treatment has increased 20 percent between 1994 and 1999, according to the Substance Abuse and Mental Health Services Administration (SAMHSA). According to SAMHSA's latest *Treatment Episode Data Set (TEDS) report*, adolescent admissions for marijuana use increased from 43 percent in 1994 to 60 percent in 1999. The report showed that in 1999, four substances accounted for 91 percent of admissions. They were alcohol, 47 percent; opiates (mainly heroin), 16 percent; cocaine, 14 percent and marijuana/hashish, 14 percent.

> 50-75% of incarcerated youth nationwide are estimated to have a diagnosable mental health disorder. Youth of color, females, and homosexual youth are most vulnerable to mistreatment and mismanagement among those suffering from mental health problems.[14]

At the same time, the local level is where treatment is provided, either directly by city or county staff (11% of all facilities), by private non-profit facilities (60%), and by private for-profits (26%).[15]

Community coalitions and environmental campaigns

With federal and private funding, dozens of local coalitions have been organized to deal with adolescent and community-wide use and abuse of AOD. Some of these coalitions have undertaken environmental campaigns that target heavy alcohol advertising in some neighborhoods, excessive granting of liquor licenses, and use of alcohol sponsorship for community events.

Drug Strategies has conducted a two-year study of community anti-drug coalitions in eleven cities. In assessing the impact of these coalitions, they concluded

> The few national evaluations that have been done do not clearly answer the core issue: Do anti-drug coalitions "work?" A central difficulty in interpreting these evaluations is deciding which measures to use in judging effectiveness. Many coalitions began with the express purpose of preventing alcohol and other drug use, particularly among young people, as well as reducing substance abuse in their communities. By these measures alone, few coalitions...can demonstrate success. However, many coalitions can show other kinds of effects which have improved various aspects of community life, ranging from elimination of billboards that advertise alcoholic beverages to cleaning up neighborhood street drug markets.[16]

The study concluded that there were six critical ingredients of effectiveness in these coalitions: broad and diverse coalition membership, a clear mission statement and strategic plan, strong, continuing leadership, diversified funding sources, training, and evaluation. Local governments are involved in all of the coalitions, but not always as the central players; in some cases they are the conveners and provide the staffing, while in others they are simply members of the broad coalition.

A special need and opportunity: younger children

In some states, new funding streams have been dedicated to early care and education programs or school readiness initiatives of various kinds. These funds tend to be allocated to programs supported by local child care advocates, with some investments in home visiting and maternal child health. But the opportunity that may be missed is a proportionate emphasis upon a particular group of younger children, the children of substance abusers, who make up a sizable segment of the 0-5 population who are subject to developmental delays, disabilities, and later on, special education.[17]

Local government affects this age group in many ways, despite the obvious and appropriate lead role of their parents in their preschool years. Child care licensing, maternal and child health programs operated by public health nurses, child welfare agencies in county-administered states—all these play a major role in the lives of many younger children. And the issue of substance abuse touches many of these programs, since the children most likely to rise to visibility in assessing at-risk factors are those from families where substance abuse and domestic violence are recurring problems. But few of these programs target substance-abusing families in any deliberate way. One assessment of parent education programs in Virginia found that there was little emphasis upon substance abuse problems, despite the fact that substance abuse was evident in many of the families, and that parents were placed in such programs due to incidents of child abuse and neglect that coincided with substance use.[18]

The opportunities for local government in addressing the needs of younger children include:

- The need for more deliberate screening of children in child care for the impact of substance abuse, both prenatally and post-natally;
- The need for residential treatment for the parents of these children who are in the child welfare system, including services for the children provided as part of an overall treatment plan for the family;
- The need for parent education and parent support programs, including home visiting, that address substance abuse problems in depth;
- The need for upgraded information systems, since AOD treatment agencies typically do not count or monitor the children of parents in treatment and child welfare agencies do not typically screen and assess parents for substance abuse problems or their developmental impact on children.[19]

Conclusion: The AOD issue is cross-cutting, strategic, and unavoidable

The problems of alcohol and other drug abuse by parents make up a significant element of family policy for local governments, for all of the reasons set forth in this chapter. If the response of local governments is to emphasize prevention aimed only at children affected by AOD problems once they become adolescents, an opportunity to develop anticipative policymaking will have been missed. And if there are few or no links from AOD problems to the other systems affected—education, health, mental health, child welfare, and juvenile justice—an opportunity to be strategic about a multi-faceted problem will have been missed. Finally, if the impact of addressing substance abuse problems on community development and renewal is overlooked or neglected, the opportunity will also have been missed to reinforce neighborhoods as places where families would want to raise their children in safe and healthy environments.

NOTES

[1] *Shoveling Up: The Impact of Substance Abuse of State Budgets.* (New York: Center for Addiction and Substance Abuse, 2001).

[2] These data are based on a new analysis of the data in SAMHSA's 2001 National Household Survey on Drug Abuse;

see http://www.samhsa.gov/news/addictedparents.html. The National Household Survey on Drug Abuse Report. (Washington, D.C.: Substance Abuse and Mental Health Administration, 2001)

[3] "$2.5 Million Available For Youth Alcohol/Drug Treatment" (Washington, D.C. Substance Abuse and Mental Health Administration, March 14, 2001).

[4] *Substance Use among Pregnant Women in 1999 and 2000,* The National Household Survey on Drug Abuse Report. (Washington, D.C.: Substance Abuse and Mental Health Administration, 2002).

[5] This chart is adapted from Nancy K. Young, Sid Gardner, and Kim Dennis *Responding to Alcohol and Other Drug Problems in Child Welfare.* (Washington, D.C. The Child Welfare League of America, 1998), which is derived from Nancy Young. (1997) "Effects of Alcohol and Other Drugs on Children," *Journal of Psychoactive Drugs.* Vol 29, No.1.

[6] These include the 15 Principles of Prevention developed by the Office of National Drug Control Policy http://www.whitehousedrugpolicy.gov/prevent/practice.html; A Center for Substance Abuse Prevention monograph, *Understanding Substance Abuse Prevention; Towards the 21st Century: A Primer on Effective Programs;* and *Lessons Learned: Strengthening Civic Infrastructure.* (Boston, Mass.: Join Together, 1998)

[7] *Principles of Drug Addiction Treatment: A Research-based Guide.* (Washington, D.C.: National Institute of Drug Abuse, 1999). *Benefits of Residential Substance Abuse Treatment for Pregnant and Parenting Women* (Washington, D.C.: Center for Substance Abuse Treatment, Substance Abuse and Mental Health Services Administration, 2001).

[8] U.S. Department of Health and Human Services, *Blending Perspectives and Building Common Ground: A Report to Congress on Substance Abuse and Child Protection.* (Washington, DC: U.S. Government Printing Office, 1999). U.S. General Accounting Office, *Foster Care: Agencies Face Challenges Securing Stable Homes for Children of Substance Abusers.* (Washington, DC: U.S. General Accounting Office, 1998). *No Safe Haven: Children of Substance-Abusing Parents.* (New York: National Center on Addiction and Substance Abuse at Columbia University, 1999). Mary Lee Allen and Jamila Larson, *Healing the Whole Family: A Look at Family Care Programs.* (Washington, DC: Children's Defense Fund, 1998). Nancy Young, Sid Gardner, and Kim Dennis, *Responding to Alcohol and Other Drug Problems in Child Welfare: Weaving Together Policy and Practice.* (Washington, DC: CWLA Press, 1998).

[9] *Child Maltreatment 2001: Summary of Key Findings.* (Washington, D.C.: Administration on Children and Families, 2001). http://www.calib.com/nccanch/pubs/factsheets/canstats.cfm.

[10] American Humane Association, *Highlights of Official Child Neglect and Child Abuse Reporting: 1986*, 24.

[11] Nancy Young, and Sid Gardner, *Navigating the pathways: Lessons and promising practices in linking alcohol and drug services with child welfare.* Technical Assistance Publication 27. (Rockville, Maryland: Center for Substance Abuse Treatment, Substance Abuse and Mental Health Services Administration, 2002).

[12] "Health, Education, Safety Experts Join White House Drug Czar to Educate Parents About Risks of Youth Marijuana Use" (Washington, D.C.: The Office of National Drug Control Policy, March 13, 2003). http://www.whitehousedrugpolicy.gov/news/press03/031003.html

[13] "Lessons from the Field: Profiling City Alcohol, Tobacco, and Other Drug Problems," (Washington, D.C. Drug Strategies, 2001). Downloaded October 6, 2002 from http://www.drugstrategies.org/citylessons/index.html

[14] Excerpted from "Handle with Care: Serving the Mental Health Needs of Young Offenders" Coalition for Juvenile Justice. Downloaded October 4, 2002, from: http://www.juvjustice.org/publications/index.html

[15] "Over One Million People Receiving Addiction Treatment," SAMHSA press release, Summary Data on 2000 National Survey of Substance Abuse Treatment Services. (Rockville, Maryland: Center for Substance Abuse Treatment, Substance Abuse and Mental Health Services Administration, August 2, 2002).

[16] *Assessing Community Coalitions* (Washington, D.C.: Drug Strategies, 2001). http://www.drugstrategies.org/commcoal/index.html

[17] Sid Gardner and Nancy Young, *Alcohol, Tobacco and Other Drugs in the Lives of Young Children.* (Los Angeles: Center for Healthier Children, Families, and Communities, University of California, Los Angeles, 2000).

[18] N. Dickon Reppucci, Preston A. Britner, and Jennifer L. Woolard, *Preventing Child Abuse and Neglect Through Parent Education.* (Baltimore, Md.: Brookes Publishing, 1997).

[19] Young and Gardner, *Navigating.*

CHAPTER 14: FAMILY SUPPORT PROGRAMS AND FAMILY INCOME SUPPORT: THE FUTURE OF FRCS AS A POLICY CHOICE FOR LOCAL GOVERNMENT[1]

Family resource centers (FRCs) make up a generic set of programs often described as *family support programs*. Other forms of these programs include school-based services, community schools, or even comprehensive Head Start programs that operate as a family support model. Their common elements have been set forth in an extensive series of reports by Family Support America and other organizations, and include:

- Staff and families work together in relationships based on equality and respect.
- Staff enhance families' capacity to support the growth and development of all family members—adults, youth, and children.
- Families are resources to their own members, other families, programs, and communities.
- Programs affirm and strengthen families' cultural, racial, and linguistic identities and enhance their ability to function in a multicultural society.
- Programs are embedded in their communities and contribute to the community-building process.
- Programs advocate with families for services and systems that are fair, responsive, and accountable to the families served.
- Practitioners work with families to mobilize formal and informal resources to support family development.
- Programs are flexible and continually responsive to emerging family and community issues.
- Principles of family support are modeled in all program activities, including planning, governance, and administration.[2]

These programs have multiplied in recent years, and prior to the current recessionary era, some practitioners predicted wide expansion of FRCs. The pressures on these programs and the policies underlying them, however, have increased in the past few years, and local government faces some important decisions about the future of family support:

- Will cities and counties fund these programs or will they allow them to operate with state, federal, and private funding only?
- Will cities and counties continue to out-station some of their own staff in mixed public-private FRCs?
- Will the network of FRCs exist as marginal projects on top of the existing system, or will they be transitioned into a primary method of carrying out city and county missions at the community level?

- Will FRCs take on what is arguably the most important kind of family
  support in contractionary times: family *income* support that connects
  working families with jobs, economic development, job skill-building,
  and the full array of income benefits that working parents are entitled to
  receive?

These policy and program questions are not always visible in local
governments, however. Many cities and counties have applauded the expansion
of FRCs without being central players or carefully assessing their impact on city
and county programs and goals, or evaluating their impact on families that need
help.

One reason that most local governments do not give family support a major
level of support is that the history of family support, as a recurring chapter in
what happens to immigrants in cities, is often overlooked in assessing its future.
Several authors and national organizations such as Family Support America
have described the rich history of family support programs. Family support as a
form of services integration is at least as old in this country as the settlement
houses of the nineteenth century and the school-based health services
established during the first major waves of immigration in the early twentieth
century. Kagan and her colleagues traced the origins of family support back
even further fifteen years ago in their seminal work *America's Family Support
Programs*: "Family support has existed in America since the village green."[3]

In more recent history, the multi-service centers funded by community
action agencies in the 1960s, HUD's Neighborhood Services programs, federal
services integration funding of the 1970's, and the school-based and school-
linked services projects of the 1980's and 1990's all predate the recent re-
discovery and re-labeling of family resource centers. The accomplishments and
failures of these earlier efforts make up an important part of the history of
service integration, providing a useful foundation for design of current efforts.
But these earlier versions of family support are not often tapped as explicit
sources of lessons to be digested, debated, and applied. The major points in
these lessons include:

- Both formal services and informal supports are vital ingredients of
  family support programs;
- Different "home bases" for family support programs exist, including
  family resource centers (FRCs), school-linked services and community
  schools, neighborhood centers, and community development initiatives;
- There are important tradeoffs (but not polar opposites, as discussed
  below) between agency-dominant and community-dominant models of
  family support;[4]
- There is a conceptual and practical tension between FRCs as universal
  programs and FRCs that target specific populations, defined by need
  (e.g. the 10-20% of births most likely to involve families with the
  greatest needs) or defined categorically (e.g. FRCs focused on children
  with disabilities).

Family resource centers also incorporate many of the values and practices of the more recent self-help, parent education and family support movements that evolved from research and practice in the child development and child welfare fields.

At the outset, I want to make my own commitment clear: I support FRCs and family support approaches, combined with public services and mobilization of community assets. I have seen good FRCs in operation, and they are greatly needed additions to the current mix of services and supports. They can also provide a tone of innovation and a spirited infusion of genuine citizen energy to tired, rule-bound institutional services.

But if we value what FRCs can do, we need to give FRCs a full chance to sustain themselves, and that involves asking harder questions of them than many of them have yet faced. At present, in late 2003, many of them do not appear likely to be given a chance at serious sustainability beyond marginal operation. The funding strategies that are supporting many of them are short-term, some of their sources are drying up or highly uncertain, and most funders have not helped them develop long-term sustainability plans in enough depth to ensure their future. Without addressing the hard questions facing the future of family support, too many FRCs will be relegated to marginal status, with just enough funding to make them one more ineffective outpost in the services landscape.

The false polarization between community and agency dominance

An unfortunate tendency in some recent discussions about FRCs is an over-polarization of the "community vs. service providers" issue, as framed by some FRC operators and those who provide technical assistance on FRCs. Some FRC proponents have argued that "the community"—a term used widely and defined vaguely—must be dominant over service providers. Some of these discussions revolve around 51% majorities on governing bodies for community members, reminiscent of the one-third set-aside for "maximum feasible participation" in the community action debates of the 1960's.

But framing these choices in such polarized terms ignores the extent to which the community is, or can become service providers. It also ignores the extent to which service providers have moved toward community engagement. To be specific with an example, out-stationing an assistant district attorney to handle child support in welfare offices is a genuine form of services integration that may have more impact on community income enhancement than dozens of community forums or bake sales.

Clearly, both extremes are inadequate: agency-only, top-down models are as unproductive of lasting results for children and families as community-only efforts that operate separately from the major funders already in the community and cannot be sustained except with external, token-level grants. But the choices aren't as simple as agencies vs. community—they involve what to do about the range of needs of families already "in the system" and those who are further "upstream" and not yet using public or nonprofit services. Saying we want to serve multi-risk families and then saying we don't want the stigma of working with families already in the system has been the inconsistent stance of more than one FRC sponsor or funder. There is a wide and deep middle ground between agency domination and community control, where most of the literature suggests the real payoffs lie, through the unique contributions each party can make to community and institutional change that improves outcomes for kids. But too few of these choices have been clearly framed in discussions about the future of FRCs.

One of the most thoughtful observers of community-based service reforms has described the connection between "the system" and FRCs well:

> Family resource centers and family support programs are bridges between professional service systems and voluntary support networks...These centers and programs bridge for families the public and private, the therapeutic and the normative, the specialized and the general, the professional and the voluntary...[5]

And the Family Resource Coalition of America (renamed Family Support America), in a 1998 summary report entitled *How Are We Doing?* said

> One of the primary roles is to build strong relationships with other community resources and services....An FRC works collaboratively with all community partners to bring together resources and activities into an integrated service system that is accessible and responsive.[6]

Bruner and FSA are right: FRCs ought to serve as such bridges. They ought to be integrators and brokers, playing roles that recall some of the newer roles for local government highlighted in Chapter 1. But too often FRCs operate largely separately from state and local government and its agencies, or accept token out-stationed staff who have little or no effect on the home agency's basic policies, rules, and operations. Those FRCs and FRC planners who speak disparagingly of "service providers" tend to have a hard time forging such partnerships, seeing the agency world as less important and more tainted than "the community."

The question of sustainability

State and federal funding prospects for expansion, or even maintenance of FRCs at current levels, appear dim. While there are some new funding programs that can be used to support FRCs, there is no interagency effort under way that seeks to tap multiple agency sources for family support; each agency is working on its own version of family support, using different definitions, evaluation tools, and intended outcomes.

Foundations that have invested in family support have been hit by the market downturn, and some have turned to new priorities. And foundations, by definition, are better suited to starting programs than sustaining them.

So what is sustainability if it is not state, federal, or foundation funding? For those who support FRCs and want to see them institutionalized, there are three strategic questions that cannot be avoided:

- The strategic question for FRCs that see their future as primarily *community-based* is how the community can support it, and whether external funding will ever be able to sustain it above token levels of funding.

- The strategic question for FRCs that see their future as *linked with local government*—cities and/or counties—is why those governments should support organizations that may duplicate their own functions while requiring additional funding to do it.

- And the strategic question for FRCs that see their future *linked to schools* is whether the education system, under enormous pressure to produce results in the currency of improved test scores, will ever provide non-trivial resources to family support programs. FRCs, seen through this narrow lens of test scores, may appear to be marginal in their effects, even though, as noted in Chapter 12, an estimated one-third of all students have barriers to learning that cannot be solved in the classroom.

Each of these scenarios demands more clarity about mission and targeting—which families should be supported, and why—beyond that achieved by most FRCs thus far. The issues of sustainability and the need for a "theory of resources" discussed in Chapter 6 are all relevant in the case of FRCs. Sustainability is about *both* funding and program effectiveness—sustainable means client outcomes that can be achieved over time, and sustainable also means that this program is fundable *because* it has shown that it can achieve those outcomes.

Local governments may wish to consider a set of scenarios for the future of FRCs, which are not mutually exclusive:

- *The child welfare services "front end" scenario*: Some FRCs have moved toward formal status as strong partners with the child welfare system, accepting and seeking as clients the families which the child protective services system believes need early help to prevent them from becoming serious abuse or neglect cases.

- *The education learning supports/school-linked services' scenario*: Perhaps the clearest description of this model has been developed by UCLA's School Mental Health Program in its "learning supports" approach. This model is also inherent in the Healthy Start projects in California that have been able to secure institutionalized funding from school districts.

- *The school readiness/early childhood development scenario:* In California, Proposition 10 (tobacco tax surcharges) funding has given new emphasis to strategies developed in North Carolina and other states which emphasize a community-driven approach to school readiness. At the same time, some communities and counties have used their inventories of local funding for early care and education programs to document that funding for these programs already flowing to their communities is 10-15 times larger than special allocations for school readiness.

- *The health/medical home/home visiting option:* These strategies are not always combined, but they all seek a closer connection between families and health and medical providers. Home visiting has been supported from both grant and institutionalized funding, the latter primarily through public health budgets. Using FRCs as an access point for health services and heath coverage for underserved families has been a common emphasis, but often without a long-term strategy for securing funding to do so.
- *The TANF/welfare leavers/working poor families option:* In this approach, family income and work supports has been viewed as more important than "soft services" family supports. Using welfare incentive funding in some cases and institutionalized TANF one-stop center funding in others, some FRCs welcome welfare clients and former welfare clients, in contrast with others who seek to avoid the stigma of serving only welfare clients.
- *Community development/building strategies:* Using Empowerment Zone funds, Community Development Block Grants, or other institutionalized sources of funding for community-targeted programs has been another approach to funding some FRCs.[7]

Each of these approaches has its advantages and disadvantages, and those will vary from community to community. In some regions, the best "handle" on family needs and strengths will be readily apparent, while in others it may require a "mix and match" strategy. But the risk of a combined approach is obvious: it may result in none of the approaches receiving a critical mass of resources and attention to have a real chance of success, with funding spread across so many geographic and programmatic areas that each ends up with a light dusting of resources, while none gets enough to make an impact. The failure to concentrate adequate resources on any one strategy to achieve results is a real risk for many FRCs that are unwilling to make the hard choices among these strategies, and as a result, seek to carry out all or most of them without adequate resources.

The critical nature of information systems

Sustainability demands robust information systems. To collect data on the outcomes of FRC programs requires much more than head count and an intake form that captures some demographic information about families. But making decisions about upgrading information systems demands clarity about mission, including answering the question "what information should we collect about what results for which clients?"

In one recent evaluation of FRCs, the most intensively served families received an average of six hours of service. Only a quarter of the intensively served FRC families also received at least one referral during this six months period. This is a dosage of service that seems inconsistent with sustained impact.[8] And this was in a project cited as well-evaluated; others may achieve even less intensity. Other evaluations that combined FRC services with home visitors and included community-wide efforts aimed at school reform reported greater effectiveness. The lesson of dosage seems clear; equally clear is the need for information systems that capture such results over time, which do not exist in the majority of FRCs.

The question of mission and resources: "On top of or instead of?"

A major issue faced by all family resource centers is the extent to which they seek to build new structures and services in their communities, in contrast with using new methods of delivering institutional services by the large public agencies that have most of the funding for children and family services. One way of phrasing this is to ask whether FRCs are intended to operate "on top of" the existing system or, over time, to replace it, to operate "instead of" the old system. The issue only arises, however, when considering whether to replicate FRCs at scale. It is irrelevant if the goal is merely funding a few of them as a small adjunct to the existing system.

If the answer is that FRCs are to operate in addition to the current system, then their future funding is inevitably competitive with the hundreds of millions of dollars of funding for existing agencies that serve some of the same families. And taking FRCs to scale will require an awesome level of funding.

No one appears to have yet done the arithmetic that would answer the question of what it takes to move FRCs from a project approach to going to scale. The arithmetic is painful for advocates of the "on top of" approach, because the funding required is enormous. For example, if the 8,000 schools in California are to be sites, with a center for every five schools, and the typical well-functioning FRC has a budget of $200,000 (assessments of the most effective ones suggest this figure is very low), it would take $320 million to take FRCs to scale. Alternatively, if FRCs were to be targeted universally on the ten million children in California (as advocates of universal vs. targeted funding would suggest they should be) and each FRC were to have a caseload of 1,000 children, it would take $2 billion. If "universalists" were to reluctantly agree that only the 20% most at-risk children should be targeted, the price tag comes down to "only" $400 million—for one state.

Previously, we cited Paul Hill's use of the term "zone of wishful thinking" to refer to reforms in which proponents have not addressed the resistance of the systems being reformed.[9] It seems possible that FRC policy may need to overcome similar wishful thinking around replication before it can escape the drawbacks of hoping for reform without a clear financial and political strategy to achieve it. Otherwise, FRCs can sit on top of an unchanged system that dwarfs its limited, marginal resources.

The literature on human services innovation, including Lisbeth Schorr's seminal 1998 book *Common Purpose*, makes clear that pilot projects can at times serve to insulate larger systems from change. Some FRCs may be at risk of playing such a role.[10] Evidence of this tendency comes in listening to senior officials of county agencies discuss "their" FRC networks, when most recent expansion of FRCs has been funded out of federal family preservation funds, one-time welfare incentive funds and new tobacco taxes. When it appeared as though major increases in child welfare caseworkers were coming in state budgets a year or so ago, some county agencies were asked how many of these new workers would be assigned to work in FRCs; the answers were typically vague or subject-changing. But the question was a fair one: if you get new family-focused funding and you don't assign any of these funds to family support programs in the community, how can you claim to be a supporter of family-focused services?

So if the "on top of" option costs too much, what is the "instead of" option? In its essence, it argues that FRCs must assume some of the functions of the current system, evolving strategically over time into the front end of one or more of the systems of services with an explicitly preventive mission. In the sustainability scenarios set forth above, several of those options are described generally. The fifth of these—family income support—needs to be considered in more depth, since lower-income families are the obvious target for FRCs taken to scale.

Family support or family income support?[11]

A fundamental issue facing FRCs and the wider family support movement is the question of whether family support initiatives should address family *income* support more intensively. Some would go further to argue that FRCs should be assessed and ultimately funded in part based on how many lower-income working families they connect with income support benefits.

Why should FRCs get into the family income business? There are at least six major answers that emerge from concrete evidence as well as arguments on ethical grounds:

- Because child development and long-term child outcomes are linked powerfully to family income;
- Because families who have recently left welfare or been diverted from it are typically working at the lowest end of the income scale in ways that affect their children directly; "most parents leaving welfare for work earn too little to support their families;"[12]
- Because there is a growing number of families who do not receive the work supports they are entitled to, based on numerous national and state–level studies;[13]
- Because a community development approach that is place-based requires a concern for the total family income flowing into a given neighborhood or community, and if working families are not receiving the benefits they deserve based on that their work and their low income, the neighborhoods they live in are unfairly deprived of a critical asset;
- Because the basic compact made in welfare reform in 1996—that welfare should no longer be an entitlement—was linked to a commitment to "make work pay," meaning that lower-income working families should be given temporary work supports as they work their

way up the income ladder, with those benefits remaining in place as long as a family stays eligible based on their income and their work;

- This argument also raises basic questions of equity with middle- and upper-income families, who are much better informed about their tax benefits than lower-income families are about what one recent study called a "bewildering array" of income support programs, each with different eligibility processes.

One in six children—12 million nationally—lived in poverty based on the 2002 Census poverty survey, which means children are more likely to be poor than any other age group. An additional 15 million children live in families with near-poverty incomes (between 100 percent and 200 percent of poverty). Yet the vast majority of poor and near-poor families have at least one adult who is employed most of the year.[14]

In a recent report on the impact of welfare reform on New York City families, the authors listed ten programs that provide direct income or income substitutes to lower-income working families.[15] Collectively, the combination of income benefits available to some working families with children amounts to more than $5,000 a year (the Earned Income Tax Credit alone tops out at $4,140 annually).

To summarize: having full access to the array of income benefits to which a family below the poverty level is entitled could mean as much as $3-5,000 annually (excluding health benefits). The average "poverty gap" for a female-headed household in an urban area in the Western U.S. is about $5,300. Thus a full-benefit income support package would reduce the poverty gap substantially and could eliminate it for some families.[16]

For a working poor family which is above the poverty level, off welfare, but still eligible for all these benefits which are set based on levels ranging from 125% to 185% of poverty, these amounts are equally important in providing the margin between inadequate and barely adequate housing or the amount between inadequate custodial child care and good child care with a developmental component. Again, for a family support program to ignore the potentially make-or-break impact of these amounts of additional income would appear to rely upon counseling or self-help to make up for cash in supporting a family. But we would never expect middle- or upper-income taxpayers to rely on counseling, instead of claiming all their available tax deductions and credits.

These numbers provide the basis for the argument that all family support programs serving lower-income, working poor families should be evaluated in part by their effectiveness in connecting families with all of these benefits. To suggest implicitly that a family support program need not concern itself with family *income* support can be justified only if one of two possibilities is true:

- Someone else is already working effectively to address the problem, or
- The problem is not important.

But neither is true. While there are FRCs and welfare one-stop centers that address some of these programs, the complicated interagency mix of work supports programs means that no single center addresses all of these. At best, they make referrals, and none has yet been identified that consistently follows up to see if the other agencies have actually connected working families in the FRC with the benefits they deserve.

For some of these programs, the time costs and complexity of assisting families are quite low. It takes about half an hour to assist a single parent who is eligible for the EITC, using a software tax program. The IRS offers volunteer services to help with this, and some FRCs have taken advantage of this help. But to seek to help families or single parents with the full array of these work supports is clearly more time-consuming, arguing for a software application or paper-and-pencil checklist for all of these programs. Such a screening tool could enable preliminary screening at initial intake of the potential that a family would qualify for these income supports, for a given family size and income.[17] In this case, it is not *services* integration that FRCs would be enabling, but integration among work support programs needed by lower-income working families.

More recently, there are new tools emerging which can be used to assemble information about most or all of these work supports. Wider Opportunities for Women (WOW) and the Annie E. Casey Foundation have recently compiled information about the WOW Family Economic Self-sufficiency checklist, which is being used in a number of states as a means of assisting families in determining their eligibility for more than one program at a time.[18]

It is important to confront an argument sometimes made by FRC operators—that their program mix should be determined by their clients and "the community." But a community cannot "choose" a program or an approach that it has never heard about. Choosing counseling over work supports may be a rational choice, but if the potential members of an FRC or its staff have never been presented the option of a comprehensive effort to link families with work supports, no choice has been made. Some FRCs have simply drifted toward doing what comes most easily, rather than what parents may need most.

Lessons from the field

During a period of three years, from 2001-2003, a colleague, Iris Alfaro, and I worked with more than twenty FRCs in a workshop process that was sponsored by the Strategies organization, an entity of the Southern California Children's Bureau. This involved work with large and small FRCs, from Northern and Southern California. The major lessons for local government that emerge from that work include:

- The importance of connecting free-standing FRCs with the agencies of local government, with which many of them are only tangentially involved; an example is how few of them work closely with welfare or child welfare agencies;

- The great difference between FRCs that emphasize referrals and the much smaller group that conduct follow-up services to see if clients referred actually got services;
- The weak state of information systems of most of these centers, which has improved in the past few years but remains unable in most centers to present a convincing case for further funding based on documented outcomes;
- Some hesitant moves toward family income support services in the past year or so, but without any FRC having yet developed a full-array approach to all income support programs—and none able to document how many families they annually connect with benefits; and
- The haphazard nature of funding, with few FRCs having developed long-term sustainability plans and most moving from one funding stream to another based on whichever is most recently available.

Conclusion

FRCs are at a crossroads. The choices they make and the choices local governments make about them will not only determine their sustainability, they will also affect the thousands of families that are or could be participants in FRC programs. The family support movement has helped focus hundreds of programs around the nation on the needs of families, but it is now critical to re-assess those needs and the capacity of FRCs to meet them, in light of new challenges to both FRCs and to the families they serve.

NOTES

[1] This section draws on a longer paper on the future of FRCs which is available at www.cffutures.org

[2] Some of the best-known of these include the Kagan sources cited below, and Family Resource Centers: Vehicles for Change, (Sacramento, Ca.: California Family Resource Center Learning Circle, 2000). Others are available at the Family Support America website: http://www.familysupportamerica.org/content/pub_proddcf.htm

[3] Sharon Lynn Kagan, Douglas R. Powell, Bernice Weissbourd, Edward F. Zigler, (eds) America's Family Support Programs: Perspectives and Prospects. (New Haven, Ct.: Yale University Press, 1987.) Sharon Lynn Kagan and Bernice Weissbourd, (eds.) Putting Families First: America's Family Support Movement and the Challenge of Change (San Francisco, CA. Jossey-Bass, 1994).

[4] Sharon Lynn Kagan and Peter Neville, Integrating Services for Children and Families. (New Haven, Ct.: Yale University Press, 1993).

[5] Charles Bruner and Carl Dunst, Key Characteristics and Features of Family Support Practice; (Chicago: Family Resource Coalition of America, 1995).

[6] How Are We Doing? (Chicago: Family Resource Coalition of America, 1998).

[7] It is also possible to add other scenarios, including reliance upon some businesses who operate their own family support programs in the form of employee assistance programs, the efforts of some unions to provide family income support services for

lower-income members, and the reliance of courts and law enforcement agencies upon case management of family violence prevention programs and parents receiving mandated family services. These are all variations of family support programs that may provide a portion of future funding needed for sustaining effective FRCs.

[8] Family Resource Centers: Vehicles for Change. (Sacramento, Ca.: The California Family Resource Center Learning Circle, 2000).

[9] Hill and Celio, Fixing.

[10] Schorr, Common Purpose.

[11] This section draws upon the work of the Annie E. Casey Foundation's Family Economic Success Project. www.aecf.org.

[12] Eileen Sweeney, Liz Schott, Ed Lazere, Shawn Fremstad, Heidi Goldberg, Jocelyn Guyer,, David Super, and Clifford Johnson, (2000) Windows of Opportunity: Strategies to Support Families Receiving Welfare and Other Low-Income Families in the Next Stage of Welfare Reform. (Washington, D.C.: Center on Budget and Policy Priorities, 2000), 1.

[13] Martha R. Burt, Nancy Pindus, Jeffrey Capizzano, The Social Safety Net at the Beginning of Federal Welfare Reform: Organization of Access to Social Services for Low-Income Families (Washington, D.C.: The Urban Institute, 2000).

[14] Ed Lazare, Shawn Fremstad, and Heidi Goldberg, States and Counties are Taking Steps to Help Low-Income Working Families Make Ends Meet and Move Up the Economic Ladder. (Washington, D.C.: Center for Budget and Policy Priorities, 2000).

[15] Hugh O'Neill, Kathryn Garcia, Virginie Amerlynck, Barbara Blum, Policies Affecting New York City's Low-Income Families. (New York: National Center for Children in Poverty, 2001). The programs included continuing TANF payments, the Earned Income Tax Credit, food stamps, Medicaid or SCHIP, child care subsidies, child support, unemployment insurance, and subsidies for attending vocational or college education aimed at increasing wages.

[16] Since these are annual numbers computed for the entire U.S. population, cost of living, family size, housing costs, and child care costs should be factored in, which would lower the actual value of these figures in some areas and raise them in others.

[17] Terminology matters in discussing family income; we are using work supports and family income supports interchangeably, but the preferred term would seem to be work supports, since it is the working status of these families that entitles them to aid and that may enable other taxpayers to recognize the merits of support for those who work.

[18] "Six Strategies for Family Economic Self-sufficiency." Wider Opportunities for Women. Downloaded from http://www.sixstrategies.org/ September 16, 2002.

CHAPTER 15: YOUTH DEVELOPMENT AS A FUNCTION OF LOCAL GOVERNMENTS[1]

Youth Development and Local Government

Youth development[2] (YD) programs are common functions for local government, though not always under that label. Parks and recreation, afterschool programs, and police prevention activities are familiar examples of cities' and counties' efforts to involve their youth in broadly based programs, while other efforts are more directly targeted on youth offenders or dropouts who are more likely to create problems for local governments.

Some YD efforts have sought independence from local government, preferring greater autonomy to closer alignment with elected officials and their bureaucracies. But in other cities and counties, local governments inevitably engage with youth, and these contacts can be both positive and effective to the extent that local leaders and their staff also engage with local youth-serving organizations.

Karen Pittman, arguably the single most thoughtful theorist-practitioner in the YD field, has recently addressed the issue of YD-local government relationships. The issue is how autonomously YD programs can and should operate, apart from the main funding streams in the public sector. As Pittman frames it, reflecting on the development of the YD field,

> [we] over-emphasiz[ed] one delivery system....To succeed, the YD movement must be linked to *the dollars, facilities, and professional and administrative services associated with public institutions*....Engaging the public systems is critical....Everyone, including those on the inside, acknowledges that these systems are slow to change. But they are where the young people and the resources are.[3]

If Pittman is right, "engaging the public systems" is critical. But with the exception of Pittman's work, one can read most of the YD literature and evaluation reports without encountering much reflection on whether and how to connect in depth with public systems.[4] The implicit message to youth and to YD organizations has been, however unspoken, "you can do this by yourselves."

But this message ignores the need to mobilize the full range of resources available to a community, beyond the resources of its youth and its YD organizations:

- The resources of public agencies
- The resources of nonprofit agencies[5]
- The resources of faith-based organizations
- The resources of the wider community, including business.

Why pay attention to youth?

In some cities, youth issues are the most visible local governmental programs affecting children and youth. Yet it is often negative perceptions and deficit approaches to "problem youth" that get most of the spotlight. Even in cities and counties with a more balanced approach, sometimes the political advantages of an emphasis on the disruptive potential of youth gets more attention than broad-based prevention efforts—even though the prevention activities may receive equal or greater priority in terms of resources. In an approach that may be characteristic, one city—which actually has a very balanced approach—describes its youth programs in the city's strategic plan in terms of their "potential to reduce disruption," rather than in terms of youth development.

In another city in the South, a multi-year reform effort began with concern by business leaders that youth roaming through the downtown area were affecting the tourist business in that city, which had major economic consequences. A thorough review of why youth were on the streets during school hours led to a deeper assessment of the city's dropout problem, which was disproportionately made up of African-American males. Over time, this entry point has led to education reforms and a demand that all school data be disaggregated racially—which it had not been in that city's past. In other cities, concerns about disruptive youth have been the entry point for a much broader discussion of why youth are not constructively occupied between the hours of 3 and 6 pm, when youth crime spikes and local businesses complain about youth congregating in the downtown and shopping areas of the city.

Local arenas for youth programs: The 4Ps

It is possible to spotlight four sets of local agencies that have special impact on youth:

1. *Police*: These functions are perhaps the most obvious areas of local agency efforts, since public safety agencies have long operated their own YD programs in athletic organizations. Some police departments have their own "youth development" units and officers trained for and assigned to those duties. Community policing aimed at youth crime and deterrence is itself a form of youth development linked with community development. Officers assigned to schools—the common formulation is "school resource officers"—can play roles ranging from direct patrol to a much more nuanced form of open contact and dialogue with youth who may never have had the opportunity to engage with police officers in non-confrontational roles.

2. *Parks and recreation*: The maintenance of parks and operation of athletics programs may not be a pure form of youth development, but some local parks and recreation departments employ youth, use youth advisory groups, perform outreach to harder-to-serve youth, and fit the definition of YD more closely than some YD organizations do.

3. *Public works*: The function of some public works departments that is most obviously related to youth is not a positive one: graffiti removal is an item in most local government budgets, and it can be a sizable one.

More positively, public works departments supervise capital budget expenditures, maintain youth facilities, and identify and make rules for public spaces that are available for youth and other community activities.

4. *Purchasing*: Decisions about which firms a city or county use as suppliers of goods and services have a youth development component, to the extent that contract requirements may include summer and year-round youth hiring, family-friendly provisions such as released time for parent-teacher conferences or athletic coaching, and willingness to consult with youth in program development of after-school and other YD programs operated by nonprofit or for-profit contractors.

One could also, if stimulated by alliterative muses, add the importance of public libraries,[6] public health services for adolescents—especially teen *parents*, planning, and, of course, public education. But the point in emphasizing these first four is that these are critical agencies that are often overlooked because they not defined as "the youth department" of city and county governments. Yet their impact can be far greater than a small 2-3 person office that does "youth issues."

YD programs vs. YD policy

But despite these several impacts on YD of local operations, as we have seen in earlier sections of this book, the inclination of local government once it decides that youth issues are important is to seek external grant funding for a series of loosely connected youth projects. The good news is that a number of cities and counties have moved from such projects toward strategic policy efforts. In fact, in reviewing Chapter 3's examples of strategic policymaking, it is clear that a significant segment of these exemplary efforts were really YD efforts initially. They moved over time toward addressing the problems of youth across agencies and strategically, rather than being trapped in grant-chasing and single-agency "projectitis."

These strategic issues include addressing

- The costs of YD programs
- Targeting YD programs—all kids or kids with problems?
- Targeting II—which kids with which kind of problems?

Costs: Doing it right or just doing it

In their report *A Matter of Money: The Cost and Financing of Youth Development in America,* Robert Newman, Richard Murphy, and their colleagues have done the most thoughtful work of any youth policy experts in costing out what quality youth development programs really require. They estimate that first-rate after-school youth programs require $3,060 annually per school-aged youth from 6 to 17.

Most local government programs would not come close to this benchmark, and most local governments do not aim their programs at the youth who need such "high-end" programs, as we will see in the next section when we look at targeting issues. The point is not that a $1,000 program cannot make an impact.

The point is that if *only* $1,000 programs are funded, either Newman and Murphy are wrong about what it takes—or many programs are not having a lasting impact. A third possibility is that such programs are in fact helpful, but primarily for those youth who are least likely to need the help, which again raises the question of targeting discussed below.

But the question about how to fund YD programs is usually addressed in a vacuum, without solid information about local sources of current or prospective funding. That is the power of a "youth budget,"which counts what city and county governments are now spending, so that grant-funded, add-on programs can be compared to the much larger base of funding already in the community.

In nearly all communities, the resources already available through existing public and private agencies are far greater than grant funding from outside the community. This is another reason to focus on the "four Ps" in local government where resources are concentrated in city and county budgets. Some YD programs have been urged by funders to develop a "theory of change" that attempts to explain how the program actually achieves the positive outcomes it seeks, showing the connection between specific interventions and resources that lead to specific improvements in outcomes. As discussed in Chapter 6, it also may be true that a clearer "theory of *resources*" is needed for YD funders and grantees alike, answering for each grantee program the simple question "if this works, who would be willing to pay for expanding it—and why should they?" Such an attempt to be clear about who might assume funding responsibility for a program will often lead to local government, since cities, counties, and school districts are often the only sources of institutionalized, non-grant funding.

Targeting issues

Which youth should local government aim their programs at? More than a decade ago, the Grant Foundation emphasized the ten million non-college-attending youth who need special attention to get into a demanding labor market, calling them the "forgotten half," in comparison with those youth who do attend college. Other subdivisions of the youth population emphasize those who "play by the rules" but do not receive targeted resources, dropouts, incarcerated youth, youth aging out of the foster care system, and other groups defined either by risk factors or special status as a result of their family situation. One recent assessment of vulnerable youth added up a total of 5 million youth 14-24—nearly 10% of the youth population—who needed extra support in making the passage from adolescence to adulthood.[7] Other groups have defined the highest-needs group as the 3-4 million "disconnected youth."

The targeting discussion, like the closely related discussion in the health care field on rationing medical care we reviewed in Chapter 5, is an uncomfortable one. Human services funders and practitioners prefer to talk about the advantages of universal programs, even while they may be funding programs that aid fewer than 1% of the total number of youth who may need a program's benefits. But programs inevitably target, whether they acknowledge it or simply serve the easier to serve youth by doing little outreach and making little effort to reach culturally diverse populations.

A related issue: in addressing targeting, some YD practitioners would argue that there may be undue emphasis on the deficits of youth, rather than their assets. The YD field has benefited greatly from the asset orientation of many institutions' work over the past decade. Yet there may be a tendency to suppress discussions of real deficits—in youth, their families, and their communities—as a result of a vague commitment to emphasizing assets over deficits. If substance abuse, clinical depression, and violence remain characteristic of a critical subset of youth, who receive far fewer resources than justified by their proportions in the total youth population, a perspective that under-emphasizes deficits may also ignore real problems that will never be addressed by loosely targeted community-wide prevention efforts.

A threshold issue for local governments in addressing targeting is whether they have identified the pyramid of need that exists in every community (as graphically depicted in Chapter 4), from the broad base of all youth at the base of the pyramid, to the youth at the top of the pyramid who require 24/7 institutional care, and all the intermediate gradations between the two. Whether deficits or assets define the pyramid matters less than whether the youth-serving programs in the community understand its broad configuration—or just do what they do without any picture of total need and where on the pyramid they are operating.

The base question is not a complicated one, and youth-serving organizations operating in a tighter funding environment would be well advised to have an answer: how do the youth you serve compare to the youth in the broader community? How do they compare to the youth with greatest need in your community?

Yet the unspoken premise of many programs remains "We open up and serve whoever comes in. This is an operating mode that largely ignores targeting issues. In contrast, the Beacon Centers in San Francisco and elsewhere have addressed targeting issues in their evaluation by asking questions about who attends the centers and how attendees compare with other students. Findings from a national evaluation of the Boys and Girls Clubs targeted youth outreach gang programs also suggest that youth-serving organizations can make an effort to identify and serve harder-to-serve youth if this goal is built into the program from the outset.[8]

Youth-serving organizations may not want to take the lead with the most vulnerable youth who are still in the community. But it is fair for public funders and others to ask what the agencies they operate and fund can contribute to the needs of those youth who are *more* at risk. Some youth-serving organizations would be able to respond that they accept referrals from public agencies of youth who are being released to the community from incarceration or diversion programs, while others have no such links to public agencies or the courts. Similarly, some agencies seek to serve the forgotten half and also take the extra step of seeing if these "disconnected" youth *become* connected, by using discrete, easily measurable indicators, (such as those used by the Taller San Jose program in Santa Ana[9]) including drivers' licenses, checking accounts, registration for adult or vocational education, enrollment in parent education classes, child support payments, and registration to vote. These are easy to verify, they are fair measures of youths' *own* actions, rather than what services are provided to them, and they emphasize the manifold ways in which youth become concretely connected to their communities. Targeting services on youth who lack these connections must be accompanied by a commitment to verify that the targeting is making a daily difference in youths' lives, not just providing services.

Targeting II: Gender and other risk factors: Who are "at-risk youth"?

In assessing who high-risk youth are, the million-plus teen-aged mothers are prime candidates, and a million more children—their babies—are near the top of the category of high-risk infants as well.[10] Teen pregnancy rates are decreasing, but these numbers are a powerful reminder that there is still a substantial number of these mothers and babies, many of whom have high odds against their success in life.

Some, but by no means all of the youth development literature tends to adopt a male model in which adolescent girls' needs and assets are not prominent. On the other side of the ledger, only 1.9 million girls, compared to 3.8 million boys, are enrolled in special education nationally, with African-American boys much more likely to be categorized as needing special education services than any other ethnic group.[11] Similarly, 83% of youth felony arrests are males.

Youth development programs that ignore these clusters of at-risk groups may be at risk of adjusting their sights so high that they are missing some of the most important groups of youth, for whom many youth development programs are irrelevant. And it may be equally important in all of these to review the numbers through a lens of gender, since male-female ratios differ substantially.[12]

Could a case be made to shift significant resources from male to female youth? Probably not within the confines of a youth development approach. But once funders and policymakers widen their concerns beyond the 11-19 year-old age span to a concern for *both* generations—the babies of these at-risk youth as well as a focus on their parent and the needs of whole families—it is more difficult to conclude that females have been given adequate attention in most youth development programs. YD programs that ignore youth parenting are at risk of becoming another categorical program in which a rigid age criterion leads to ignoring two-generation problems. But their premature parenting may be one of the most important defining characteristics of why these youth face problems and why their children will as well.

It is not necessary to argue against early childhood investments to make the case for disconnected youth. Once an intergenerational perspective is taken, the two become critically overlapping priorities for a substantial number of these youth (and their younger children). And sadly, many more of these youths are likely to become parents as a function of their age and their disconnectedness itself.

In addition to its importance in targeting decisions, for YD programs to make common cause with early childhood programs (and the variety of state and federal funding sources that target young children) seems a better political and fiscal strategy than seeing priorities for younger children as invariably competitive, given the presence of approximately three-quarters of a million children attached to the 3 million 16 to 24 year olds who are most "disconnected." It would be a powerful signal that proponents of such a strategy have risen above simply proposing one more categorical program, and that they have a broad fiscal agenda as well, for the targeting discussion to explicitly include the children of these disconnected youth and young adults. A larger number of these disconnected youth are parents than are incarcerated; yet in some recent proposals, considerably more attention is given to serving disconnected youth who are incarcerated than those who are parents—or those who are, sadly, both.

The fiscal argument for targeting these youth would be even stronger if one started with the high risks faced by the sizable number of these youth and young adults and "backed into" a strategy of helping young parents. Funding for this two-generation strategy could make a sizable down payment on a larger program for those disconnected youth most able to break the intergenerational cycle of disconnection, or to continue it. And public will might be mobilized in a way that could combine the clout of two sets of advocates and providers, rather than creating yet another point of contention among health, education, and human services groups.

This point is intended to be more than a plea for non-categorical thinking. While recognizing that funder groups separately oriented to early childhood, school reform, and youth initiatives are both a reality and a necessity, a two-generation approach would also set a tone for the communities in which we work, and would confront their own worsening fragmentation. If funders sought to bridge some of these gulfs in their own problem definitions and grant conditions, local grantees might have an easier time putting the pieces together. A move toward defining disconnected youth and their children as challenges that are co-equal and inextricably linked would demonstrate how bridge-building in communities could work against the erecting of more walls of competitive funding. Local governments could, in fact, issue challenges making clear that they would support some of the agencies that do the best job of connecting their early childhood strategies with their disconnected youth, who are often the parents least likely to get recruited into parent-child programs. Those communities not funded as part of an emphasis on disconnected youth would still end up with closer ties between these two overlapping groups, which may equip them to seek and secure other funding.

The effectiveness challenge

As argued in Chapter 3, strategic policy includes a concern with its effectiveness. But in youth programs, inadequate resources, untargeted programs, and fragmented projects are common. Most local governments do not place much emphasis on any reasonable test of effectiveness in making a difference in the lives of the youth they try to help. The challenge to local governments is to decide what outcomes they should demand, if any, and how quickly they should look for them.

In a recent assessment of the YD field, Gary Walker of Public-Private Ventures has argued that mentoring and after-school programs, especially when provided by "brand name" organizations such as Boys and Girls Clubs and Big Brothers/Big Sisters, are the models of "as good as it gets" programs, with a track record of effectiveness that goes well beyond broader and more diffuse efforts at youth development.[13] But this recommendation comes into direct conflict with the idea of working to reduce fragmented grants, because such programs are rarely part of a community-wide strategy to respond to the full array of youth needs. Rather, they represent direct responses to the needs of specific groups of youth, effective because they have chosen to work in a focused way with a finite number of youth, without addressing issues of scale.

The issues of effectiveness also spotlight a critical gap at the community-wide level of YD: a consensus among youth-serving agencies and their funders of how progress will be measured at the community-wide level. As noted in Chapter 4, what is often missing is a score card of some kind that says these 10-15 indicators are what we will look at annually to assess whether the problems of youth in our community are getting worse or better. Within such a scorecard, some communities have begun trying to develop a "dashboard" of performance measures that can be used to more frequently measure progress, if not success. If a YD coalition meets regularly but never reviews progress against agreed-upon measures, the coalition will lack a culture of accountability that says "how did we do this month/this quarter?"

The good news is that the effort to identify risk and protective factors has yielded an impressive list of indicators, but the other news is that there are still very few communities that are regularly measuring a core list of indicators or investing in filling the gaps for the indicators they still don't collect at all—like true dropout rates, civic participation measures, or social capital-building among youth.

Innovative roles for local government

It is possible, drawing upon the 15 roles for local government presented in Chapter 1, to describe a number of roles in supporting youth development functions which would correct for the inadequacies of scale, dosage, targeting, and effectiveness of local governments' current support for youth programs. These include:

1. Prevention programs: a countywide or citywide network might want to convene a "prevention summit" of all the disparate programs (which would first require a full inventory or matrix of these efforts—a major product in itself, since you can't glue together pieces that you can't find) aimed at different kinds of risky behavior, with youth taking a prominent role in convening the summit and capturing its lessons. This could break through the fragmentation of separately funded prevention efforts aimed at dropouts, use of alcohol, tobacco, and other drugs, violence, gangs, teen pregnancy, and the other problems associated with categorically defined prevention efforts.

2. Providing add-on resources to strong youth development organizations (YDOs) to ensure that they could improve their effectiveness and increase the dosage of services they provide by "gluing" on components now missing from YDOs, e.g. adding health services to after-school programs, adding parent services to youth programs for teen parents, or adding academic enrichment to arts and recreation programs.

3. Providing support for "key bridges" where youth move from one system to another—from child welfare to juvenile justice, from mental health to special education, from afterschool programs back to schools—at those key points where a "handoff" needs to be made from one system to another. These are the very points at which youth often get lost between the cracks of the systems, and efforts to build better bridges between systems may ensure that the resources of more than one system are available to help youth.

4. Seeking state support for greater discretion to blend separate funding streams for youth programs based on locally-determined outcomes. A foundation for "glue funding" efforts in California is the Youth Pilot Project, or AB 1741, which funded six counties beginning in 1993 to blend state-only funding for several children and family programs. While the effort met with considerable frustration and was not adequately staffed by the state during most of its tenure, it was based on a clear principle that is certain to be rediscovered: *state discretion to blend funding streams should be increased to the extent that local (county) agencies accept accountability for well-specified outcomes.* Since it is much easier for states in budget difficulty to grant discretion than funding, it is possible that efforts like the California model could win wider support.

5. *Youth budgets:* Newman and Murphy describe a group of organizations which have already begun inventorying the resources available to youth programs, using a Youth Budget format. Los Angeles County, Philadelphia, Contra Costa County, and numerous other sites have developed children and youth budgets as a context for decisions about grant funding and which programs need more intensive evaluation. A youth budget can spotlight the absence of priorities in some local governments, by raising questions during the budget cycle that include:

   • Which programs are growing most rapidly in spending or in client enrollment, e.g. foster care?

   • Which programs have the highest longer-term payoffs from current spending?

   • Which programs have the strongest or weakest evidence of their effectiveness, based on both national best practices and the quality of the evaluation and information systems developed by grantees?

   • Which programs are currently most visible as a result of recent events or a media spotlight?

In many budgets, these analyses are implicit or simply missing; a youth budget raises these questions to visibility. It also opens the prospect of YDOs learning about and commenting on those parts of the local budget that are not labeled YD—the sheriff's budget or the public works budget, which may represent considerably more staff and spending than small setasides for YD programs.

6. Some observers of the present budget crises in state and local government have predicted a new wave of legal action aimed at state and local public agencies, since an increasing number of those agencies will be moving into violation of legal requirements and compliance mandates in child welfare, juvenile justice, mental health, special education, developmental disabilities, and other areas where legal mandates are in force. To the extent that this prediction is borne out, it may benefit cities and counties to focus their work with vulnerable youth on those areas where federal and state mandates are strongest, or at least to recognize that different mandates exist in different program areas and can at times provide added leverage for resources.

7. Entire books have been written on the issue of youth participation in programs, and some of these approaches have already been referenced in Chapter 4's discussion of information and values tools. "Youth mapping" is just one example of the dozens of models of roles for youth participation in planning, operating, and evaluating services for youth *by youth*.[14] In some cities and counties, this emphasis has moved past formation of a token youth council to active involvement of youth across the government, in ways that represent genuine policy change.

Why should local governments be more strategic in supporting youth programs?

Urging local governments to adopt a broader strategy is uphill work, but so was civil rights in the early 1960's and so is reforming systems in the 21st century. In tight fiscal times, it may seem even easier for cities and counties to duck behind budget problems as an excuse for their inability to fund youth–serving organizations. But in tight times, the case for bad programs also grows weaker. A recent *LA Times* editorial, appearing on October 28, 2002 and calling on the new Police Chief to attack the gang problem and stop funding ineffective programs like DARE, suggests that the media will respond to a political message that calls for shifting scarce resources from weak programs to stronger ones—and investing the resources required to be able to tell the difference.[15]

In fact, as noted in Chapters 3 and 5, it is both a fair question and a valuable diagnostic to ask a city or county how much they have shifted in the current year's budget from the worst programs to the best ones—and how they tell them apart. If funders asked this question more often, public agencies would have to work harder to come up with an answer, or to acknowledge that when budget cuts happen, they take the easy road—they cut programs across the board and make no distinction between programs with strong claims and those with weak ones.

So the first incentive for a YD approach is that local governments would have better credibility with funders and possibly the media if they supported *effective* youth-serving organizations and shifted funding away from their less effective youth-serving programs. A second, closely related incentive is that funded community-based agencies may provide critical ingredients that can make a public agency's own programs more effective. If a youth-serving organization can provide cultural competency or outreach to a geographic area where the county has no staff, the county is adding to the effectiveness of its own investments in programs.

Here some of the clearest examples are those cities and counties such as Santa Cruz and Los Angeles that have taken the lead in outstationing their own staff or working with outstationed community-based agencies to provide probation services in schools and other locations. These models have the potential of meeting youth agencies more than halfway toward the community side of service delivery, showing the clear incentives for public agencies to deliver their services in different ways.

A third set of incentives for YD efforts in local government would seem likely if a group of funders—or a single, well-placed one—announced it was preparing to fund cities or counties that were willing to adopt YD principles in their budgeting and planning for human services programs. In tight budget times, for good or ill, local governments would see such a "hook" as a welcome one that might eventually generate other external funding. If funders were willing to set the bar well above local governments' rhetoric about YD, and demand specific evidence that YD approaches were being used to link separately budgeted line items beyond one or two pilot projects, it might screen out the grant-chasers from those local policy leaders who are really willing to explore what taking YD seriously would mean.

A fourth set of incentives flows from the long-standing hypothetical argument for prevention programs: they save money later. Intuitively, policymakers can understand the argument that YD programs save downstream costs. But budgets do not rest on intuition alone, and YD evidence is less weighty than its proponents sometimes admit. As the 2002 National Research Council study summarizes its review of available evaluations of YD programs,

> Even with the most rigorous methods of evaluations, there is limited evidence that measures the impact of these [youth development] experiences on the development of young people and therefore limited evidence on why program effects are or are not obtained from the evaluations reviewed.[16]

The argument about costs and cost savings has to be approached carefully, since the evidence suggests that good YD programs are *not* cheap, and their costs increase to the extent that they seek to serve the most disconnected youth. Newman and Murphy's estimates of the costs of solid YD programs [over $3,000/year/per youth] end up with costs considerably higher than most city and county-funded programs. The NRC compilation of programs models cites the unit costs for only a few programs; Teen Outreach is $500-700/youth/school year; other after-school models are described as costing up to $1,000/school year, plus training and facilities costs.

Moreover, the politics of local government sometimes operates to spread benefits as widely and thinly as possible, which can result in a dosage far below what it takes to make a difference. While YD staff may be less expensive than public agency staff because they are neither unionized nor fully provided with benefits, ensuring adequate training may reduce the differential. Moreover, it hardly seems consistent to argue the merits of lower wages and benefits for YD staff, and then try to make the case that they are essential workers with unique skills.

So the cost savings argument belongs in the mix of approaches to making the case for closer YD-local government links, but care should be taken that it is not the only ammunition used. The community base, the ethnic diversity, and the outreach potential of youth-serving agencies all strengthen the basic argument for closer ties.

A final argument rests on the need for a continuum of care for higher-needs youth, which public agencies have difficulty serving with their own limited resources. If public programs are mandated to serve the youth "at the top of the pyramid," i.e., those whose institutional care, intensive needs, or incarcerated status makes them unavoidable clients of local public agencies, then one important argument for youth agencies is that they make up a major component of the continuum of care for the youth "lower down the pyramid." Those youth whose needs are not as intensive, but who may end up in these higher categories without prevention and intervention, are more typical clients for most YDOs.

This is not the same thing as a vague argument that prevention is good and will eventually save money. It is a far more specific argument that youth-serving agencies have the potential to identify and serve youth who are not yet in intensive caseloads.   But the argument rests upon youth-serving agencies' willingness to do so and to document that they do.

Youth-serving agencies are not just able to do a better job than public agencies at the prevention job, with youth who are not yet in the highest-needs categories. They also have the potential to be a critical part of after-care and community transitions. This alternative goes further "downstream" to targeting youth re-entering their communities from incarceration or foster care. Such a role also requires evidence that agencies can accept handoffs of youth from the more intensive systems as they transition back into school and independent roles in the community. This may require agencies to segment their services into "open-door" modes for a broad segment of youth and more intensive services for transitioning youth.[17]

So to sum up: the potential exists for youth-serving agencies to become a more closely integrated partner with public agencies, both in prevention roles for youth lower on the pyramid of need, and in aftercare and transition roles for higher-needs youth after intensive treatment or incarceration. This "bookend role," as it might be termed, would involve agencies operating on either end of the public systems, as crucial supplements able to perform functions that public agencies can't or won't.

These comments about the need for youth agency ties with local government are not made without awareness of the challenges of working with cities and counties, especially in tight budget times. In addition to their budget constraints, officials and staffs in the public agencies of these governments are often resistant to serious pursuit of an effectiveness agenda, because examining the effectiveness of what they are now doing and funding may lead to painful admission that present programs are neither measured nor effective. As mentioned already, cities and counties continue to invest in low-dosage, loosely targeted programs because it spreads the political benefits more widely than targeted, intensive programs.

But resisting the demand for accountability for results is certain to become more difficult as budgets remain tight and evaluation results improve. For funders to offer to help those cities and counties that are willing to undertake this work is to place bets on the most forward-thinking local governments, rather than to accept the narrowest workings of the political system as immutable facts of life in all local governments.

Beyond the mantras

In any field, a set of mantras or often-repeated slogans sometimes become a partial substitute for critical thinking. In the YD field, some of the recent mantras are

- "youth grow up in communities and families, not programs"
- "problem-free is not fully prepared."

For the 600,000 children and youth in out-of-home care, we all hope and pray that they are living in some kind of community, and that the new family (or agency) that has taken them in will keep them safe and developing better than they were in the family from which they were removed. But these youth are definitely growing up *in a program*, and it is the community's legal responsibility to make sure that program does what it is supposed to do.

The concept of problem-free as a minimal base of achievement is a good one, and so is the idea that fully prepared is a higher level to be aspired to by communities. But with very few communities actually measuring whether *either* minimal or higher levels are now being achieved, it seems essential to get beyond the slogans to actually caring enough to count, and to develop a "short list" of outcomes measures in the form of a community score card for youth that is issued annually, debated widely, and taken seriously in resources decisions.

Youth development connections with the larger array of needs

Finally, any serious effort to develop youth development strategy raises (as suggested in the comments above on teen pregnancy and the children of parenting youth) a question that cannot be answered within the confines of youth development: how do these goals and resources compare in importance with all the other goals and resources in the broader arena of children and youth policy in a given state or community?

We get to youth development as a priority from one of two assumptions:

- a sense of urgency—something bad is happening, or we have the opportunity with new funds or new leadership to make something good happen if we act now, and this program area presents unique opportunities, or

- a sense of general inadequacy in the YD field in comparison with other, "better resourced" areas such as child development or in-school programs, that leads us to say this is a neglected area and we should try to put more resources into this area of need.

But part of the problem may be considering the YD field separate from its close connections with other fields, including:

- as noted, the needs of children of teen parents as a second (or third, or fourth) generation problem;

- the dropout-creating potential of high-stakes high school testing and graduation requirements; and

- the impact of disconnected, unprepared or underprepared youth on the state's economy and the families affected by this low earning potential.

To the extent that segmenting YD as a subfield that is treated separately worsens fragmentation and thus ineffectiveness, a narrow approach to YD may itself become part of the problem. At the very least, YD grant-making should look to the outer margins of the YD arena, assessing opportunities for new bridge-building, and rewarding those agencies that do the best job of partnering with organizations outside the YD field whose programs touch on or flow from YD issues.

Conclusion

The gains achieved by youth development programs in the past decade are impressive. New emphasis and new resources have been focused on the needs and assets of adolescents, national and local organizations have made sizable improvements in their capacity to operate and evaluate stronger programs, and youth themselves have been more actively engaged in planning, operating, and assessing programs aimed at improving their life outcomes.

But in the decade ahead, building on these gains will demand major new efforts to clarify the targeting issues and the role of public agencies at the local level. As much as federal and state leadership could help to improve YD programs' scope and effectiveness, the focus of most policy action seems likely to remain at the local level. In response, funders may want to increase their efforts to create new incentives for local governments and public agencies to address these issues, and to spotlight the best practices of those that have already begun to move in these directions.

NOTES

[1] A portion of this chapter draws upon work sponsored by the Walter S. Johnson Foundation on youth development programs in California.

[2] Youth development is defined by the Carnegie Council on Adolescent Development as the process through which "adolescents actively seek and are assisted to meet their basic needs and build their individual assets and competencies."

[3] Karen Pittman, *Youth Development: Issues, Challenges, and Direction.* (Philadelphia, Pa.: Public-Private Ventures, 2001), 33-42 [emphasis added].

[4] An important recent exception to this has been the work of the John Gardner Center at Stanford with Pittman and others to inventory and assess what other states have done to develop policy frameworks for youth development at the state level. While one can question how much these state coordinative efforts remain program-driven vs policy-based, clearly some states have made recent efforts to connect separate YD efforts. Yet little of this work addresses the role of *local* government, which is much more closely involved with the daily lives of youth. Thaddeus Ferber and Karen Pittman, with Tara Marshall, *State Youth Policy: Helping All Youth to Grow Up Fully Prepared and Fully Engaged.* (Takoma Park, MD: The Forum for Youth Investment, 2002).

[5] Some observers of the youth development field combine YDOs and nonprofits [NPOs], but it makes more sense to distinguish between smaller community-based organizations and larger, nationally connected organizations like the Boys and Girls Clubs and the Y's.

[6] Chapin Hall and The Forum on Youth Investment both recently issued reports on libraries and YD opportunities. Julie Spielberger and Samuel Whalen, *The Public Libraries as Partners in Youth Development Initiative: An Interim Report of the Evaluation of a Wallace-Reader's Digest Funds Initiative* (Chicago: Chapin Hall Center for Children, 2002) Downloaded at
http://www.chapin.uchicago.edu/ProjectsGuide/NewPublication.html

[7] Nicole Yohalem and Karen Pittman, *Powerful Pathways: Framing Options and Opportunities for Vulnerable Youth.* (Tacoma Park, MD: The Forum for Youth Investment, 2001), 3.

[8] Carolyn Marzke, Evaluation of the Boys & Girls Clubs of America TEENSupreme Career Prep Pilot Program: Year 1. (Washington, D.C.: Policy Studies Associates. 1999).

[9] Personal communication, Taller San Jose staff, Santa Ana, Ca.

[10] In 1996, one-quarter of teen births nationally were not first births; so the number of mothers understates the total number of younger children in these families.

[11] Rosa Smith, "Black Boys: The Litmus Test for 'No Child Left Behind.'" *Education Week*, October 30, 2002.

[12] In some cases, that would require substantial additional analysis, because the data do not distinguish between male and female counts in some of these programs—a finding that in itself signals the lesser importance given to gender, resulting in a default to a focus on males.

[13] Gary Walker, *The Policy Climate for Early Adolescent Initiatives.* (Philadelphia: Public Private Ventures, 2001).

[14] The John W. Gardner Center at Stanford University has compiled a variety of sources on youth mapping and youth involvement, as well as links to other organizations that play such roles. http://gardnercenter.stanford.edu/resources/yell_bib.shtml

[15] An op ed article in a very different newspaper, the *Orange County Register*, was similarly critical of DARE [February 9, 2003], drawing upon the GAO report issued in January 2003.

[16] National Research Council, *Community Programs to Promote Youth Development*. (Washington, D.C.: National Academy Press, 2002) 194.

[17] A parallel and closely related issue is whether family resource centers have a useful role to play in accepting referrals from child protective services agencies of families whose children are not removed to out-of-home care (or who may be returned home from foster care), but who may need both family support and continued monitoring of child safety. This is addressed in Chapter 14.

CHAPTER 16: THE ROLE OF LOCAL GOVERNMENT IN THE FUTURE

What will be the role of cities and counties in the intergovernmental system of the early decades of the 21st century? Some observers have projected further decline for central cities, reflecting their political shrinkage in favor of areas of the nation that added new members of Congress in the reapportionment following the 2000 census. But counties in the South and West, and those cities that are able to expand their geographic areas, as David Rusk has explained, are likely to grow in political influence as their growth in elective power and numbers increases.

At that point, the prognosis for children and youth diverges, with those local governments that are gaining in older voters likely to differ from those with increasing numbers of lower-income, younger residents. Santa Ana, California, with one of the highest percentage of residents under 20 in the nation, cannot easily be compared with Miami, Florida, with 21.9% of its residents over 60. In demographic work performed as part of the development of a report card for Santa Ana, one of the clearest findings was the city's strong reliance on county funding for many of the programs in the city aimed at children and youth. Such cities are necessarily intergovernmental in their advocacy.

Clearly, the fiscal future of cities and counties will be strained. As the nation moves through and beyond the recession and under-employment of 2001-03, with prognoses of state budget deficits for several years in the future, local governments do not appear likely in the short run to return to an expansionary era. Looking out further, the structural deficits of cities and some counties also seem unlikely to change in the foreseeable future. However, those cities that have locational advantages, and those counties in which suburban and business growth remains a factor, may do considerably better. And, writing in a county that is somewhat notorious for experiencing the largest public bankruptcy in American governmental history, it seems important to add that those counties in which policy leadership includes appropriate measures of fiscal prudence and oversight are likely to do better than those that are still hoping for a repeal of the business cycle.

All of these fiscal issues are heightened in importance by the impact of accelerating changes in demography and in science and technology. The kinds of services that are delivered to children, the way those services are delivered, the gaps in technological access among different groups of children and youth— all these issues of the near future will further challenge local governments' ability to meet the needs of children and families, while at the same time providing those governments with additional tools to serve a changing mix of children and families.

An overview of future issue trends

At the end of Chapter 1, we previewed some of the developments that may affect local government as it responds to children and family needs and aspirations. Those included:

- Immigration as it affects both population and service needs;
- Overall demographic change that will shrink the youth cohort in relative size;
- Technical changes and political demands for greater program effectiveness will increase the pressure for results-based accountability in local government funding and services;
- Privacy and confidentiality issues will be raised as a temporary barrier to expanded information services to clients and program accountability;
- Various forms of teledemocracy or cyberdemocracy will be attempted, without yet affecting the fundamental operations of government in most localities;
- Pressures for privatization of services will continue, with greater accompanying capacity for local governments to hold privatized services accountable for results that go beyond lower costs;
- Educational choice as a value will be joined by greater concern about parents' early education choices and the impact of low-quality early care and education on school readiness; and
- Extensive debates will intensify over the use of biotechnology for social control of youth and others whose behavior is defined as anti-social.

These trends can be grouped into three broad categories:
1. Those that are primarily *demographic* in nature: immigration, intergenerational issues;
2. Those that are *technological:*   results-based accountability systems, new forms of governmental participation, and biotechnological social control; and
3. Those that are *political and ideological*:   privacy, educational choice, and the ethical uses of technology.

The final set may also be grouped under a fourth category—those which are significantly *ethical* in content (although all of them have some ethical content). Several of these issues underscore the extent to which ethical frameworks may help local governments address these issues more thoughtfully. The arenas of data privacy, biotechnology, and cyberdemocracy are unavoidably ethical in nature.

Looking at the political horizon

Politically, it is very risky to prognosticate about political issues more than a year or two away. But if we call upon local government to be more strategic, while restricting our own horizons for strategy to the next biennium, we are guilty of a kind of planning hypocrisy. So we will try to look out over a longer span of time, into the next decade or so.

Haves and have-nots

If the economic divide between higher and lower-income Americans continues to increase, whether measured in income or wealth, that divide is likely to continue to increase in visibility as a major issue. In recent years we have experienced a mini-crisis of confidence about the integrity of American business leadership, in what some have called "the Enron era." But it is impossible to see how long-term this may be, and whether it will spill over to a greater reliance upon either public or civic, third-sector solutions to the problems of children and families.

What seems likely to have more lasting impact is the reaction to the family income gap. It is hard to imagine the organizations representing lower-income working parents—and those that will come to realize they should—will remain inactive as that gap remains stagnant or widens. The shape of the state and local recovery of the mid-2000's will obviously have much to do with the perception that working parents and other low-income citizens are falling further behind. The debate over tax cuts may shift from a discussion about *whether* to cut taxes to a discussion about *what kind of tax cuts should be made*, with more of a spotlight on benefits that affect these lower-income working families, and thus the localities in which they live.

Older and not-yet

These political/economic issues intersect with intergenerational issues. The shape of the economy will in part determine the fiscal space for consensus between younger and older workers and retirees—or those who want to retire, but can't. The intergenerational issues are coming to a divide, and the evidence will continue to come in, either in support of the optimism of Theodore Roszak (discussed in Chapter 9) and his fellow "half-fullers," or confirming the pessimism of those who predict a bitter zero-sum game between retiring boomers and those still working.[1]

For local governments, there may be more than a ray of hope in the demographics of aging. That is because most of the costs of aging are borne by state and federal budgets. If local governments are able to take advantage of the "compassion dividend" that Roszak and others predict (described in more detail in "A Modest Proposal" in Chapter 9), the elderly may prove to be a net positive economic factor in some cities and counties. For others, however, the evidence of older voters' compassion is still sparse, and school bonds and community facilities may be at risk, especially where the demography of taxpayers and service-users differs widely.

Technology matters here, too, for it is the longer-living activism of older residents of cities that can affect whether they want new recreational facilities as opposed to needing health care facilities. If their biomedically-aided longevity means that their longer productive work lives add to the net sum of their volunteer contributions, it may neutralize some of the resentment younger workers may feel at having to support Social Security and Medicare contributions for older retirees. But at the lower end of the economy, the costs of prolonging work lives may overwhelm both older and younger residents, especially with health cost increases.

School choice and the middle ground

The debate over educational choice will not diminish, including expansion of the growing middle ground between public schools and vouchers, with an array of charter and other variations on public school accountability and innovation. Although school choice is a fundamental issue for some, with religious overtones, as noted in Chapter 10, there is wider middle ground available than on issues like abortion and the death penalty. In some cities, such as Indianapolis, it has been local leadership that has begun to define and shape the middle ground between extremes of the educational status quo and full voucher-based school choice. That city's Mayor's authority to approve new charter schools is an extraordinary example of mayors moving into school reform and expansion of the middle ground options.

New York City's performance-based school budgets are another middle-ground reform that moves toward greater local determination without going all the way to charter schools or a voucher system.[2] Since 1997, a select number of schools have developed budgeting reforms that moved some decision-making closer to the individual schools, with new flexibility to target better-documented school funding to locally-chosen goals, with the capacity to follow up and see if the goals were met. The reforms included new software enabling local districts to compile information on students' academic performance and schools' individual budgets.

To the extent that the public schools learn to make tactical retreats for the sake of their own strategic defense, they may be able to satisfy their upper-income critics. But it will take significant changes in resources, especially investments in teaching, to quiet some of their other critics who focus on poor students who don't learn.

Choice also affects school readiness, as the educational options available to parents of younger lower-income children mirror the inequity of those for school-aged children. As discussed in Chapter 12, the children who most need high-quality preschool options are those who get it least often. Parents have more choices in early care and education, but unfortunately the evidence is that many parents whose children need higher-quality care will not get it.

Charitable choice and the middle ground

Both shifts in the composition of federal courts and the multiple models of faith-based organizations which are emerging seem likely to expand the challenges to local governments arising from charitable choice options in federal and state legislation. The exploration of middle ground options in Dionne and Chen's recent compilation makes clear that many different forms of faith-based organizations' work with local government are still legally available.[3] Some of these potentially intersect with Roszak's projection of the volunteer boom he sees resulting from a more active elderly population. Even Marvin Olasky, the "inventor" of "compassionate conservatism" in its most recent form, argues for an "arms-length handshake" as a middle ground between full use of public funding by faith-based organizations and spurning all public funds.[4]

Immigration

Immigration issues are linked to the intergenerational issues, through the unmistakable arithmetic that shows that more workers will be needed to fuel the retirement and health costs of the boomers. But there will continue to be communities whose majorities experience a sense of loss as their population changes to become more globally diverse. As any foreign traveler knows, one experiences an inevitable disorientation when the street signs are mostly written in an incomprehensible language, which already characterizes some American communities for some of their long-time residents.

Immigration of high-skilled workers is perceived very differently than immigration of lower-skilled workers—even though the economy may depend upon both. Taking the housekeepers, nannies, gardeners, child care and nursing home aides out of a community would have at least as great an impact on the local economy as a loss of well-educated computer programmers or biotechnology professionals. And as those job titles indicate, it is often children and families who would most directly feel that absence.

For local governments, the legal authority of the federal government in immigration issues is a reality, but the consequences of federal decisions can still affect local politics and regional economies in ways that lead to new pressures for cities and counties. The children and families connected with immigration may be perceived as net assets or liabilities; numerous school districts impacted by immigration have learned to cite the dozens of languages spoken by their students as a challenge to their academic achievement. And the cultural differences in the ways families raise and discipline their children, as we have already noted in Chapter 9, can have great effects on children's services.

As immigration issues shift their geography from border states, New York, and Florida to a much wider cross-section of the nation, local governments become engaged in states where immigration issues have not been a major political issue. Food processing in the Midwest, construction in the Northeast, and several other industries with national scope are increasingly affected by legal and illegal immigration. In her masterful book, *The Middle of Everywhere*, Mary Pipher uses Lincoln, Nebraska as her setting and shows how broadly this heartland community has been affected by immigration.[5]

Privatization

A recent assessment of those states and localities that have gone furthest with privatization in the child welfare field[6] concluded that

- The varieties of privatization make it very difficult to generalize about it as a single phenomenon, since privatization includes managed care, reliance on nongovernmental community-based helpers, reliance on private for-profit firms, and several other variations;
- In the child welfare field, privatization has been affected by a lack of baselines and benchmarks, weak information systems on both client outcomes and costs, the difficulties of monitoring contracts to private and nonprofit providers, a lack of specific outcomes used to monitor contractors, start-up costs, and a lack of capacity in some jurisdictions to provide the contracted services;

- Problems also occurred with cost differentials, as higher-cost children with more serious problems affected rate-setting and risk pools in ways that undermined the purposes of privatization; and
- The assumption that privatization to the community level would lead to greater use of non-child welfare funding sources proved over-ambitious, with difficulties attracting funding from other agencies not under the control of the child welfare system and problems with Medicaid managed care providers not allowing some costs and reimbursements.

This assessment concluded

> There has been some success...on the other hand, many other aspects of these efforts proved inadequate. The financial methodologies frequently were unworkable, if not disastrous. Monitoring and evaluation posed significant difficulties, both for private agencies that were expected to comprehensively monitor and report on program achievement, and for public agencies that were attempting new quality assurance roles. Finally, outcome and performance measures proved to be a major hurdle for most of the programs. The desired results were often not clear, and the performance targets frequently were unspecified or were developed in the absence of validating data...Privatization cannot succeed simply by transferring to private agencies the constraints that have characterized public agencies' service provision to poor children and families.[7]

The pressures for privatization of local government functions are likely to increase, but it is to be hoped that the lessons of past efforts will improve the quality of the efforts undertaken. Freundlich and Gerstenzang emphasize that

> Public agencies should not expect to save money through privatization. Cost savings are highly unlikely, given the real costs of developing, implementing, and overseeing a privatization initiative and the costs associated with providing a full array of services to children and families under expectations of higher quality.

The technological issues

Those challenges that will emerge from technology—participatory options, social control options, the challenge to privacy—all pose difficult choices for local governments. Much of the public policy around these new tools and issues will develop outside the sphere of local government, and federal and state policy responses will constrain local governments' actions, as they always do. But there is already evidence that different cities and counties will react differently and that there is enough policy slack in the system to permit such variations, just as there is with issues of educational choice. Some of the most important decisions about use of these tools will be made in the non-public sectors, by private and civic sector leaders, potentially in concert with leading local governments. Roszak notes that most biotechnology is being financed by private laboratories, not the federal government, and thus local firms "fly under the radar" of federal regulation thus far.[8] Local governments may have to make the rules that govern uses of such research, as they have for environmental regulation in areas like sewage release into the oceans, in the absence of state or federal regulatory authority.

Cities which are more familiar with biotechnology, for example, may find it easier to experiment with new uses of such technology than those for which these tools are unfamiliar and threatening. Cities with extensive computer industries may find it financially easier to experiment with cyberdemocracy, as has already been seen in some areas such as Silicon Valley.[9] Such cities are also likely to be those that use technology for job training and location efforts, such as those described by Blackwell and her colleagues.[10]

The social control policy choices will be some of the most difficult, although in several areas policy has been overtaken by practice. It is undeniable that use of pharmacological medication is widespread in nursing homes, as a means of keeping patients more docile and easier to "manage," as several assessments have concluded.[11] The leap from using calming drugs in nursing homes to using them in prisons and juvenile detention facilities is not a great one; in one county a senior administrator was removed after media attention to his excessive use of prescriptions for children and youth in the mental health system. The use of electronic detention is widespread already, and the enormous costs of incarceration are likely to fuel a continuing search for cost-cutting options.

A concrete example of the use of such tracking has occurred already in several after-school programs that are using scanner cards which youth use to register each time they attend the program. The cards enable program staff to determine which programs are attracting the most youth; if linked to characteristics on intake forms, they can also achieve an additional purpose: comparing youth who attend with those who do not.[12]

These policy debates may include ethicists, as urged and hoped for in Chapter 5—or they may not. But the issues are ethical at their core, because they involve both how we will treat children who cannot make decisions for themselves and how we will treat persons who have lost some of their personal rights to freedom through illegal behavior or actions deemed illegal by the larger society. But as we debate how to decide these issues, the ability of science and technology to control behavior through understanding the neurochemistry of the brain is multiplying much faster than the political arena's understanding of how to approach these issues.

Cyberdemocracy options

At this point, the jury is still very much out on the net effects of what is variously termed e-democracy, teledemocracy, or cyberdemocracy. Local governments are definitely making increasing use of the Internet and establishing their own increasingly dense websites. But the disagreement is over what political effects may result from a less-used feature of cyberdemocracy: voting and deliberative democracy. In the experiments with online voting, the tradeoff that Arthur Applbaum cites—between deliberation and directness—is evident, but which side "wins" remains unclear.[13] Clearly, it is possible to conduct annual, weekly, or even daily plebiscites on local government, using survey software and the ability to instantly tabulate "votes." But the question remains how rapidly and how deeply opinions are formed that underlie those votes, and whether "instant, shallow opinions" should be valued as a net contribution to government.

Local governments are likely to experiment with these techniques, without yet investing major political capital in them. But outside local government, the prognosis is less optimistic at the moment, as several observers note in expressing concern over the fragmenting and narrowing effects of online advocacy. Whether we are yet faced with a nation "Surfing Alone," to twist Robert Putnam's phrase, in ways that reduce the bonds among large communities in favor of fragmented pseudo-bonds within

---

Which is the Real City Council?

It would not be difficult to arrange a parallel or "shadow" city council made up of all the citizens who logged on and voted on a matter pending before the elected Council. And it would not be difficult to "certify" on-line voters as a representative group, or to filter out multiple votes, if participants agreed to a random verification of 10% of all voters. A correction could be made for non-universal Internet coverage, as is now done in phone polling, and links to public access sites like libraries could reduce the effects of partial Internet access. Using survey software, regular tallies of "votes" could be posted. At that point, the virtual "council" could grow to represent hundreds or even thousands of local residents, which would have to be taken very seriously by the elected Council.

---

smaller, virtual communities that may rarely come face-to-face, is unknown. But it has become a definite concern.[14] Add to this is the concern voiced by those who have analyzed the "digital divide" that still takes the form of far less Internet usage by lower-income, more diverse groups, and the problems seem to be multiplying.[15]

On the services side, however, technology is moving more rapidly, in other arenas:

- Carrying out new outcomes accountability through web-based client information systems that seek to track children and parents each time they "log into" a services site. In California, several counties have used software firms to begin tracking tobacco tax-funded services to younger children from birth to enrollment in elementary school. The potential for providing much-needed services is obvious, but thus far, concerns have been expressed about considerably more data collection going into these systems than useful data analysis and policy implications coming out of them. In each county, there has been a debate about the impact of this technique on privacy, which has been handled in part by uniform parent consent forms and interagency protocols on the agreed uses to which the data may be put.

- Developing software which can input information about a family's composition, income, and other eligibility criteria and determine the likelihood of the parents' and children's being eligible to receive up to a dozen different work or income supports or in-kind benefits.[16]

Yet a dose or two of realism is also needed. Jerry Mechling supplies some of it:

> ...if the e-government agenda were a trip to the moon, we would have just cleared the gantry a few seconds ago.....we are still a long way from our final destination....We have made scant headway on concerns about the impact of e-government on privacy, security, equity, and the very legitimacy of our institutions of governance.[17]

Mechling discusses the impact of citizen contact management that can manage all contacts of residents with their local governments. He mentions the concerns of those who have decried use of the Internet in communities where many families have no connections to the Internet, and cites governments' complaints that they cannot invest in expanding access at current prices of hardware and connectivity. But his conclusion is still upbeat, over the longer term:

> Government bureaucracies will ultimately become flatter, faster, and more customer friendly. Services will become better integrated and customized, with rich self-service options.[18]

How will these trends affect local government?

Some of these trends will increase the resources available to cities and counties, while others will increase the services needed by their residents. All, however, will create new demands for policy that is less reactive. Local governments will benefit when they are staffed and led by officials who deliberately exercise a continuing "search" function in looking for new ways of doing things, while maintaining sufficient skepticism about making sure that their governments are doing the right things, rather than merely doing the latest things. Although it is difficult to staff small and medium-sized local governments with "futurists," the role is an obvious and critical one for statewide and national organizations like the National League of Cities, the U.S. Conference of Mayors, the National Association of Counties, and the International City Management Association.

NOTES

[1] My own belief is that the organizations representing older voters will find it very difficult to go beyond slogans to making full common cause with those representing children and families—but I hope I am wrong and Roszak is right. I'd much rather live in the country he foresees.

[2] Debra Viadero, "N.Y.C School-based Budgeting Linked to Test Score Gains." *Education Week*, August 7, 2002. The Final Report of the Evaluation of the Performance Driven Budget Initiative is available from the Institute for Education and Social Policy of New York University.

[3] E.J. Dionne and Ming Hsu Chen, (eds.), *Sacred Places, Civic Purposes.* (Washington, D.C.: The Brookings Institution, 2001).

[4] Marvin Olasky. *Compassionate Conservatism*. (New York, The Free Press, 2000), 186.

[5] Mary Pipher, *The Middle of Everywhere*. (New York: Harcourt, Inc. 2002).

[6] Madelyn Freundlich and Sarah Gerstenzang *An Assessment of the Privatization of Child Welfare Services: Challenges and Successes* (Washington, D.C.: CWLA Press, 2003).

[7] Freundlich and Gerstenzang, *An Assessment*, 293-294.

[8] Roszak, *Longevity Revolution*, 214-15.

[9] Sunstein, *Republic.com.*

[10] Blackwell et al., *Searching*, 162-172

[11] "Too Many Drugs Prescribed for the Elderly?" CBS News, July 21, 2001. M. Fouts, J. Hanlon, et al., "Identification of Elderly Nursing Facility Residents at High Risk for Drug-Related Problems. *The Consultant Pharmacist*. 12(10):1103-1111. (American Society of Consultant Pharmacists, Inc. October 1997).

[12] Ed Finkel, "Plastic Card Tells a Dangerous Truth*," Youth Today*. (Vol. 12, No. 7. July/August 2003).

[13] Arthur Isak Applbaum, "Failure in the Cybermarketplace of Ideas," in Elaine Ciulla Kamarck and Joseph S. Nye, (eds.), *governance.com: Democracy in the Information Age*. (Washington, D.C.: The Brookings Institution, 2002).

[14] Sunstein, *Republic.com.*

[15] *Online Content for Low Income and Underserved Americans: The Digital Divide's New Frontier.* (Los Angeles: The Children's Partnership, 2000).

[16] The Wider Opportunities for Women website has supporting materials for this calculation at http://www.sixstrategies.org/files/SSS%20calculator%20supporting%20materials.doc

[17] Jerry Mechling, "Information Age Governance: Just the Start of Something Big?" in Kamarck and Nye, *governance.com*, 141-142.

[18] Mechling, "Information Age,"155.

CHAPTER 17: PUTTING IT ALL TOGETHER: THE CHALLENGE OF LEADERSHIP IN LOCAL GOVERNMENT

This book, and the realities it is based upon, pose a new set of challenges to local government: to rise above the project-driven approach to children and family policy and become more strategic, to look at the new tools that are available in developing such policy, and to weigh the impact of the four forces described in Section 3 on city and county policy toward children and families. These tasks demand a different kind of leadership, which is already visible in some cities and counties, but which will need to become much more active in most local governments than it is today.

Leadership is partly recognizing long-term self-interest—rising above today's short-range view of the possible to seeing what is necessary over the longer haul. At the same time, it also requires taking risks to transform the political will to make children and family policy a higher priority for local policy.

Leadership requires awareness of the tools discussed in Chapter 4, combined with the willingness to use both the information and values tools that are available. Leaders with these attributes have several qualities:

- A hunger for good data.
- A willingness to push staff and line agencies to produce better information.
- A wide range of contacts in the community who can supplement numbers with stories of people's lives, the neighborhoods they live in, the racial and cultural forces that affect them, and the barriers to opportunity that hold them back.
- An understanding of how to build consensus, going beyond weather-vane, poll-driven politics.
- An understanding of trends enabling them to be anticipative, rather than solely crisis-driven.
- A keen sense of how to respond to inevitable crises by using them to widen public understanding of issues and problems and mobilize new resources.
- An awareness of how timing affects decisions: both the action-forcing events such as elections, annual budget cycles and State of the City addresses and the deadlines and cycles inherent in programs that rely on different "clocks" to determine whether clients are making progress.[1]

Assembling the pieces

Taking the prescriptions of this book seriously is not a task that can be assigned to a junior staffer or to a single, one-day strategic planning retreat.

These tools and strategies must be infused throughout the government; if they simply devolve to a lower-level staff unit, they will become one more pro forma filter through which local policy making must pass, like an environmental review for a new development or an amended capital budget item for a new child care center.

Again, Angela Blackwell and her colleagues offer a vision that helps explain where we are going. In a section on leadership, they write

> As issues become increasingly complex and intertwined, isolating a single solution to an individual problem becomes virtually impossible. To challenge racial and economic disparities, leaders must understand this complexity, articulate integrated visions, and strategize accordingly.[2]

"Integrated visions" is exactly what is needed for children and family agenda to emerge in local government, not isolated projects or motherhood policy statements. Leadership able to develop those integrated visions and carry them on into implementation is not impossible, but today it is less common than it needs to be. Blackwell and her associates describe some of the leadership development programs that have aimed at creating more collaborative leaders who understand the tools of 21st century analysis as well as the art of consensus-building across diverse populations and electorates.

Technocracy, jazz, or muddling?

Given the emphasis in this book on more strategic public policy, it may be important to again stress the point that this does not mean that policy leaders should rely upon technocratic, quantitatively driven analysis. A much more dynamic, interactive policy process is needed, not a static, one-time adding up of all the factors affecting children and families to produce a new set of policies.

In their book, *The Future of American Progressivism*, Roberto Unger and Cornel West describe a form of improvisation in public policy that they liken to jazz. Echoing an older literature on "muddling through" as the craft of public management, West refers to the critical need for experimentation:

> The United States is rich and powerful because it is a country of experimenters. Motivated, sustained, and cumulative tinkering with institutional arrangements is an indispensable tool of democratic experimentalism, of improvisational reform, of jazzlike public action.[3]

These more informal ways of describing what is needed are helpful as a corrective to a mechanistic, "by the numbers" approach to public policy making. But here is the difference: When we know that at least 5,000 students are at risk of dropping out of a city school system, and we have a good idea of who they are by the 1st or 2nd grades, launching a program for 100 of them with great fanfare and no idea of how to sustain it is not muddling through or jazz improvisation—it is playing a few bars and calling it a performance. It is not strategic, nor is it experimental—it is merely tactical. Moreover, it is a tactic that diverts resources and energy from larger, longer-term solutions. Such small, partial visions lack ethical integrity, they lack budget sustainability, and they lack any serious claim to be real strategies.

The leadership balancing act: Behn's three myths

Robert Behn, in his excellent study of leadership in the Massachusetts welfare program in the 1980's, sets forth three different "metastrategies" of leadership. Behn concludes that all three are inadequate, if they are pursued separately.[4] He refers to three myths: the "policy myth" that if the policy is right, it will be implemented right (he also calls this the "Legislator's Conceit"); the administration myth that once the administrative systems have been set up, everything will work as expected, and the "leadership myth" that a manager with the right goals and mission can achieve that mission without policy or administrative changes.

In addressing the needs of children and families, Behn's three elements are useful in making clear that a robust leadership strategy does demand all three elements. Narrow reliance on policy change, administrative systems, or mission-driven leadership by themselves will be unlikely to pull together the disparate components of strategic policy in a way that ensures their effective implementation to achieve consensus goals. All three elements are needed because of the highly scattered and fragmented pieces that make up the portfolio of current children and family *programs*, which do not yet constitute *policy*. The tendency is for position to affect stance, with policy staff tending to ignore implementation, administrative staff tending to ignore leadership, and leadership tending at times to ignore both because of the supposed clarity of the goals they have set.

Timing adds a fourth layer of complexity and challenge. Behn refers to Rosabeth Moss Kanter's powerful observation: "Here is an irony: change requires stability."[5] Kanter is referring to continuity of leadership, without which leadership can degenerate into an "innovation *du jour*" approach, with lots of innovation, but little that lasts. Term limits can have an effect on the legislative dimension of innovation, creating an apparent premium on "new things" and downgrading anything that takes longer than four years. While civil service and management appointees with tenure at the top of agencies can provide a greater measure of continuity, such continuity can be rare in some cities and counties, with a decided effect on policy. In a recent conversation with the staff of a mayor with 1½ years left on his term, the prospects of implementing a longer-term set of policies was dismissed as *too* long-range.

Yet making strategic policy for children and families, especially for the youngest members of that broad population, is by definition longer-range than the next grant cycle, the next budget, or the next election. It requires thinking, working, and setting priorities that last longer than any of these cycles. If there were no elected leaders who had ever done this, we could simply say that standard asks too much and is unrealistic. But there are such leaders, as we have seen throughout this book, and they have shown how the longer view can prevail.

Leadership in children and family policy as shared power

Local government in all its functions is often an example of what Bryson and Crosby call a "shared power model" of political influence, in which no one power center dominates so much that others are likely to accede to its goals simply because it is dominant.[6] And when the special issues of children, youth, and families are added to the mix, the shared power model becomes even more relevant, since

- Local government is part of an intergovernmental system in which other levels have critical roles;
- Local government shares its power at the local level with many other sources of influence outside the sphere of governmental control, including parents, private health providers, early care providers, court systems, and nonprofit, community-based, and faith-based organizations; and
- Local government inevitably faces a wide range of conflicts among stakeholders over underlying values about how children and families should be treated, as discussed in Chapter 5, and some stakeholders become more fully engaged when "their" issues come into visibility.

By definition, then, in the children and family arena, local government exercises leadership in horizontal, shared power modes far more often than it exercises anything like direct control. The use of horizontal power places an even higher premium on longer-term efforts, since it often takes longer to build trust and win credibility with those who are one's elected peers than those whom one controls or can easily dominate.

In a shared power environment, an advantage can go to the leader with a clear voice. "The best megaphone," as Cliff Johnson of the National League of Cities puts it, belongs to the mayor, who can use it to convene, to advocate, to spotlight new efforts, to call for shifting resources from the least effective to the most effective programs—who can, in short, provide a vision of strategic planning and services that goes beyond cheerleading to genuine leadership. None of these roles are about dominating with raw power; all are about using a skillful blend of information and values to make a difference.

Collaborative management and *collaborative leadership* are the brand names of what city and county officials must do to respond to the needs of children and families. Robert Agranoff and Michael McGuire have written an excellent book on the challenges of collaborative public management and the tools used to bring it to fruition.[7] While focused on economic development, its conclusions bear relevance for much of the children and family agenda as well. Their book makes the case that local officials who understand these tools can achieve better outcomes using networks of organizations they do not control, but which they need to succeed.

Agranoff and McGuire make a case that several important tools of collaborative management create value in networks, including:

- what they term "groupware"—the intergroup development of information flows that facilitate group cohesion;
- social capital—including the ingredients of trust among members of the group;
- shared learning in the sense that Senge and others have refined in referring to "learning organizations;"
- negotiation skills, citing Bardach's powerful phrase "to collaborate is to negotiate;"[8]
- information itself, as a currency of collaboration that enables members of a group with dissimilar mandates and resources to communicate with each other about their environments and the effectiveness of their shared efforts.[9]

Leadership as the mobilization of information

The literature on local government leadership has become very articulate about models and modes of collaboration over the past decade or so. But what that literature still seems to under-emphasize is the power of information to shape a policy agenda and thus to set the goals for collaboration. As I have written elsewhere, collaboration can drift into becoming an end in itself, rather than a means for achieving important shared goals.[10] The goal-setting dimension of collaboration depends heavily upon the quality of information—information about current conditions and about the effectiveness of current programs in altering those conditions. Those elected and appointed officials who understand this can play multiple horizontal roles, with the assurance that they will bring to the table a critical resource that few other players possess: useful information that enables a spotlighting of what is happening to children and families and which programs really work.

That is the invaluable function played by tools such as a local report card and a children and family budget, which can add up "the trees" of fragmented data in new ways that make the forest visible for the first time to many of the players in collaborative networks. To know the real dropout rate for specific ethnic groups, rather than the publicly released aggregate numbers, to know how many kindergartners and first graders are "held back or "held out" because they are not ready for school by a school system's arcane definitions, to know the correlation between a school's test scores and its families' income levels–these are sources of influence, if not power. If local government leaders passively rely upon public and private agencies to bring this data to the table, they are far more likely to get canned, sanitized data than information that can frame solutions as well as spotlight problems.

So leadership becomes a constant search for both nuggets of information and for the overall patterns that make isolated data into useful policy knowledge. A recent book on a leading American politician concluded that he simply had no innate curiosity. This is a drawback that would be a potentially fatal flaw in local political thickets, where knowledge can be influence on its way to becoming power.

As Lisbeth Schorr has said of the best evaluations, the best leaders use both "stories and numbers." They can communicate using both quantitative aggregates and sub-sets of data with narrative power, and the narratives themselves, the stories that translate the data into people's lives in ways that move them to action.

The Risks and Gains in the Politics of Local Children and Family Policy

If developing strategic policy for children and family issues were all politically uphill, running impossible risks, it would be unrealistic to urge city and county officials to move into such a precarious arena. Gladiator movies are fascinating to watch, but if there is nothing but lions, tigers, and large, angry mercenaries in the arena, few elected officials will rush to the lists. Nor should they.

But there are risks and gains beyond the immediate political dangers of venturing into strategic policymaking. Notable among them are the costs of timidity, irrelevance, and being surpassed in leadership visibility by other elected officials or other organizations outside government. If the premise is accepted that children and family issues are growing in visibility and importance, then the political risks of ignoring them may be greater than the risks of seeking to build a new consensus about how to respond to them. To be dismissed as irrelevant—especially if state legislators, officials in other communities, and local business and civic leaders have begun forging a new consensus—is not a recipe for long-term political success. To risk marginalization may be more dangerous in the longer range than to risk becoming involved in issues of controversy.

In Chapter 3, I reviewed the political, economic, and ethical arguments for local leaders to become more strategic in addressing children and family issues. Chapters 12-15 argued that four cross-cutting policy areas—education and school readiness, substance abuse, family support, and youth development—are unavoidable issues that will cost local leaders credibility if they are ignored or dealt with through fragmented and ineffective programmatic responses. And in the prior chapter, in looking at the future of local governments' efforts to deal with children and families, I discussed a set of political issues—immigration, economic inequality, the aging of the voting population, school choice, and responses to new technological challenges—that all seem likely to keep various versions of children and family issues in the political spotlights.

But there are other elements of the calculus of risk and gain. Leadership sometimes gets forfeited. When it does, one of two things can happen: governments get taken to court or people get tossed out of office. In some states, the mechanisms for doing both are conjoined, and the results can be upheavals like the California recall election of 2003.

In other states and localities, the legal route gets taken when negotiations with the executive and legislative branches get stalemated. In chapter 11, we reviewed the legalities of regionalism, and in chapter 15 we briefly reviewed the legal prospects of compliance enforcement affecting youth programs, in which we predicted that legal action would be taken against budget cuts that cross the line from deep cuts to deliberately opting out of compliance with the state's own and federal laws and regulations. In both of these cases and others, a failure of leadership is sometimes evident in legal action adopted as a near-last resort by advocates and providers.

So leaders are those who take risks, but they are also those who see risks coming further down the tracks than others with shorter sight. Knowing that you are headed for legal action may be a spur to policy action. At the same time, in some localities, a legal thicket may be exactly the briar patch you wish to be thrown into, as a way of advocating with state and federal agencies. I have known local agency heads who admitted that their frequent prayer was "Please, Lord, let them sue me."

Leadership from outside local government: The challenge to advocates

Yet the fact remains that in some cities and counties, there will simply be no elected leader or agency head who understands or cares enough about these longer-term challenges to make them a priority. In such cases, as we have argued throughout this book, the matrix of roles for government becomes a template available to those outside government—advocates who can use it to assess what their local government is doing, and what it is failing to do.

In fact, in some cities and counties the real leadership for a children and family agenda may come from the edges of the public sector, or even completely outside local government. Roles that may once have been framed as advocacy are now increasingly framed as social or civic entrepreneurship, and that function that can be played inside or outside local governments.[11] Our premise in this book is that the leadership role can and should be played inside government, but if it is not, the issues will not disappear. Then the leadership may have to come from outside.

For advocates, providers, community leaders and residents, the challenge is seeing the field of children and family policy whole—watching the forest as well as the trees, branches, and leaves—and avoiding the narrowly categorical debates that allow local government to spread marginal resources across one more underfunded program and declaring it a victory. Some of the very tools suggested for use by local governments can help advocates and providers in this task:

- Using report cards that cut across multiple indicators of children and family needs;
- Relying on asset inventories and children and family budget breakouts to understand what the real stakes are across the entire budget, rather than a single-program focus that ignores the larger base of spending;
- Resisting grant-driven planning in favor of redirection of much larger existing resources;
- Citizen participation "ladders" that increase the ability of outside groups to reject token roles for substantial ones;
- Consensus-building tools that can be used among different interest groups of providers and community members to forge a new action

agenda shared by groups that may have worked competitively in the past.

Each of these tools can provide local groups with more information, planning ammunition, and a better seat at the table in discussing options for strategic choices. A separate book could be written about these options for advocates, and an excellent overview of the state of children's advocacy has recently been written.[12]

Local Government: Not always central, but invariably indispensable

It is possible to summarize the argument of this book with two conclusions—one verifiable, the second an assertion:

- Local government is not always centrally involved in children and family policy.
- For children and family policy to be fully effective in meeting its goals, local government *must* be integrally involved, whether through its own actions or under pressure from outside forces.

The first of these is not difficult to prove, as the budget percentages cited in Chapter 1 make clear. When only 5-25% of your budget is focused on a set of issues, and the issues are disaggregated so that they come to you in separate programs rather than as a cluster, often those issues will not rise to the level of priorities for resources or time. Those cities and counties whose exemplary performance has been cited in this book *are* models, but they are not norms, and should not yet be described as though they were.

But without local government leadership, the children and family agenda will suffer. Local government is at the delivery level, and it can mobilize local resources in ways impossible at the state or federal levels. It can contribute to community building efforts, in part by making better connections between community building and children and family agendas.

Paradoxically, perhaps, the neighborhood movement needs stronger local governments to carry its agenda to scale and escape its own traps of token-funded projects. Only a strong local government can offer the recurrent "deal," which is always an important option: more devolution and discretion (and eventually, more resources as well) at the community level in return for more accountability for results. That is the deal that cities and counties are continuously re-negotiating with state and federal funders, as the pendulum swings from devolution to centralization. And that deal mirrors the deal cities and counties can make with the communities within their boundaries.

Conclusion: Not the last word

The last word in this book is to emphasize once more the need for words and deeds to come from local government, not its former practitioners. The multiple roles and the new tools available to leadership which are set forth in this book present a better array of options than local governments have ever had for the purpose of taking children and family policy seriously. But it will take local officials who are willing to be new kinds of leaders to chose those roles and use those tools.

There is a serious downside if those deeds and actions do not happen, which can be seen in bold relief in actions taken by some cities and counties already:

- A retreat into privatization of the worst kind, often under-regulated by governments that have withdrawn both their oversight and a portion of their funding from privatized functions, driven solely by short-run cost savings;
- A reliance upon community-based and faith-based initiatives that never rise above the level of projects to full strategic policy;
- A retreat that leaves the field of policy to fragmented, categorically-minded advocacy and provider groups who may find it very difficult in some communities to build genuine, working coalitions across their various interests;
- A reliance upon state and federal leadership that has been visible only in a few states, and seems even less likely with the fiscal strains of the next few years of intergovernmental relations.

These are not hopeful prognoses. But the more optimistic, even inspiring lessons are those from the opposite kinds of cities and counties. Those are the sites where leadership has resisted the partial view and seen the full forest, in the midst of which there is a living space filled with children and families who have been given, and who have themselves created, a far greater potential to make their communities good places to live and grow and contribute.

Let me close by recalling, as I did in the preface, how much I honor those who are inside city and county government, where I spent a valuable part of my own professional and political life. They are in an honorable profession—however much their worst counterparts may from time to time dishonor it. They are making hard choices, often without the resources they need, except for the most important resource of all: leadership.

Several years ago, in speaking of local leadership in my county government, I made a speech concluding with these remarks: "With a gross domestic product of over $100 billion, our county does not have a resources problem—it has a leadership problem."

This comment infuriated an elected leader who was in the audience, as well as several other county officials and supporters of the incumbents. I take very little satisfaction from the fact that a few months later the county went bankrupt because its leaders had stopped leading, refusing to make hard choices, and ended up with *both* a resources and a leadership problem, to the tune of $100 million in continuing annual debt payments.

That bankruptcy was very public, in contrast with the thousands of small victories and battles that will be waged today and tomorrow across the nation in cities and counties by those who make local government work: a zoning variance granted for a child care center, a transit line opened up for reverse commuters, a literacy program for new immigrants at their children's school. In the final analysis, these are projects, not policy. But it will be the leadership at the local level that converts these projects into policy that can make a difference in the lives of children and families at the local level of our nation.

NOTES

[1] These include, for example, children's developmental clocks that give such urgency to early intervention, the child welfare clock that determines how long parents have to convince a judge to return children who have been removed and the welfare clock that determines how long a parent may receive benefits.

[2] Blackwell, et al. Searching, 195.

[3] Roberto Mangabeira Unger and Cornel West. The Future of American Progressivism. (Boston, Mass.: Beacon Books, 1998), 20.

[4] Robert Behn, Leadership Counts. (Cambridge, Mass.: Harvard University Press, 1991).

[5] Rosabeth Moss Kanter. The Change Masters: Innovation and Entrepreneurship in the American Corporation. (New York: Simon and Schuster, 1983), 122-123.

[6] John M. Bryson and Barbara C. Crosby. Leadership for the Common Good. (San Francisco, Ca.: Jossey-Bass, 1992).

[7] Robert Agranoff and Michael McGuire. Collaborative Public Management: New Strategies for Local Governments. (Washington, D.C.: Georgetown University Press, 2003).

[8] Eugene Bardach. Getting Agencies to Work Together. (Washington, D.C.: The Brookings Institution, 1998), 238.

[9] Agranoff and McGuire. Collaborative Public Management, 179-181.

[10] Sid Gardner. Beyond Collaboration to Results. (Phoenix, Az.: Arizona Prevention Resource Center, 1998).

[11] Douglas Henton, John Melville, Kimberly Walesh. Grassroots Leaders for a New Economy. (San Francisco, Ca.: Jossey-Bass, 1997).

[12] Carol J. DeVita and Rachel Mosher-Williams, eds. Who Speaks For America's Children? The Role of Child Advocates in Public Policy, (Washington, D.C.: The Urban Institute Press, 2001).

AUTHOR BIOGRAPHICAL SKETCH

Sid Gardner is President of Children and Family Futures, a non-profit firm that works on children and family issues, with special attention to children affected by alcohol and other drugs.

Mr. Gardner served for ten years as Director of the Center for Collaboration for Children at California State University, Fullerton. He has also served as a program officer of the Annie E. Casey Foundation, as a Hartford City Council Member, on the staff of the White House Domestic Council, as Director of State and Local Affairs for the Children's Defense Fund, as Deputy Assistant Secretary of the U.S. Department of Health, Education and Welfare, and as an Assistant to the Mayor of New York City. He has taught at seven universities in California and Connecticut, and has published widely on the topics of services for children and families, collaboration, and ethics and public policy.

Mr. Gardner received his B.A. from Occidental College and has Master's degrees from Princeton University's Woodrow Wilson School and from Hartford Seminary. Mr. Gardner is a California native, a Vietnam veteran, and lives in Irvine, California with his wife, Dr. Nancy Young, a stepson, and an adopted son and daughter. He has an older daughter who is married and has one son.